Petals and Bullets

Dorothy Morris

*New Zealand Nurse in the
Spanish Civil War*

The Cañada Blanch / Sussex Academic Studies on Contemporary Spain

General Editor: Professor Paul Preston, London School of Economics

Margaret Joan Anstee, *JB – An Unlikely Spanish Don: The Life and Times of Professor John Brande Trend.*

Richard Barker, *Skeletons in the Closet, Skeletons in the Ground: Repression, Victimization and Humiliation in a Small Andalusian Town – The Human Consequences of the Spanish Civil War.*

Germà Bel, *Infrastructure and the Political Economy of Nation Building in Spain, 1720–2010.*

Germà Bel, *Disdain, Distrust, and Dissolution: The Surge of Support for Independence in Catalonia.*

Carl-Henrik Bjerström, *Josep Renau and the Politics of Culture in Republican Spain, 1931–1939: Re-imagining the Nation.*

Kathryn Crameri, *'Goodbye, Spain?': The Question of Independence for Catalonia*

Mark Derby, *Petals and Bullets: Dorothy Morris – A New Zealand Nurse in the Spanish Civil War.*

Michael Eaude, *Triumph at Midnight in the Century: A Critical Biography of Arturo Barea.*

Francisco Espinosa-Maestre, *Shoot the Messenger?: Spanish Democracy and the Crimes of Francoism – From the Pact of Silence to the Trial of Baltasar Garzón.*

Soledad Fox, *Constancia de la Mora in War and Exile: International Voice for the Spanish Republic.*

María Jesús González, *Raymond Carr: The Curiosity of the Fox.*

Helen Graham, *The War and its Shadow: Spain's Civil War in Europe's Long Twentieth Century.*

Angela Jackson, *'For us it was Heaven': The Passion, Grief and Fortitude of Patience Darton – From the Spanish Civil War to Mao's China.*

Gabriel Jackson, *Juan Negrín: Physiologist, Socialist, and Spanish Republican War Leader.*

Xavier Moreno Juliá, *The Blue Division: Spanish Blood in Russia, 1941–1945.*

Sid Lowe, *Catholicism, War and the Foundation of Francoism: The Juventud de Acción Popular in Spain, 1931–1939.*

David Lethbridge, *Norman Bethune in Spain: Commitment, Crisis, and Conspiracy.*

Carles Manera, *The Great Recession: A Subversive View.*

Jorge Marco, *Guerrilleros and Neighbours in Arms: Identities and Cultures of Antifascist Resistance in Spain.*

Martin Minchom, *Spain's Martyred Cities: From the Battle of Madrid to Picasso's* Guernica.

Olivia Muñoz-Rojas, *Ashes and Granite: Destruction and Reconstruction in the Spanish Civil War and Its Aftermath.*

Linda Palfreeman, *¡SALUD!: British Volunteers in the Republican Medical Service during the Spanish Civil War, 1936–1939.*

Linda Palfreeman, *Aristocrats, Adventurers and Ambulances: British Medical Units in the Spanish Civil War.*

Linda Palfreeman, *Spain Bleeds: The Development of Battlefield Blood Transfusion during the Civil War.*

Cristina Palomares, *The Quest for Survival after Franco: Moderate Francoism and the Slow Journey to the Polls, 1964–1977.*

David Wingeate Pike, *France Divided: The French and the Civil War in Spain.*

Hugh Purcell with Phyll Smith, *The Last English Revolutionary: Tom Wintringham, 1898–1949.*

Isabelle Rohr, *The Spanish Right and the Jews, 1898–1945: Antisemitism and Opportunism.*

Gareth Stockey, *Gibraltar: "A Dagger in the Spine of Spain?"*

Ramon Tremosa-i-Balcells, *Catalonia – An Emerging Economy: The Most Cost-Effective Ports in the Mediterranean Sea.*

Maria Thomas, *The Faith and the Fury: Popular Anticlerical Violence and Iconoclasm in Spain, 1931–1936.*

Dacia Viejo-Rose, *Reconstructing Spain: Cultural Heritage and Memory after Civil War.*

Richard Wigg, *Churchill and Spain: The Survival of the Franco Regime, 1940–1945.*

To Roberta 'Bobbie' Taylor,
a living embodiment of the principles
and spirit of Dorothy Morris

Petals and Bullets

Dorothy Morris

New Zealand Nurse in the Spanish Civil War

MARK DERBY

sussex
A C A D E M I C
P R E S S
Brighton • Chicago • Toronto

Canada Blanch Centre
for Contemporary
Spanish Studies

2 4 6 8 10 9 7 5 3 1

First published in Great Britain in 2015 by
SUSSEX ACADEMIC PRESS
PO Box 139, Eastbourne BN24 9BP

Distributed in North America by
SUSSEX ACADEMIC PRESS
Independent Publishers Group
814 N Franklin St, Chicago, IL 60610, USA

Published in collaboration with the Cañada Blanch Centre for Contemporary
Spanish Studies, London.

British Library Cataloguing in Publication Data
A CIP catalogue record for this book is available from the British Library.

Library of Congress Cataloging-in-Publication Data
Applied for.

Paperback ISBN 978-1-84519-684-4

Typeset & designed by Sussex Academic Press, Brighton & Eastbourne.
Printed and bound by CPI Group (UK) Ltd, Croydon, CR0 4YY
Printed on acid-free paper.

Contents

The Cañada Blanch Centre for Contemporary Spanish Studies   viii
Series Editor's Preface   x
Acknowledgements   xiv
List of Illustrations   xvi

Introduction: A Life Devoted to Nursing   1

1   The Morris Family Yacht   8

2   Good Bombing Light   28

3   Hospital Inglés de Niños   58

4   With Horsebox and Lie-Low   93

5   Wearing the Snood   121

6   The Conscience of the World   139

7   'Brazen and Tyrannical'   159

Notes   169
Bibliography   183
Index   188

The Cañada Blanch Centre for Contemporary Spanish Studies

In the 1960s, the most important initiative in the cultural and academic relations between Spain and the United Kingdom was launched by a Valencian fruit importer in London. The creation by Vicente Cañada Blanch of the Anglo-Spanish Cultural Foundation has subsequently benefited large numbers of Spanish and British scholars at various levels. Thanks to the generosity of Vicente Cañada Blanch, thousands of Spanish schoolchildren have been educated at the secondary school in West London that bears his name. At the same time, many British and Spanish university students have benefited from the exchange scholarships which fostered cultural and scientific exchanges between the two countries. Some of the most important historical, artistic and literary work on Spanish topics to be produced in Great Britain was initially made possible by Cañada Blanch scholarships.

Vicente Cañada Blanch was, by inclination, a conservative. When his Foundation was created, the Franco regime was still in the plenitude of its power. Nevertheless, the keynote of the Foundation's activities was always a complete open-mindedness on political issues. This was reflected in the diversity of research projects supported by the Foundation, many of which, in Francoist Spain, would have been regarded as subversive. When the Dictator died, Don Vicente was in his seventy-fifth year. In the two decades following the death of the Dictator, although apparently indestructible, Don Vicente was obliged to husband his energies. Increasingly, the work of the Foundation was carried forward by Miguel Dols whose tireless and imaginative work in London was matched in Spain by that of José María Coll Comín. They were united in the Foundation's spirit of open-minded commitment to fostering research of high quality in pursuit of better Anglo-Spanish cultural relations. Throughout the 1990s, thanks to them, the role of the Foundation grew considerably.

In 1994, in collaboration with the London School of Economics, the Foundation established the Príncipe de Asturias Chair of Contemporary Spanish History and the Cañada Blanch Centre for Contemporary Spanish Studies. It is the particular task of the Cañada Blanch Centre for Contemporary Spanish Studies to promote the understanding of twentieth- century Spain through research and teaching of contemporary Spanish history, politics, economy, sociology and culture. The Centre possesses a valuable library and archival centre for specialists in contemporary Spain. This work is carried on through the publications of the doctoral and post-doctoral researchers at the Centre itself and through the many seminars and lectures held at the London School of Economics. While the seminars are the province of the researchers, the lecture cycles have been the forum in which Spanish politicians have been able to address audiences in the United Kingdom.

Since 1998, the Cañada Blanch Centre has published a substantial number of books in collaboration with several different publishers on the subject of contemporary Spanish history and politics. An extremely fruitful partnership with Sussex Academic Press began in 2004. Full details and descriptions of the published works can be found on the Press website.

One of the areas covered most intensely by the series has been the role in the Spanish Civil War of the International Brigades. An early contribution included a fascinating biography by Hugh Purcell and Phyl Smith of Tom Wintringham, the commander of the |British battalion. The series has centred particularly on the medical services of the brigades and medical advances in the war with important volumes by Nick Coni, David Lethbridge and Linda Palfreeman. The role of the nursing services has been investigated fruitfully by Angela Jackson, and her work is now complemented by Mark Derby's multi-layered and moving biography of an extraordinary New Zealand nurse, Dorothy Morris. His book constitutes a splendid complement to Angela Jackson's life of the left-wing nurse Patience Darton.

Series Editor's Preface
by Angela Jackson

Mark Derby begins his book on the life of Dorothy Morris with a particularly pertinent quote relating to a problem faced by certain biographers, myself included, when writing about the lives of those who have been habitually referred to in a rather snide manner as 'do-gooders'. It poses the question, if you can't resort to celebrity, sex or scandal, what exactly can you do to convey the passions filling the lives of these altruistic, and often eccentric, oddballs? This quandary is faced even more acutely when writing about women who have not lived their lives in the public eye, but were extraordinary nonetheless. Without recourse to the media coverage and political records of the famous, source material can be limited and hard to find. Fortunately, the faults and frailties that are revealed both wittingly and unwittingly in the oral testimonies and other archival documents unearthed by the biographers of lesser-known women often yield a more extensive analysis than might at first be expected.[1] How rewarding it can be when these characters are finally revealed as far more than mere stereotypical heroic figures in the history of 'women worthies'![2] Though strongly individualistic, they do frequently share certain attributes: enough grit to be regarded as somewhat abrasive and, in those days before the women's liberation movement, the guts to give orders to all and sundry in the name of efficiency, even at the risk of being regarded as 'mannish'. Like Patience Darton, an English nurse who also served in Spain, Dorothy Morris took pride in maintaining the high standards of her nursing training as far as possible, despite primitive war-time conditions, and wished to pass on her skills to the local women for whom even washing an unknown male patient was a socially radical action. Both found that not everyone approved of their attitude.

In our present era of anti-heroes, such heroines, warts and all, are still worthy of our admiration. Dorothy Morris was one of the women who willingly volunteered to go to Spain and face all the dangers of carrying out arduous duties in the midst of a bitter conflict, despite the fact that the war was regarded by many people in those days as just another 'quarrel in a far away country between people of whom we know nothing'.[3] The challenges they met there, and then later in other countries, were many: the sudden burden of responsibility; the difficulties when caring for patients and refugees under totally inadequate conditions, exhaustion and ill-health. Over and above any fears for their own safety, they frequently suffered the emotional trauma of loss, not only of the patients and refugees whose lives could not be saved, but also of brothers, husbands and lovers who died in battle. The way in which the majority dealt with these challenges was, indeed, heroic. Both Dorothy and Patience were among the foreign volunteers who were able to glory in the sight of almond blossom but suffered the grief of devastating personal loss.

The title of the biography perfectly reflects Dorothy's experiences of war and her appreciation of beauty: she was as well aware of the horrors of warfare as of the importance of cultural activities in grim refugee camps. This duality is also reflected in the poignant contrast between the happiness of the children she saw playing in the streets of Murcia by the light of a brilliant moon and explosive flares of aerial bombardment, and the sadness surrounding the last call-up of young men, not much more than children themselves, who died in vast numbers during the last few months before Franco's victory.

Mark Derby has skilfully blended a variety of sources to contextualise the life of Dorothy Morris. To Dorothy's own letters with their perceptive comments and descriptive delights he has added the views of her family, friends and colleagues. The collection of images helps to convey a sense of the rich history of the times in which she lived: a history which is explored in a clear and well-expressed style by the author, drawing on a wide range of archival material. Readers will find much of interest in his description of New Zealand society and the political atmosphere which influenced Dorothy's early years. The poverty she saw there goaded her to action, just as similar injustices at the other side of the world in Britain spurred other mettlesome women to volunteer for Spain. The chapters concerning Dorothy's experiences during the Spanish civil war give a highly personalised perspective on the work of the International Brigade medical services and make an important contribution to the record of the daunting tasks undertaken by the Society of Friends in Spain to help thousands of refugees, many of them children. Dorothy's organisational skills developed through her role working alongside other stalwart women with close links to *los cuáqueros* and led her to refugee work on an unimaginable scale during the Second World War. This gives Mark Derby the opportunity to explore the role of the United Nations Relief and Rehabilitation Administration (UNNRA).

Although her comments on the political situation were often astute, and she was more than ready to give outspoken opinions on the failings of politicians, like many women who became deeply committed to the cause of the Spanish Republic, Dorothy Morris was not a member of any political party. She also can be counted amongst the overwhelming majority of the women who, whether firm believers in a particular party political doctrine or not, always looked back on their time in Spain as having been worthwhile, despite the suffering they saw there and the defeat of the people whose cause they had supported so devotedly. Dorothy, apologising for resorting to such melodramatic terminology, really felt that she had been in the 'fight against the forces of evil'.

Mark Derby's biography has much to offer the general reader along with those carrying out specific research in the fields relating to her life or within the wider context of gender studies. His excellent book is a welcome addition to this series on contemporary Spanish history, offering us a vivid and sensitive portrayal of a dynamic woman.

Notes

1   See for example Angela Jackson's biography of Patience Darton, *For us it was Heaven: The Passion, Grief and Fortitude of Patience Darton from the Spanish Civil War to Mao's China* (Brighton: Sussex Academic Press, 2012), drawing on sources such as correspondence between Patience and the International Brigader, Robert Aaquist; Paul Preston's *Doves of War: Four Women of Spain* (London: HarperCollins, 2002), which includes an exploration of the honest admissions made by Nan Green in her memoir *A Chronicle of Small Beer: The memoirs of Nan Green* (Nottingham: Trent Editions, 2005).

2   The history of 'women worthies' is a term that has been used by histo-

rians such as Natalie Davis and Gerder Lerner to describe a type of 'compensatory history' found in certain studies of notable women.

3   Neville Chamberlain, radio broadcast, 27 September 1938.

Angela Jackson is the author of several books on the Spanish Civil War including, in this series, *British Women and the Spanish Civil War* (2002) and *For us it was Heaven: The Passion, Grief and Fortitude of Patience Darton from the Spanish Civil War to Mao's China* (2012)'

Acknowledgements

Dorothy Morris's extended family, including her niece Mary Stapylton-Smith, and her god-daughter Jane Taylor and her family, have supported this project fully from its inception. That support, more than anything else, convinced me to proceed with this book.

Roger Steele and his colleagues at Steele Roberts Publishing painstakingly transcribed Dorothy Morris's letters into digitised text, thereby supplying the book's first, and best, passages.

Pamela Wood and Judy Yarwood, lecturers in the history of nursing at Monash University and the Christchurch Polytechnic Institute of Technology respectively, were patient and generous to a researcher knowing nothing whatever about their subject.

Donald Davis, archivist of the American Friends Service Council in Philadelphia, delivered numerous gems from his superbly organised records.

Michael O'Shaughnessy spent an afternoon thoughtfully excavating his own longstanding researches into New Zealand connections with the Spanish Civil War.

Bernard Wilson made repeated trips to the Friends Library in London on my behalf, unreservedly shared his influential research on Mary Elmes, and gave crucial advice and encouragement.

For their help in translating research materials from French, Spanish and Catalan, I am indebted to Diana Burns, Farrell Cleary, Cristina Gomez de la Torre, David Jorge and Saioa Lopez Polin.

For many other instances of support, I am grateful to Harry A'Court, Susan Armstrong-Reid, Rosemary Bailey, Serge Barba, Pedro Belmont, Patrick Butler, Angeles Carceres, Marta Casulleras, Madeleine Claus, Geoff Cowling, Roger Dennis, Nigel Derby, Rosamunda Droescher, Kate Godfrey (Enfield Local Studies and Archive), Julia Holderness, Roger Kelly, Daan Kolthoff, Amanda Leinberger (Archives and Records Management, United Nations, NY), Carmen Gonzalez Martinez, Mack Morum, Gordon Ogilvie, Robert Ostrycharz, staff and Old Girls of Rangi Ruru School, Anna

Rogers, Jeremy Rose, Tanja Rother, Alan Swain, Alvaro Toepke, Antonia Viñao and (by no means least) David Worsfold.

Linda Palfreeman and Angela Jackson each brought a deep knowledge of Spanish Civil War medical volunteers to bear when editing the text.

A generous grant in aid of publication was provided by Unions Manawatu. To John Shennan and his colleagues George Larkins, Roger Middlemass and Alan Millar – salud, compañeros.

I have been privileged to work on this project with Paul Preston, an internationally acclaimed historian of the Spanish Civil War. My publishers in Britain, represented by Anthony Grahame, and in New Zealand, by Robbie Burton, have been both exacting and encouraging during the complex, trans-hemispheric publishing process.

As ever, thanks above all to my family.

List of Illustrations

Picture section after page 74.

1 The stalwart crew of the *Lucky Lady* gold dredge pose on board their vessel at Bannockburn Creek near Cromwell, 1901. Young engineer Geoffrey Morris is fourth from right.

2 Proud parents Rebecca and Geoffrey Morris with their first children – Dorothy (then aged about six) and Geoff junior.

3 A large crew and not a lifejacket in sight. The Morris children and friends set out for Quail Island in Lyttelton Harbour, *c.* 1914.

4 Rangi Ruru school prefects, 1920. Dorothy Morris third from right.

5 The Morris family in repose at Flackley Ash, *c.* 1925. From left Frank, Dorothy, their aunt Selena, Ruth, their mother Rebecca, Roger, and their father Geoffrey. The two boys wear the distinctive uniform of Christ's College, Christchurch.

6 A newly trained nurse, Dorothy relaxes at home in Lyttelton, *c.* 1930.

7 Dorothy Morris, studio portrait, *c.* 1926.

8 The Malecon, Murcia, southern Spain, *c.* 1937.

9 The villa that became the English Children's Hospital, Murcia, 1937. Several patients stand on the front steps.

10 Sylvia, a Spanish nurse aid whose surname is unknown, with two of her patients including a tiny 'starveling'.

11 Nurse aid Irene Caelon with a refugee woman and young patients at the Children's Hospital.

12 These cheerful and sturdy convalescents are shown on the hospital's front steps.

13 Dorothy with an unidentified patient on the hospital roof, early morning, 1938.

14 Stylishly wrapped in winter coats, Mary Elmes (centre), Dorothy Morris and their driver Juan stand next to their delivery van, Perpignan, 1939.

15 La Coume, the French farmhouse that became a Quaker-owned refuge, *c.* 1940.

16 This small oil painting was one of Dorothy Morris's dearest possessions. It is likely to have been painted by a Spanish Civil War refugee in Perpignan, *c.* 1939, and shows a residential street in that region.

17 Dorothy in her last years in Christchurch, with her great-nephew Ben, 1981.

Photos 13 and 14 courtesy of American Friends Service Council, Philadelphia US; no. 15 courtesy of Fondation Krüger, Mas de la Coume, Mosset, France; no. 16 courtesy of Jane Taylor. Other photos courtesy of Morris family collections.

Spain veined with bloods and metals, blue and victorious,
proletariat of petals and bullets,
alone, alive, somnolent, resounding.

FROM 'WHAT SPAIN WAS LIKE", *Spain in My Heart* (1938), PABLO NERUDA

Introduction
A Life Devoted to Nursing

*"Here in our modern culture – where evil is sexy, goodness is
dull, and organised goodness is dullest of all – can we find a
way to make organised altruism interesting?"*[1]

This is an account of a life devoted to nursing, and to providing aid
to refugees, orphaned children and other civilian casualties of warfare. It is the story of a woman raised in fortunate circumstances in
New Zealand who chose to pursue her career elsewhere, often under
conditions of extreme discomfort, danger and distress. Making
Dorothy Morris's life appear interesting and even significant in a
cynical and self-interested era poses more than the usual challenges
to a biographer.

The moment which made this challenge seem worth the effort
occurred in the reading room of the Alexander Turnbull Library, New
Zealand's central repository for manuscripts and other unpublished
archive materials. Some years after Dorothy's death, her relatives
decided that this library should hold the letters she had written to
New Zealand from the many countries, battle zones, hospitals and
apartment rooms in which she had spent her working life. There are
more than 80 pages of these letters, mostly handwritten in an
emphatic and blessedly legible script, but also typed under a succession of institutional letterheads. They comprise a piecemeal
first-person account of a life of extraordinary dedication, adventur-
ousness and political commitment, traversing some of the defining
events of the twentieth century.

The broad outline of the part Dorothy played in those events was
already known to me. In 2009 I had published a book on New
Zealanders' response to the Spanish Civil War, and this included a
few pages on Dorothy's service with the International Brigades,
drawn mainly from contemporary newspaper reports.[2] Her letters

supplied a great deal of extra information about this watershed period of her life, and also revealed a range of further activities I had known nothing about at all.

Yet the problem of depicting organised altruism remained. A nurse and refugee aid worker, even one who had treated frostbitten antifascists in the Sierra Nevada and saved malnourished babies from typhoid fever, did not present a self-evidently engaging and compelling subject for a book more than half a century later. What persuaded me to make Dorothy Morris's letters available to a surfeited present-day readership, together with the background and other information needed to make full sense of them, was the tone in which they were written. She had studied at university before training as a nurse, spoke several languages, read widely, and had clearly been accustomed to defending her viewpoint within her large and opiniated family. Her letters to them are vividly descriptive, fiercely polemic and historically fascinating, and many are phrased with a journalist's eye for the telling detail. They convey Dorothy's experiences at the core of contemporary world events, but also her unsentimental and astute attitude towards the political forces behind those events. Reading her letters, I developed a sharply defined impression of a woman whose altruism was motivated by well-informed political convictions, and of a skilled and self-sacrificing health professional who was also assured, poised, and determined to provide herself with the delights of spring blossom and tailored clothing.

Professor Paul Preston and his UK colleagues encouraged and supported me to make Dorothy Morris's letters available in edited form, and her relatives and friends were endlessly generous in supplementing the information they contained. Even so, the letters were found to omit much crucial information, and to have other deficiencies of content which required effort and further support to overcome. Many had been written during wartime and were subject to the routine ignominies of military censorship. Dorothy was a naturally expressive and emphatic writer, and even though she aimed to stay within official guidelines, she must have posed many dilemmas for the Republican censors. "I rather fear that several of my recent effusions mayn't have got out", she told her family shortly before leaving Spain. "I find it cramps my style considering the censors, kind though they usually are! I feel not able to settle and describe things for you in more detail."[3]

Even more disappointing for present-day readers is the realisation that an unknown but undoubtedly sizeable portion of Dorothy's correspondence failed to reach its intended destination. Several of her letters refer to others posted earlier but for various reasons never delivered. In London at the height of the Blitz, she received, "the devastating news that my Christmas letters and parcels to you and to one or two old friends have all been lost en route to NZ. . . . When I think of how I'd pulled myself together and written a quite full account of my French adventures and journey as a refugee and my small doings in England etc. I could weep. I've no copy either. I'll try to do it all again tho' I have so little time these days".[4] Seventy-odd years later, I could weep as well at the irreplaceable loss of this 'full account' of the adventures and travels of a refugee aid worker in German-occupied France.

While Dorothy was running a hospital in southern Spain during the civil war itself, her outbound letters were often given to colleagues and visitors leaving the country, for posting outside Spain's borders. "Posting them in the ordinary way is generally all right ultimately though we know they have sometimes hazardous trips and then of course they have to wait a while to be censored."[5] Inward mail deliveries were equally haphazard and many of the letters sent to her relied on hand-delivery by sympathetic visitors from London. "We know that we don't get all [the letters] that we should, here," she wrote. "The wonder is, considering conditions, that we get the number we do. We are duly grateful for them but sometimes sigh for the piles of lost ones . . . It will be like the grave giving up its dead if I ever get all the accumulation that must be somewhere".[6]

A further swathe of Dorothy's letters to her family was destroyed, regretfully but deliberately, after her death by her sister Ruth, who eventually found herself unable to store the entire surviving correspondence for lack of space.[7]

Repairing these unfortunate gaps in the biographical record of a widely travelled woman who spent almost her entire working life outside New Zealand required concerted research in the archives of at least eight European countries and the US. All of that work, however, was carried out without me leaving my office in an attic room of my house in Wellington, New Zealand. I am grateful to the specialist staff within those archives for their expert, patient and willing efforts on this project. Numerous other non-professional researchers provided much further vital information to a total stranger, without any expectation of reward. This book could not have been written without their remarkably generous contributions.

With the distinguished exception of journalist Geoffrey Cox's riveting eyewitness account of the battle of Madrid, this book is the first full-length account of a New Zealander's participation in the Spanish Civil War.[8] It therefore adds to the body of information on the foreign volunteers in that conflict, and more specifically, provides a participant's report on elements of the Spanish Republic's wartime medical and aid services, now widely agreed to have influenced the Allies' provision of those services during and after the Second World War. Dorothy herself was in no doubt that the experiences she painfully acquired as a battlefield nurse, children's hospital director and emergency aid supervisor during the civil war gave her the practical and theoretical foundation for a later career in Britain's wartime welfare service and with the United Nations Relief and Rehabilitation Administration (UNRRA).

The letters on which this book is based were not, however, written in calm retrospect but usually dashed off or typed in the heat of the events they describe. Their primary purpose was simply to inform and reassure Dorothy's closeknit and affectionate family of her wellbeing in the midst of world-shaking experiences. Even though her episodic account of those experiences was not shaped with an eye for posterity, it nevertheless contains historically valuable insights, thanks largely to Dorothy's perceptive, intellectually independent and forthright view of the political turmoil surrounding her.

She also seems to have occasionally written from Spain with the intention of reaching a readership beyond her own family, in order to influence the public impression of the civil war created by the timorous and parochial New Zealand press. Two substantial feature articles describing her arrival in Spain, the establishment of emergency hospitals and the tactics of the contesting military forces appeared in her country's leading newspapers during 1937. At that time no New Zealand newspapers had correspondents reporting directly from Spain, and their civil war coverage was either reprinted from British newspapers or provided by international news agencies. Dorothy's vivid and urgent front-line dispatches provided a refreshing counterpart to those detached and irresolute reports. The two conservative mass-circulation dailies which accepted her non-professional contributions are likely to have done so purely on the basis of their news value and readability. The stories appeared along-side other war news from impeccably objective sources, but with the added appeal of a local connection and the authority of direct experi-ence.

It seems likely that Dorothy wrote these articles as letters to her family, but with instructions to forward them to the newspapers in the hope of winning greater public support for the Republican posi-tion. Her model and inspiration for this practice was Sir George Young, the improbable British aristocrat who organised and person-ally led the emergency medical service which first employed Dorothy in Spain. Sir George had earlier worked as a journalist and diplomat, and he was fully aware of the importance of public opinion, fundraising tactics and the role of the media to the effectiveness of his hastily assembled medical aid team. He wrote a number of on-the-spot articles for the British press on the work of his mobile field hospitals, and Dorothy seems to have followed his example in addressing her compatriots.

The image of Dorothy Aroha Morris which emerges from her surviving letters is of an attractive yet contradictory character. She was a gifted and outstandingly dedicated nurse, sternly upholding the high standards imparted during her New Zealand training, yet also a warm-hearted internationalist willing to adapt to local condi-tions and customs, even in the face of opposition from fellow foreign volunteers. For much of her wartime career her altruism was organ-ised through two admirably inclusive and idealistic institutions – the Quakers and the UNRRA, a precursor of the UN itself. She thought highly of both these employing bodies, but always from the perspec-tive of an outsider, and with a wry, clear-eyed recognition of the obstacles to practising humanitarianism under the burdens of large-scale bureaucracy and imperfect human nature.

One constant and lifelong motivating force was Dorothy's non-aligned democratic socialism, acquired as a trainee nurse in

Christchurch and seemingly reinforced by all her later experiences elsewhere. Writing from southern France in late 1939, on the brink of a Nazi invasion, her leftwing sympathies were applied just as actively to analysing her distant and comfortable homeland as to her immediate surroundings. A redistributive Labour government had been re-elected in New Zealand for a second term, and Dorothy's well-meaning but more conventional parents had evidently expressed anxieties about its more daring policies. She poured scorn from afar on their ambivalence:

> It seems to me that you are all suffering from the temporary inconvenience of eggs being broken to make the omelet . . . As the World goes today, you have only one choice – either the omelet made at the cost of temporary discomfort . . . or the starvation of Fascism. I know what I'm talking about . . . I nursed the rich in England for long enough to find out something of what they are up to . . . which is why I am here now. I often wish I could send some of my Catalans or Spanish to leaven the NZ stock a bit. It seems in retrospect too intolerably soggy and dull to survive.[9]

These are not the musings of a dilettante safely insulated from the real-world consequences of her political philosophy. In London two years later, under daily threat of a devastating air attack, Dorothy's observations of wartime British society led her to similar conclusions:

> The struggle behind the lines at this moment is this, put simply – Who, when the war is ended, shall own the 'assets' of the Empire? The STATE, meaning I suppose everybody in one way or another, or a select small body of 'Big' industrialists, controlling a few huge combines to whom & which the rest of us will be ant-slaves. Here in England one can watch that fight going on every day, & sometimes it is very, very interesting.[10]

Dorothy continued to find British politics interesting after the war, even as its society developed in the direction she least liked, and she chose to remain living there until near the end of her long life. That decision places her in the expansive company of voluntary expatriates from New Zealand who distinguished themselves on the other side of the world. Although never noted for humility, she insisted that her achievements as a nurse and refugee worker were merely a small part of a much greater collective effort, and not worthy of individual merit, and she forbade the publication of a biography in her lifetime.

Almost 20 years after Dorothy's death, her acts of organised altruism can be recognised as uniquely and internationally significant. At the time of writing, emergency medical response teams from many countries, including New Zealand, are assembling in equatorial Africa to confront the threat of the Ebola virus. The members of those teams demonstrate that the organised altruism of dedicated medical professionals, prepared to place themselves in harm's way on behalf of the most vulnerable sections of the world's population, remains profoundly important and, to this onlooker, wholly admirable.

In her own way and her own era, Dorothy Morris played a similar part at the centre of international crises. The vivid, unsentimental manner in which she describes her actions and motives ensures their continuing relevance.

Chapter I
The Morris Family Yacht

May is a foreboding month in the New Zealand city of Christchurch. Autumn turns towards winter, knifing nor' west winds sweep down the streets from distant snowfields, and the sky begins to darken from late afternoon. In 1932 the advent of May brought more than its usual discomforts to the city. The economic depression that had turned millions out of work worldwide had reached its most unsparing stage in New Zealand. Of the hundreds of people who thronged Cathedral Square, Christchurch's geographic centre and social hub, a great many showed the pinched features, shabby and inadequate clothing and subdued manner of the long-term unemployed.

The Square, a broad, paved concourse over two hundred yards wide, was dominated by its handsome cathedral, built sixty years earlier to announce the Anglican faith and optimistic expectations of the city's leading settler families. Christchurch's major streets all fed into the Square and it was the natural site for meetings and public gatherings. In particular, it was the main junction for the city's network of tram routes. At any time a dozen or more clanging electric trams, with double poles swaying overhead, nosed in and out through the crowds.

By mid-afternoon on Friday the sixth of May, four or five thousand people filled the Square, many more than usual for that time of day. Their extra numbers, and turbulent mood, were explained by the uniformed policeman and three or four tin-hatted 'special constables' – untrained volunteer law-enforcers – who leaned from the running board of every tram. Some days earlier the tramway workers' union had reached an impasse with its members' sole employer, the Tramways Board, which proposed to cut either their hours or their workforce. The union opposed both options, and the Board responded by sacking twelve of its members. With the city's rate of unemployment at its highest ever, the 'trammies' would ordinarily have been forced to accept such an action without complaint. However, the twelve included one man with more than seven years of exemplary service, the union's popular and charismatic president Jock Mathison. For his members, this sacking represented unjust victimisation for their temerity in negotiating over the cutbacks, and they promptly voted to strike until the men were reinstated. The Board stood firm and the city's trams, a vital component of a community in which few could afford a car, were soon being driven by strikebreakers, accompanied by a party of regular and 'special' police to guard against violence or sabotage.

At about three o'clock that Friday afternoon the striking tram-workers marched in formation the few blocks from Trades Hall to Cathedral Square. Many of them were ex-servicemen, and the body of 200 had no difficulty keeping in step as they swung into the Square four abreast. The crowd already gathered there broke into a chorus of the *Red Flag* to show their support, and followed it up with marching songs from the Great War.

Not everyone joined in the cheers and singing. The strike supporters, who included other unionists, rural relief workers and the unemployed, were surrounded by onlookers and shoppers, housewives and schoolboys, and they were closely watched by a small contingent of uneasy policemen. Trams came and went, and the booing and hooting grew louder, especially at the sight of the 'specials'. A small radical element among the protestors ran alongside the trams, hurling insults at the 'scab' crews and their passengers as they dismounted.

The police tightened their grip on their batons as they struggled to keep the crowds clear of the tram tracks. They were hugely outnumbered, and had no hope of reinforcements while their colleagues were assigned to guarding suburban routes for the evening rush hour. Suddenly a rock flew from the crowd, thumping off the side of a moving tram. Police rushed to make an arrest but the crowd closed ranks in front of the culprit, and he disappeared before the officers could reach him.

It was a leaderless protest, surging back and forth with no defined goal, a "ballet of the headless mob", in the words of the historian of these events.[1] As the afternoon wore on the mood in the Square, wrote one reporter, was "gradually growing more ominous in tone".[2] By four o'clock, with tempers fraying on both sides, a new tactic emerged as a group of women suddenly sat down in the path of a temporarily stalled tram. Police formed a 'flying-V' wedge formation, broke through a crowd of onlookers and arrested several of the women, then others who came to their aid. The detainees were hustled towards a corner of the Square where a row of taxis was parked, ready to convey them to police cells.

An agitated crowd surrounded the vehicles, demanding the release of the prisoners. Their shouts grew deafening and the police maintained tight ranks, with inspectors ordering their men to lash out at any sign of violence. The instant the last of the cabs was packed with handcuffed protestors, their white-faced drivers were ordered to head for the police station with all doors locked. One car, nudging though the dense and angry crowd, struck an ill-clad man a glancing blow from its bonnet and knocked him to the ground. The crowd gave a roar and surged towards the vehicle. A police inspector barked a command, his men raised their batons, and began to bring them down indiscriminately on heads and shoulders. Bodies fell to the paving stones, women screamed, bystanders fled for safety.

Among the hundreds of passersby who witnessed this ugly conclusion to the tramworkers' protest was a slim, dark-haired nurse in her late 20s. She worked at a nearby hospital, and may have been starting or finishing her shift as she passed through the Square that evening. The sight of underfed men and women being "severely handled by police", her friends learned late in her life, "coupled with her sympathy for the plight of workers on poor wages, turned her towards a more radical political view."[3]

Dorothy Morris was born several hundred miles south of Christchurch in the very centre of the lower South Island, in a small goldmining settlement named for the bigoted 17th-century Puritan Oliver Cromwell. In the 1860s gold was discovered in this region's fast-flowing, snow-fed rivers, and miners converged on it from across the world, including several hundred hardy and determined Chinese. A makeshift town soon appeared in an area with no prior history of permanent settlement.

The landscape surrounding Cromwell is quite unlike the conventional tourist impression of New Zealand. The terrain is harsh, nearly treeless and largely infertile, hemmed in by mountains and with a climate that veers between seasonal extremes. When, many years later, Dorothy arrived in the high sierra to the west of Madrid, she may well have experienced an eerie sense of recognition. Cromwell's first permanent residents were attracted there only by its mineral prospects, and they endured its hardships in the hope of earning enough to leave.

The town's fortunes fluctuated, as goldrush settlements tend to do, but as the 20th century began large sums were made by using floating steam-powered dredges which scooped up bucketsful of silt and gravel from the riverbeds and extracted their precious metal with the equipment they carried on board. Among the more than 100 dredges in operation was the optimistically named *Lucky Lady*, whose dredgemaster, or first mate, was a well-spoken engineer of English descent named Geoffrey Morris. Photographs of his vessel show a cramped deck dominated by crude machinery and massive pulleys hauling looms of exposed wire cable. Keeping this equipment in working order called for mechanical expertise in tiring and sometimes dangerous conditions. A competent engineer like Morris was a crucial and much respected member of the dredge's crew.

Geoffrey Morris was the son of a Sussex doctor who had migrated to New Zealand after serving in the Crimean War. He evidently had no desire to follow his father's profession and at a very young age went to sea, travelling around the world on steamships as an engineer. When that life lost its appeal he came ashore and found work on the Cromwell dredges.[4]

The tall, bearded and commanding ex-seaman married a local girl, Rebecca Pretsch, the daughter of an immigrant from Silesia, on Germany's Swiss border. Karl Pretsch was a skilled painter and decorator who had worked on palaces in Russia until a disagreement with an employer drove him to migrate as far away as possible. He eventually served as one of Cromwell's early mayors, and his surname remains well known throughout the central Otago region.[5]

In 1904 Dorothy became the couple's first child. The Maori-language middle name they chose for her, Aroha, suggests that the Morrises were an unusually progressive and tolerant family for their time. Maori people had never been numerous in the Cromwell region, and became rarer still after the big gold dredges attracted fortune-seekers from across the world. However, Geoffrey had at least one close friend from the small local Maori community, and he and his wife eventually chose Maori middle names for three of their children.[6] Their firstborn was named with one of the most potent and evocative words in the Maori language. 'Aroha' means love, or compassion – qualities that their daughter would come to demonstrate in ways her parents can never have imagined.

When his daughter was aged four, Geoffrey Morris received an exceptional opportunity to better his circumstances and advance his social position. He accepted the job of superintendent engineer for the port of Lyttelton, where he and Rebecca would eventually raise four more children, and where they would spend the rest of their lives.

Like Cromwell, Lyttelton was a small settlement with a population of only a few thousand, and it proved a delightful place for the Morris children to grow up. The port lies in a deeply indented sound to the south of the city of Christchurch. Lacking navigable harbours of its own, Christchurch was entirely reliant on Lyttelton for its shipping access, although the Port Hills, a steep range lying between the city and the harbour, posed a formidable obstacle. The problem was overcome in the 1860s by a rail tunnel through the hills, which emerged on the Lyttelton side to reveal a natural amphitheatre sloping down to the water's edge. Almost every house on the little town's steep streets could boast a view of the forested sound and the profusion of wharves, jetties, cranes and warehouses strung along the inner harbour.

As a man of newly steady means and a prominent position in Lyttelton society, Geoffrey Morris bought a large house to the west of the main harbour. He named it Flackley Ash, after the family home of his English forebears. (The original house of that name, near the East Sussex coast, is now a rural hotel and restaurant.) The new Flackley Ash stood on a headland above sheltered Magazine Bay, the town's most popular swimming beach and the site, from 1906, of its municipal bathing sheds. Soon after their arrival the first of Dorothy's brothers was born, and named after his father. Two more sons and a final daughter were eventually added to the family.

Especially in their early years in Lyttelton, the Morris family regularly returned to Cromwell for holidays with their relatives, a journey taking a full day by train and bullock cart. In this way Dorothy acquired a permanent love of the barren and austerely beautiful Central Otago landscape. As a young girl, however, she also received a painful and lasting lesson there on the status of her sex. Her father had formed a close friendship with a leading figure in Cromwell's close-knit community of Chinese miners, a massive man named Ah Foo. He came from the far north of his country, near Mongolia, and towered over his slender southern kinsmen. He claimed that he was the son of a minor noble, and that he had murdered his cousin during a lover's quarrel and fled from China to escape retribution.

In the days before Dorothy and her parents had left Cromwell, Ah Foo doted on his good friend's baby daughter, presenting her with tiny gifts and carrying her on his well-padded shoulders. Several years later, after the move to Lyttelton and the birth of Dorothy's first brother, the family made a return visit. Dorothy was walking through Cromwell's main street beside her aunt Kitty, who was pushing baby Geoff in a pram, when the familiar form of Ah Foo loomed up. Dorothy greeted him with a child's delighted recognition. He ignored her completely, bent over the pram to salute the first male Morris offspring, and pinned a small enamel brooch onto his smock. Both girl and aunt felt greatly irate at being passed over for an infant, and the brooch was flung into the Kawerau River.[7] Despite her many later attainments, Dorothy retained the galling memory of this incident throughout her life.

The decade after the Morris family's arrival in Lyttelton was the most commercially vigorous and exciting in the history of the port. The entire country enjoyed mounting prosperity in the early 1900s, and the tonnage of shipping entering Lyttelton in the years before World War One was not surpassed until the next boom period of the 1950s. Every year from 1906 a million pounds' worth of wool from the great sheep stations of Canterbury and Otago passed over the docks. An ever-increasing volume of fuel oil flowed in the opposite direction to feed a booming market for motor vehicles. Nearly all of these cargoes were carried by steamships, since the great age of the three- and four-masted trading barques had recently ended. However, Lyttelton continued to host fleets of smaller sailing vessels carrying freight and passengers between other ports around the country. This period also saw the start of a regular passenger ferry service between New Zealand's two main islands, and daily steamer services to the coastal communities surrounding Christchurch.

The port's most distinguished regular arrivals were the Shaw Savill luxury liners *Athenic, Corinthic* and *Ionic* which, from 1905, paid four to six visits every year, staying for several days each time. Lyttelton throbbed with activity on those occasions. The dockers worked the wharves until midnight, loading goods and supplies onto carts hauled to and from the warehouses by huge and obedient horses. While their crews packed the waterfront pubs, the ships' officers spent festive evenings as guests of local families, including the hospitable household of the newly appointed superintendent engineer. The small, salty and self-contained town was filled with music, strangers, coloured lights and activity whenever a ship was in, and throughout Dorothy's schooldays a ship was in every fortnight or so.

The only major and ongoing constraint to expanding the port's operations was the limited depth of water in the channel running out to the open sea. As ocean-going steamers grew ever larger and deeper of draft, fewer of them were able to reach the Lyttelton docks due to the constant silting-up of the seabed. From the start of the new century the Harbour Board employed its own steam dredge in the hope of overcoming the problem, and Geoffrey Morris was engaged to supervise this and the Board's other steam-driven equipment. A bigger dredge arrived six years after his appointment, and two years later this was also superseded by a purpose-built steam-dredge, the most advanced in Australasia. It remained in constant daily use on the harbour for the next half-century.

This long, low and hardworking vessel, with its decks strewn with heavy equipment and its twin funnels magnificently snorting steam, became one of Lyttelton's most familiar and affectionately regarded sights. She was named the *Canterbury*, after the province surrounding both the port and the city of Christchurch that it served, and spent her days chugging between the harbour entrance and the wharves, scooping up the heavy clay spoil and hauling it back to dump at sites selected to create precious flat land for new port facilities. She could also be enlisted for ceremonial and other duties. In 1914 she was strung with bunting to farewell departing troops, and three years later her powerful pumps were called upon to put out a serious fire on board a naval vessel. The unlovely but efficient *Canterbury* was Geoffrey Morris's pride and joy. The history of the Harbour Board records that, "He and his family took a personal pride in her appearance, keeping her clean and her brasswork polished, so that she became known, humorously, as 'the Morris family yacht'".[8]

A 1912 photograph of senior Harbour Board staff indicates the social distance Geoff Morris had travelled since his days eight years earlier as a grimy engineer on board a Cromwell gold-dredge. To the left of Captain Thorpe the harbourmaster, he stands trim and erect in a suit and waistcoat, with his neatly trimmed beard and moustache evincing competence and kindliness. Unsurprisingly, he became a Lyttelton borough councillor some years later.[9]

Geoffrey Morris was also a formidable walker, and on weekends and holidays he would lead the whole family on long rambles across the Port Hills. The young Morrises also like to travel right around the harbour in their heavy and capacious wooden rowboat.[10] They joined enthusiastically in the harbour's pre-war social life. On public holidays, parties of picnickers from throughout the Canterbury region arrived to take hired launches to secluded bays that at that time had no other access. The annual New Year's Day regatta filled the inner harbour with sails, flags and steam-whistles while crowds descended on the hotels and boarding houses, and prominent homes, including Flackley Ash, were filled with houseguests.

The big, shipshape, wooden house was distinguished from its neighbours by a 40-foot flagpole on the lawn. It had a flourishing garden which Geoffrey senior spent much of his weekends digging with a long-handled shovel, and which supplied his household with flowers and fresh vegetables year-round. The children kept chickens and rabbits, which also found their way into the copious meals cooked by their mother on a basic coal stove and gas ring. The house, like all others in Lyttelton, had no electricity until well after the First World War, and was lit with candles and kerosene lamps. Yet it was warm, welcoming and comfortable, and often filled with the music of a wind-up gramophone.[11]

The most notable visitors in this era were the members of the several Antarctic expeditions led by Robert Scott and Ernest Shackleton, who chose Lyttelton as their point of departure. The two men made a joint expedition to the ice in 1901–4 and Shackleton headed two later voyages, while Scott's ill-fated final expedition departed in 1910. These were intensely exciting and romantic adventures, equivalent to the voyages of Drake and Raleigh in the past, or to lunar excursions in more recent times. Robert Scott, in particular, became a great favourite of Lyttelton society during the several weeks he and the crew of his ship *Terra Nova* spent preparing for their departure in the spring of 1910.

By all accounts a very charming man, Scott, after his day's work among huskies, Siberian ponies, motorised sledges and tons of supplies, was welcome at the homes of all the town's leading citizens. His officers and men, including second-in-command Lt. Evans, Dr Edward Wilson and Lts Bowers and Oates, also received invitations to a round of private and municipal banquets, receptions, concerts, dinners and balls.

On 26 November the overloaded *Terra Nova* was at last ready to depart for the ice, and lay at anchor in the harbour mouth. Captain Scott was ferried out to his ship in the Harbour Board's pilot boat, accompanied by his wife of two years, who had come to farewell him. Also on the boat that day was the six-year-old daughter of the port's superintendent engineer. "Lady Scott wore a big black hat . . . and because I was so short I could see under the hat and the tears were trickling from her eyes. I was the only one in the whole wide world to see and know."[12] The *Terra Nova* discharged Scott and his team, and some months later she was welcomed back to Lyttelton with a chorus of "shrieks and screams from every horn, whistle and siren in port".[13] It was not for almost another year that the town, and the rest of the world, received the devastating news that Scott, Bowers, Evans and Oates had all perished in their attempt to reach the pole.

Similarly dramatic events later in 1913 would have had less impact on a young schoolgirl, but they foreshadowed some of the concerns that would later direct Dorothy's life. Lyttelton's dock workers, the 'lumpers' who manhandled cargoes to and from the ships' holds, were staunch unionists and when a strike broke out on the Wellington wharves and quickly spread to every major port and mine in the country, they did not hesitate to support it. The sight of the nation's wharves suddenly inactive and under the control of their workforce provoked profound political trauma in a country heavily dependent on the export of its primary produce.

In Lyttelton itself the dispute was conducted with relative decorum. The wharfies drew up a roster and picketed the wharves day and night to ensure that nothing was loaded or unloaded without their consent. Yet they gave that consent willingly, and filled the blackened wicker baskets themselves, when the public hospitals grew short of coal for their boilers, so that the water taps threatened to run cold. To discourage violent disagreements between supporters and opponents of the strike, the strike committee went to each of the port's pubs in turn and instructed their licensees to close their doors for the duration of the dispute.

The government, however, preferred sterner measures. In the larger port cities to the north, rioting, gunfire and sabotage had broken out, and no chances were taken that Lyttelton might resort to the same tactics. A British naval vessel steamed up the harbour and trained its big guns on the town, and its armed ratings patrolled the wharves with fixed bayonets and a machine gun. Meanwhile strike-breakers were being recruited, and to ensure their safety farmers' sons from the rural hinterland were enrolled as mounted 'special consta-bles'. Seven hundred of these eager volunteers were assembled in Christchurch and armed with makeshift batons fashioned from pick handles. Very early one morning they rode out of the city and over the Port Hills, and in three separate columns clattered down the streets of the sleeping port to the wharves. The greatly outnumbered pickets were caught unawares and offered no resistance, and soon the cranes and carts were again hard at work, this time at the hands of scab labour.

It was an ignominious defeat for the radical unions nationally, but in Lyttelton at least the strike had an intriguing after-effect. Just a fortnight after the mounted men's early-morning coup, a by-election was held for the local parliamentary seat. It was won by a dapper young socialist named James McCombs, who represented the newly formed Social Democratic Party, an immediate forerunner of the NZ Labour Party, and had been a firm, though judicious, supporter of the strike. The 'special constables', still on duty at the port, tried to prevent his victory speech but McCombs went on to represent Lyttelton until his death 20 years later. His widow Elizabeth, of equally socialist persuasion, then became the town's next MP.

The young Dorothy Morris may not have realised it, but her

parents were surely aware that they lived in a politically progressive community. By 1914 both Christchurch and Lyttelton were Social Democratic Party strongholds, and the party's opposition to compulsory military service, and later to conscription, tempered the patriotic fervor that swept the country once war was declared.[14] The port was placed on a war footing, and many of its ships were requisitioned for military service, but an undercurrent of radical opposition was always present. The tiny and uninhabited Ripa Island, lying opposite the port on the far side of the channel, became a defensive fortification equipped with artillery and used for gunnery practice. Yet it was also a detention centre for the dozens of young men who refused to submit to compulsory military service and, it was rumoured, were subjected by their guards to great brutality.

Dorothy's formal education had begun some years earlier, and unpromisingly, at a local convent school. She left abruptly and unhappily one day when the nuns insisted that her father, an unbeliever, would go to hell. Lyttelton's other primary school took care of her education until she entered high school, which entailed a long and multifarious daily return journey. Her morning began with a mile-long walk to the railway station, a half-hour train journey that included the pitch-black tunnel through the Port Hills, a tram to Cathedral Square and a final walk to the Girls High School. Again, her initial choice of school proved an unfortunate one, as she apparently felt unable to fit in with the large classes of city girls. Thereafter she attended a small and exclusive girls' school with the mellifluous Maori name of Rangi Ruru, founded in the 1880s by a large family named Gibson. Most of the eight Gibson daughters became teachers at the school and one of them, Helen Gibson, served as its principal for almost 50 years, including the duration of Dorothy's enrolment there. The cost of an education at Rangi Ruru was beyond the means of a Harbour Board engineer, but one of Dorothy's aunts offered to pay the fees.

Dorothy entered Rangi Ruru in 1917, when its roll numbered only about a hundred girls.[15] Its curriculum and customs were modelled on the grand English public schools, and its class sizes, equipment and out-of-school activities were all superior to those the state education system could afford to provide. Rangi Ruru students received a thorough academic grounding, and Dorothy became a naturally fluent and expressive writer. In her final year she was among the prizewinners in a nationwide essay competition.[16] She especially loved history and English, and gained a basic knowledge of French that she would later appreciate and develop. Academic subjects were supplemented with music, drawing and dancing, and with compulsory classes in cooking and hand sewing. Games were important, especially hockey in the winter months and swimming in summer, an activity at which Dorothy, who lived above a popular swimming beach, unsurprisingly excelled.

Rangi Ruru girls were taught to prepare themselves for an elite station in life. Their personal conduct was strictly regulated and no girl was permitted beyond the school gates unless wearing gloves and a hat – white or cream in summer and navy blue in winter. Despite an inherent independence of spirit, Dorothy appears to have thrived at this school. She formed lifelong friendships with several fellow pupils and by 1920 became a prefect, entitled to wear on her tie a silver badge bearing the school's entwined initials. School photos show a tall, slim and graceful girl with glossy dark hair, olive colouring and a strikingly purposeful and confident bearing.

That confidence and purpose can be ascribed to her fortunate blend of personal and social influences – an upbringing as the responsible eldest child of a close-knit and highly regarded family, within a hard-working waterfront community where class distinctions were permeable and where diligence and competence conferred high status. Dorothy had also been born in a country where women gained the vote ahead of the rest of the world, and was raised and educated among impressively able female relatives, teachers and other exemplars, some of whom appeared happy to live as single women.

Predictably, for a capable student with professional aspirations, she moved on to university after leaving school. Christchurch's only university was then officially known as the Canterbury College of the University of New Zealand. Dorothy's time there was undistinguished. Her academic record was patchy, and she left after her second year with papers in English and education but without completing any qualifications. This uncharacteristically lacklustre performance was probably due to the lack of any clear goal or purpose for her higher education.

It must have sparked heated discussions around the Flackley Ash dining table when Dorothy announced her intention to abandon university studies and instead enter Christchurch Hospital's nursing school. Nursing was then regarded as a questionable occupation for a well-educated girl from an upwardly mobile family. While New Zealand nurses had made considerable progress in elevating the status of their work from a calling to a medical profession, a 19th-century odour of bedpans and low-paid drudgery still clung to it.

The wider Morris family could claim a tradition of medical practice, and this may have helped to influence Dorothy's choice of career. Her paternal grandfather had been a well-respected rural GP, and two of her aunts ran a private nursing home. Yet their experiences were not all of the kind to allay parental fears. One of those aunts had nursed in North Africa during the First World War, and been so badly injured there by a shell-shocked patient that she was sent to a hospital in England to recover.

Geoffrey Morris, in particular, probably hoped to see his firstborn child enter a more prestigious occupation, but she had made up her mind and eventually prevailed. The referees for her application to enter nursing school were her much-respected family physician, Dr Upham, and Mina Holderness, the principal of a small private girls' school where she had taught since she gave up university. The application was accepted, and she was enrolled in Christchurch Hospital's nursing school as a 'probationer' in late 1926. At age 22, she was somewhat older and certainly better educated than most of the intake.

During their statutory three-month probation period, nurses were known as 'pinks' for the colour of their uniform. After an intensive initiation, the 'pinks' sat a comprehensive exam designed to test their suitability for nursing. Dorothy's results enabled her to progress to the grey uniform of a 'pupil trainee'.[17] She entered upon her three-year training at a particularly opportune time and place. Christchurch Hospital was well equipped and picturesquely sited alongside the Avon, the willow-lined stream that winds through the centre of this famously Anglophile city. More significantly, it was the first hospital in the country to create a Preliminary Training School for its nurses.

In the previous century, and despite the best efforts of reformers such as Florence Nightingale, nursing was typically regarded throughout the English-speaking world as a job requiring little more expertise than a housemaid's. In 1878, a decade after it opened,

Christchurch Hospital expected of its nurses only that they be literate, "treat the patients with kindness, and see that all patients are in bed after the doors are locked, and put the gas down after retiring for the night."[18] Nurses were then entitled to a daily pint of beer, although whether this was for the betterment of their health or for smoother labour relations is not clear.[19]

In 1891, however, in advance of any other hospital in the country, Christchurch Hospital established an in-house training school for its nurses, equipped with a model ward. A purpose-built nurses' home opened in 1895. All student nurses were required to live in this two-storeyed brick building for the duration of their training. As well as practical experience, they were given regular lectures by the resident surgeon and matron. On completion of their training, those who achieved a satisfactory standard were issued with a certificate of competence by the Hospital Board, New Zealand's first formal nursing qualification.[20]

The Nurses Registration Act of 1901 made the training and certi-fication system developed in Christchurch mandatory throughout the country, and established the world's second (after South Africa's) nationwide system of registration for nurses. Nurses registered under the Act were required to be aged at least 22, and to have had an adequate combination of classroom teaching, professional training and varied practical experience. This system was not without critics, both from within and beyond the profession. Since nursing training remained firmly based within specific hospitals rather than an educa-tional institution, it more nearly resembled an apprenticeship scheme than a fully professional field of study. Senior nurses, familiar with the earlier and less formal training, resented the greater degree of control now exercised over the all-female nursing workforce by doctors, at that time still an overwhelmingly male profession.

Despite these lingering anxieties, New Zealand's pioneering system produced nurses whose capabilities at least matched, and generally exceeded, those of colleagues in other countries. Some years later Dorothy described her nursing school training to a vastly expe-rienced English aid worker, who was impressed by its emphasis on medical knowledge over menial toil. "To train as a nurse in her country had not been the heavy weather that it is in ours . . . This did not mean that her standards were lower".[21]

The workload was undoubtedly heavy, however, by comparison with the present day. In the 1920s it was not uncommon for trainee nurses to work a year without a day off.[22] One who trained at Wellington Hospital described the experience as, "Very much along military lines. The ward sister was the equivalent of the sergeant-major. There was a great tradition of Florence Nightingale, of giving service and dedication and all that sort of thing. We were almost brainwashed."[23]

Christchurch's longer-established nursing school gave its students rather more latitude and responsibility that those in other centres. Dorothy's English colleague gained the impression that the school was, "like a college, where there was plenty of time off for surf bathing, tennis and social life."[24] In her first year of study a new school building opened, where she was provided with board, a uniform and laundry service as well as her tuition. These services were all supplied free – indeed, as a member of the nursing staff she received a weekly wage, starting at a meagre 12 shillings a week, but increasing yearly.

In this period, before the use of effective antibiotic drugs, one of the most crucial nursing roles was to ensure cleanliness and prevent infection, especially when assisting surgery. Training emphasized practical skills more than theoretical knowledge, and students were schooled in rigidly enforced hygiene practices, which later proved life-saving when Dorothy worked at improvised operating tables under primitive conditions that would have horrified her instructors. She and fellow trainees were given classes in preparing invalid foods, instructed to vigilantly monitor patients after treatment, and developed skills to manage, without medication, those who were restless or sleepless.[25]

As Dorothy became accustomed to the routines and expectations of her new role, she would have noticed that one facet of the hospital's work was becoming ever more demanding. The North Canterbury Hospital Board, which administered Christchurch Hospital and the various smaller hospitals in the region, had statutory responsibility for care of the "ill and destitute". These included the unemployed, deserted families and those incapable of earning their keep due to sickness or old age. The hospital received a state subsidy towards the cost of providing charitable aid to these distressed members of its community. In the prosperous years of the early 1920s, their numbers were relatively small and the wider community could comfortably accommodate the cost of their care. By the time Dorothy's training began, however, economic depression was making its presence felt across the Canterbury district, and the numbers of "ill and destitute" became both more numerous and more dependent on hospital aid.

During each year of Dorothy's training, the numbers receiving charitable aid increased, especially during the winter months when no casual farm labour was available. This aid was distributed on the frigid principle that individual applicants were assumed to be at fault for failing to provide for themselves. There was no automatic state payment for those out of work, and able-bodied male applicants were required to labour on relief schemes designed to absorb their numbers. Hospital Board doctors examined the men to determine their capability to carry out relief work, and many applicants concealed illness, injury or incapacity in order to be passed as fit, since relief work paid better than charity and provided a degree of companionship.

Christchurch's make-work schemes were more generous than those in other centres, since the city was the first in New Zealand to elect a Labour-dominated city council.[26] The council opposed the belt-tightening policies of the ruling conservative government and instead borrowed money to maintain its services and pay relief workers standard wages. On her train journeys to the family home in Lyttelton, Dorothy could now see large gangs of men labouring to widen the bridle track over the Port Hills to form a route suitable for motor vehicles. Barrows and hand tools were favored over earth-moving machinery.

A key figure in city administration during this fraught period was Elizabeth McCombs, the wife of Lyttelton's long-serving MP. She and her husband James were founding members of the Labour Party's national executive, and from 1921 Elizabeth also held a seat on the Canterbury Hospital Board, Dorothy's employing body.[27] The well-educated and confident Mrs McCombs, with close links to the temperance and Christian Socialist movements, was the most prominent female Labourite in a city with a strong tradition of well-to-do lady reformers, who made use of their status to relieve the circumstances of more needy women.

For those who could not qualify for relief work, the main source of unemployment relief was the quaintly named Benevolent Committee of the Hospital Board, which provided weekly vouchers for food and rent. By the late 1920s the demand for these was so great that the Board's offices faced serious overcrowding each Thursday. "Every inch of room was taken up and the office staff had to push through the throng to shepherd the applicants into the committee room or to the ration room . . . Many of the people were almost at the end of their tether and the long wait in a close atmosphere was obviously telling on their nerves."[28] The unemployed found it deeply humiliating to advertise their poverty by standing in ever-lengthening queues for their weekly handout, but it was a ritual they could no longer avoid. Some Christchurch families were found to be living on potatoes and food scraps, with boxes for furniture and sacking for bedding. Their children went barefoot throughout the winter. These circumstances added a variety of illnesses to the strains already borne by the long-term unemployed.

At the end of her three years of training, and after passing all of the hospital's own examinations, Dorothy qualified to sit the final state nursing exam. In 1929 she passed it with honours, and was then entitled to wear the five-pointed star medal of a New Zealand registered nurse. The 'Lady Superintendent' of the nurses' training school provided a note to her file advising prospective employers that, "Miss Morris was a capable and trustworthy nurse who will with further experience be very satisfactory either in private Hospital or public institution." The note added, with some prescience, that, "with added experience, she should prove capable in administrative work."[29]

For a year after her graduation Dorothy remained at the hospital where she had trained, worked in the women's surgical ward and the outpatients' department. She then resigned, probably with the aim of making a better income in the private health sector. Her friends were aware that she hoped to travel overseas, and the rate paid in small private hospitals reduced the time needed to realise this goal. She soon found work in the city's leading private surgical hospital and nursing home, the Limes Hospital in central Christchurch. This had a total of just 18 surgical beds, and six registered nurses were employed there under the direction of a matron, Mrs Williams.

Patients came to the Limes from "the city's elite families", and discretion was demanded of each of its staff.[30]

Outside the Limes' imposing entrance, the situation of the poorest continued to worsen. On one day in April 1931, over 600 people applied for relief at the Hospital Board offices.[31] A month later police were called to clear the crowd outside.[32] By 1932 over 10,000 people were applying to the mayor's relief depot each week. A maternity hospital noted an increase among its working class patients in "serious cases due to ill-nourishment on the part of mothers".[33] A large section of the unemployed had by this time reached the end of their resources, with their possessions and savings exhausted.[34] The mental stress of this predicament was acute, and men became so broken in health that their nerves gave way and they voluntarily admitted themselves to mental hospitals.[35]

This was the fraying state of the city's social fabric when the Christchurch Tramways Board announced in early 1932 that it would dismiss twelve of its employees, including the union president, and precipitated an unprecedented strike. The Tramways Board was composed almost entirely of conservative citizens from the business community, the one exception being the ubiquitous Elizabeth McCombs, the sole female board member and the only Labour Party representative. Hers was also the only dissenting voice when the board passed a vote to sack the twelve men.

In the 80 years since European settlement was established there, Christchurch had not faced a single conflict as great as the potential public unrest over the tramways strike. The land wars between Maori and settler in the previous century had convulsed other parts of the country but left the Canterbury region undisturbed. By the early 1930s, however, many of the unemployed had united under organisations led by hardened radicals such as Sidney Fournier, who hinted at plans for more militant forms of protest. "We are peaceful now," he told one meeting, "but we may not be in a few weeks' time."[36] Their numbers included veterans of World War One who had grown bitterly disillusioned about the fruits of their sacrifice. One was reported as saying, "We all heard that 'King and country' cry, and we humped our packs right through Egypt and France. Now it's all over, do we have to hump them through our own country? It's hard – damned hard!"[37]

Just weeks before the tramways strike was called, other New Zealand cities had seen protests by the unemployed erupt into mass violence. In Auckland a huge but peaceful demonstration rapidly became a riot after police batoned an unemployed leader to the ground during his speech. The dutiful, shuffling body of unemployed men was suddenly transformed into a gleeful mob that surged down the city's main shopping street, smashing plate glass and flinging the contents of window displays to the crowd. An Act was immediately rushed through Parliament to empower the government to declare a police state, and major centres quickly recruited volunteers to augment their regular police forces, as they had done during the waterfront disputes in 1913.

In Christchurch about one thousand of these 'specials' were enlisted and issued with steel army helmets and yard-long wooden batons. Most were professional men, office workers and shop assistants, and some patrolled the streets wearing bowties. The tram strike was their first opportunity to encounter outright public disorder. In the early morning of Friday the sixth of May, they had helped arrest 16 strikers at the central tram depot, who were hoping to prevent strikebreaking drivers from moving the ponderous vehicles out of the sheds. In Christchurch Square that afternoon the regular police kept a squad of 'specials' in reserve but out of sight. They were understandably wary of their inexperienced colleagues' ability to manage a large and fractious crowd whose motives may have ranged from simple curiosity, or support for the sacked unionists, through to an eagerness to take part in whatever looting might eventuate.

As it happened, it was the crowd's disparate and uncoordinated character, at least as much as skilful policing, which ensured that when violence suddenly broke out in the Square, it was contained and relatively minor. Yet for Dorothy, the sight of unarmed and undernourished people clubbed to the pavement by police batons was an unforgettable lesson in the exercise of power. "These years in the early 1930s with their unemployment, poverty and illness greatly affected her attitude to living and authority", wrote a close acquaintance late in her life.[38]

This mettlesome attitude was demonstrated, in this period, while Dorothy was on a country bus trip. She noticed a Maori man sitting beside the road ahead, waiting for a lift. His leg was wrapped in a bloodstained and filthy bandage, and he was evidently trying to reach medical help. The bus driver passed without stopping. On the return journey the injured man was still there, patiently waiting for transport. Again, the driver made no attempt to stop. According to family memories of this incident, Dorothy then rose to her considerable height and ordered the driver to pull up. "I would," the man protested feebly, "but I can't. There are no spare seats." Dorothy instantly offered to give up her own seat and walk, and this tactic succeeded in shaming the driver into collecting the unkempt-looking and needy passenger.[39]

Dorothy continued nursing the wealthy invalids of Christchurch for a further two years, until she achieved her aim of saving the cost of an overseas trip. Her New Zealand nursing file ends with a letter of recommendation from the former Lady Superintendent at Christchurch Hospital. "This is to recommend Miss Dorothy Morris to anyone requiring the services of a qualified and experienced general nurse. . . . She was a reliable, competent and trustworthy nurse whom I have no hesitation in recommending to anyone desiring her services . . . Miss Morris is leaving New Zealand. We would be grateful for any help extended to her during her sojourn abroad."[40] Within days of the date of that generous letter, the thirty-year-old nurse of radical temperament departed by ship for Europe. Her family cannot have guessed, as they waved her goodbye from the port where she had spent most of her childhood, that she would not return permanently for almost 50 years.

Chapter 2
Good Bombing Light

The original and legendarily well-appointed Selfridge's department store in London's West End is "about the size of Cathedral Square", Dorothy informed her mother in November 1935, employing a standard for comparison familiar to most New Zealanders. As her first Christmas in her new country approached, she clearly hoped to compensate for spending it so far away from her family by emphasising the advantages of her location. Selfridges was "all highly decorated for Xmas", she wrote, with "spruce trees with twinkling coloured lights all along and round it . . . Inside the size of the place and multitude of departments and goods is beyond my pen to describe. I wandered in to the provision department today. The hampers are wonderful beyond words – 10/- up to 10 guineas worth – and every kind of food in the world is there."[1]

Access to these delights was convenient, since Dorothy's address at that time was the Grosvenor Court Hotel, just around the corner from Oxford Street. Although quite unaffordable on a nurse's salary, the hotel was the home of her current patient, the managing director of a large furnishing firm. Along with many other foreign-trained nurses working in London, Dorothy had joined a so-called nursing co-operative, an agency which supplied trained nurses for private cases. New Zealand nurses generally found it easy to obtain jobs in this way, as their training was considered to produce better graduates than the English nursing schools.[2] The work was demanding – nurses were required to 'live in' with their patients and remain on duty 20 hours a day. Generally, however, their accommodation was luxurious.[3] Dorothy was "very comfortable in this hotel", she told her family. "My patient's a pleasant soul. I may be here 2 or 3 weeks yet but don't definitely know. I should think he will be away by Xmas."[4]

Nursing "members of the richer classes", as she later described them, was evidently a short-term arrangement for a nurse who was capable of appreciating the trappings of wealth (her patient had promised her handsome discounts on his firm's products), while remaining acutely aware of economic injustice.[5] In the same letter in which she exclaimed at the treasures to be found in Selfridge's, Dorothy noted the "real bombshell" that resulted from the recent general election in her own country. A Labour government had been elected there for the first time, on a platform of fundamental economic and social reforms including a universal free healthcare system. Conscious of her more conservative parents' somewhat ambivalent attitude to this unprecedented political bombshell, she confined her enthusiasm to noting that the New Zealand Labour Party's win had dominated the British press to an extent unusual for such a small and distant former colony. "The *Times* had a good deal to say – NZ had the 'second leading article' two days running – 1 before and 1 after [the election], and other papers have commented in their various ways, and agree that things must be very interesting to watch!"[6]

Dorothy was much less restrained when reporting political developments elsewhere in Europe, where fascist and other parties of the extreme right appeared to hold in contempt the League of Nations' prohibition on warfare between its members. In the month before her letter was written, Mussolini's Italy had launched a grotesquely unequal military strike on Abyssinia, employing tanks, bombers and poison gas. Both countries belonged to the League of Nations, yet the League appeared incapable of enforcing its authority to prevent the conflict, in part due to the wavering of key member countries such as the UK. Her host country's weak-kneed and apparently hypocritical stance infuriated Dorothy. "The news has been thick and fast lately," she wrote, "but tonight there are hints that [Mussolini] is losing ground and if only sanctions can be more firmly applied, he is definitely done for. It is typical of England, I'm afraid, that with all the talk and the lead she has given, none the less the Govt are still allowing the Anglo Persian Oil Co. to supply Italy with petrol in vast quantities. I don't wonder that no country is able to understand or trust England."[7]

These and other profoundly disturbing indications of a slide towards dictatorial government across Europe were, in the mid-1930s, subjects of nightly discussion among progressive Londoners.

They included members of the high-minded and women-only Lyceum Club in Piccadilly, such as Evelyn Isitt, the London correspondent for the liberal daily, the *Manchester Guardian*. This very tall, arresting and well-connected journalist, a lifelong advocate for women's rights, was a New Zealander who had lived in London for 25 years. By 1935 she held a regular salon at the Lyceum Club for fellow expatriates. Dorothy met her in this politically fraught period and was impressed by the older woman's example of holding an influential position in a male-dominated profession without abandoning her liberal sympathies or her regard for her country of birth.[8]

When Spain elected a popular front coalition in February 1936, this news, as with New Zealand's election, drew international attention. The narrow Republican victory ran counter to the rising tide of totalitarian rule in the region, and also promised to transform Spain's economy, one of the most impoverished and feudal in Europe. This optimism was shortlived. Less than six months after the historic election, in early July 1936, a group of high-ranking generals, supported by the Catholic Church, large landowners and the radical right, attempted to overthrow the new government through a military coup. The uprising was fiercely resisted, and sections of the military disobeyed the orders of their generals and remained loyal to the government. After several weeks of chaotic street fighting, and as elements of the population chose, or were compelled, to support one side or the other, the failed coup degenerated into a stubborn and vitiating civil war between Republicans, who remained loyal to the government, and Nationalists, who supported the generals. Each side controlled wide areas of the country, roughly equal in extent. The Nationalists held much of the north and west of Spain, including the main agricultural and food-producing regions, and a smaller area in the southwest, on the Mediterranean coast. The Republicans retained control of the largest cities, the eastern coast and central Spain. The country had been ruptured internally, just as Europe more generally was in the process of dividing along ideological battle lines.

From the outset of the civil war Germany and Italy began supplying apparently limitless convoys of trained troops and advanced weaponry to the Nationalists, who were led from early 1937 by General Franco. Lacking other allies, the Republicans faced early defeat from the overwhelmingly superior forces ranged against them.

They were granted a reprieve by the intervention of military advisers from the Soviet Union, and also of largely untrained volunteer troops from more than 50 countries, who became known as the International Brigades.

Dorothy, an unhesitating supporter of the Spanish Republic, found it deeply galling that the government of Britain, along with that of France, did not promptly intervene to support Spain's elected government in its defence against the coup. These two countries, the most influential members of the League of Nations, took a cautious and non-committal position, as they had done over Mussolini's actions in Abyssinia. They justified their strategic inaction by declaring that the agonies visited upon Spain were a purely civil matter for that country to resolve unaided. This chaste diplomatic posture ignored the fact that the conflict had already become intensely internationally significant, since Germany and Italy were using Spain as the testbed for their advanced military hardware and tactics. Nevertheless, British and French diplomats drew up a multi-national Non-Intervention Agreement banning signatory countries from supplying weapons to either side in the civil war, or permitting their territories to be used for the transit of war materials from elsewhere. This discreditable document, giving scrupulously equal treatment to Spain's democratically elected government and its rebel opposition, was signed by most European governments, including Germany and Italy, who were already openly flouting it.[9]

While Britain's government stood carefully aloof from events in Spain, the British public assembled a massive movement of popular organisations to defend the country's newly elected and vulnerable Republic. Anti-fascist, peace, political, women's and religious groups all gave their support to Aid Spain campaigns, and submerged their political differences in favour of a loosely affiliated popular front. "Like many idealists and activists of her generation," wrote a friend much later, Dorothy "became involved in the struggle in Spain."[10]

Medical aid, it was soon apparent, was the most desperate need of the Spanish people. The German and Italian aircraft flying daily bombing sorties over Madrid were delivering the first intensive aerial bombardment of an urban population in history. Massive casualties were being inflicted on combatants and civilians alike, while survivors lost their homes and added to the rising tide of civil war refugees.[11] Within a fortnight of the military rebellion, at a large meeting at Friends House, the London headquarters of the Quakers, the Spanish Medical Aid Committee was formed. In the following weeks the committee recruited several teams of volunteer doctors, nurses, orderlies and drivers, as well as ambulances and medical supplies. Its first ambulance unit left for the Aragon front in August 1936. A Scottish unit with six ambulances left the following month, and several others soon followed.

Each of these hastily assembled medical teams included several nurses, whose motives for volunteering varied widely. Although some were politically sympathetic to specific elements within the embattled Republic, others were impelled by sheer curiosity and vague idealism. "The opportunity to become involved in a foreign country at war seemed unmatched for adventurous nursing", thought the London-based, Australian-born nurse Elizabeth Burchill, as she signed up for one of the ambulance teams.[12]

Through the last months of 1936 Dorothy spent anxious hours considering, planning and discussing her intention to work in Spain. The deciding moment occurred during a mass meeting in support of Republican Spain at the Albert Hall. Donations were solicited from the audience, and Dorothy wrote a cheque on the spot and on the back added a note saying, "she wished it could have been more but she was only a poor nurse from New Zealand on a working holiday in England." This message was read out from the stage in the course of the meeting and its author was invited to volunteer to serve in Spain.[13]

Her opportunity to do this arose soon afterwards, in early 1937, when she read in the monthly *Nursing Journal* the brief notice, "Wanted – nurses for Spain. Apply Southern Spanish Relief Committee". This London-based organisation was newly formed to co-ordinate the activities of several other aid bodies, including the Save the Children Fund and the service committee of the British Quakers. Dorothy applied to the address given in the advertisement, and thus met one of the most colourful, gifted and ultimately productive of the many impressive individuals working for Spanish relief and medical aid.

Sir George Young was an eccentric of a type regrettably rare among Britain's minor aristocracy. An Old Etonian and baronet, he had studied political science before working as a diplomat in several countries, including Spain. He later became a journalist and in 1933 published *The New Spain*, a book urging international support for the great social changes foretold by the growing political support for a Republic. Sir George was fluent in Spanish as well as several other European languages, and had acquired a deep knowledge of the history and culture of the country he dearly loved. His regular visits to his villa at Torremolinos, near Málaga in the far south of the country, had made him known among customs officials as 'el hidalgo inglés' (the English lord). He was a highly distinctive figure, as his normal attire within Spain included a flowing white cloak, white corduroy breeches and a broad-brimmed hat. The British nurse Frida Stewart saw him arrive in the city of Valencia dressed in this manner and "clinging to a wicker chair, strapped to an antiquated motorbike ambulance". She formed the view that, "There's no doubt about him being courageous and cracked!"[14] This intriguing character was deeply concerned at the conflict rending his adopted country, and he made use of a lifetime of diplomatic and other contacts to create the London Universities Ambulance Unit, which derived its name from its primary funders. Sir George was also generous in providing his own resources, and he proposed to convert his Torremolinos villa into a hospital.

Despite his unconventional outward appearance, the former diplomat acted systematically and professionally to develop an appropriate medical response to an unprecedented and fast-changing crisis. The nurses he recruited were required to be fully trained and in excellent health, since they might be exposed to infectious diseases and other physical dangers. Before they left Britain they were inoculated against typhoid and typhus, at that time a painful procedure. No salary was offered apart from daily pocket money of a few pesetas, almost the smallest unit of Spanish currency. A knowledge of Spanish language was not required, but Dorothy's competent French would have been a distinct advantage. According to her fellow applicant Elizabeth Burchill, nurses appointed to Sir George Young's teams were expected to avoid expressing political views, a precaution that recognised the extremely tense and bitter divisions within the groups they would be serving. In its untested formative stage, the Universities Ambulance Unit proposed to operate as an entirely non-partisan organisation, providing medical aid to all who needed it regardless of military or political affiliation. Perhaps the most demanding expectation of all was the requirement that nurses should, "display cheerfulness and fortitude at all times amid the chronic shortages of almost everything."[15]

On 6 February 1937 Sir George publicly announced his intention to send an ambulance unit to the southern fronts of the civil war.[16] It was to be based initially in Málaga, the region where his connections were strongest. This traditionally languid, Arab-inflected coastal city, close to the narrow strait separating Spain from Morocco, was a popular winter retreat for England's wealthy. "There was a whole neighbourhood populated only by rheumatic businessmen from London, Liverpool and Glasgow", noted a Russian journalist in the following month.[17] The city also had an entirely separate local population of desperately poor labourers, dockworkers and fishermen. This glaring inequity, and the anarchist sympathies of its working people, had given Málaga the reputation of "the most revolutionary town in Spain".[18] When its local military posts obeyed the generals' call for a nationwide uprising in mid-1936, hastily formed anarchist militias had put up vigorous and effective armed resistance. The generals' revolt was crushed in Málaga and most of its surrounding province, and by January 1937 the city was still under the control of anarcho-syndicalist labour organisations.

In that month a major military offensive was launched against the city by the Nationalist army, supported by Moroccan and Italian troops, Italian artillery and tanks, and German and Italian aviation. As many as three bombing raids a day struck the town, and the Youngs' villa at nearby Torremolinos was an early target for destruction. The attack was headed by General Queipo de Llano, whose enthusiasm for his assignment reached psychopathic levels. In radio propaganda broadcasts he advised the malagueños to "start digging graves", and made lurid predictions about the reprisals his Moroccan troops would take against the town's female population. "These Communist and anarchist women, after all, have made themselves fair game by their doctrine of free love . . . Kicking their legs about and squealing won't save them."[19]

By the first week of February the fall of Málaga appeared imminent, and Sir George was forced to amend and accelerate his plans to deal with the evolving tragedy. In advance of the final assault on their city, some 150,000 malagueños abandoned their homes and set out eastwards towards the Republican-held city of Almería. De Llano gleefully promised that they would be bombed along the way. On 8 February the city finally fell to the rebels amid scenes of extreme brutality and bloodshed. Journalists and other observers were banned from entering Málaga while the Nationalist forces carried out the 'cleansing operations' they had foreshadowed. The ambulance unit's plans to base a field hospital in the city had to be abandoned, although the need for emergency medical aid was evidently greater than ever.

The speed and unpredictability of the deteriorating military situation had far outstripped the capability of Sir George's personal fundraising efforts, and he came to rely heavily on support from sympathetic agencies, in particular the Quakers. His collaboration with the Society of Friends would be close and long-lasting, and Dorothy Morris would also form an enduring relationship with this immutably pacifist institution. The *cuáqueros*, as they are known in Spanish, had a long tradition of aiding refugees, especially those displaced by warfare, and immediately after the outbreak of the civil war the Quakers formed a London-based committee to consider how best to serve the needs of Spain. The aid they supplied, although explicitly non-ideological, went predominantly to Republican-held territories since the Nationalists occupied the major food-producing areas and therefore had less need for emergency relief supplies.[20] From late 1936 Quakers, their staff and colleagues began feeding large numbers of refugees relocated to Catalonia from besieged and bombed Madrid. Many were found to be suffering from tuberculosis, anaemia and other illnesses related to malnutrition. In December 1936 Edith Pye, a Quaker midwife with experience of working with refugee women and children during and after World War One, led a relief expedition to Barcelona bringing several tons of supplies, including cocoa. (The Quaker-owned chocolate maker Cadbury–Fry was reliably generous in donating its products.) By February 1937 the Friends and their partner agencies were extending these efforts to south and central Spain, where Sir George and his team were also headed.

After satisfying the ambulance unit's organisers that she could meet their daunting standards, Dorothy's departure for Spain was extremely rapid. She was permitted to bring a single small suitcase, and told that she could not advise even her immediate family about her departure, for fear of alerting Franco sympathisers in Britain who might seek to disrupt the unit's plans. Instead, she was instructed to arrange for her mail to be forwarded to her from London at intervals. Just days after the fall of Málaga the first unit, comprising a fully equipped ambulance and two cars, left London for Spain. Sixty-five-year-old Sir George led the team in person, accompanied by his assistant Peter O'Donovan, his Spanish chauffeur-mechanic, and a US woman co-driver whose name is not recorded. The head nurse was Violetta Thurstan, a formidably competent Englishwoman with wide experience as a nurse and hospital administrator in Poland and Russia during World War One. She is said to have left her home in Devon and enlisted for Spain within a week of learning that nurses were needed there.[21] Thurstan was supported by three qualified younger nurses – Margaret Crichton from Perth in Scotland, a Mennonite named Sinclair Cavell, and 32-year-old Dorothy Morris.

At Dieppe, their port of arrival in France, the first obstacle was encountered. Customs officials found an irregularity in the passport of the team's only Spanish member, which threatened to take some days to resolve. Violetta Thurstan was asked to go on ahead by train, initially to Valencia, where the Republican government had relocated when Madrid appeared likely to fall to a three-pronged Nationalist attack. This was an extraordinarily risky journey for a single woman to make at the height of wartime, but Thurstan proceeded as instructed. At Valencia she discussed with government officials what relief needs were greatest. She was told that in Almería, to the east of Málaga, a torrent of distressed refugees had created scenes of utmost desperation, and was provided with a letter of introduction to the city's governor. After a further 40-hour journey she reached Almería and found that the Valencian officials had not exaggerated. "Food is terribly short," she wrote to Lady Young, "there are long queues of people waiting for bread and yesterday the doors were shut because there was no more, and women with little babies had to go away crying . . . A bomb has just gone off and the streets are so crowded that everyone gets into a panic. I have been told to sleep with a torch ready to my hand . . . and make a dash downstairs if anything happens."[22]

These safety measures were necessitated by the Nationalist naval vessels that were shelling the city every morning, as well as by nightly bombing raids. Any medical facility the ambulance unit planned to establish would require some security from these attacks, and the city's governor referred Thurstan to a building a few miles out of town along the Alicante road. Known as the Villa Maria, it appeared suitable for an emergency hospital.

Once the passport difficulty was resolved, the main body of the ambulance unit took a full week to travel from Dieppe to Alicante, due to petrol shortages and their heavy load of supplies. At Perpignan, 20 miles from the Spanish frontier, they collected still more supplies sent ahead by rail. These included spare tyres for their vehicles, and a stock of butter, which Dorothy noted was scarce in Republican-held Spain.[23] In Alicante the convoy left one car and part of its supplies, and moved on through the Sierra de los Filabres mountain range. This was Dorothy's first time in Spain, and she encountered sights and experiences far removed from the tourist trails. "We did a long day's trip down through Murcia and behind Cartagena to Almeria," she reported later to a Christchurch newspaper. "200 miles of wild hills and arid country under a hot sun . . . We passed on the way many, many refugees coming up from Malaga – pathetic bundles on donkeys trailing along the dusty endless road that we were tearing down at 50 miles an hour."[24]

These panic-stricken refugees were victims of one of the most notorious barbarities of the civil war. As de Llano had vowed would happen, the thousands of fleeing malagueños, mainly women, children and the old and infirm, were repeatedly attacked by Nationalist forces as they struggled the 200 kilometres towards Almería. Some rode donkeys, as Dorothy noted, but most were on foot, carrying their possessions in cloth-wrapped bundles and lacking any protection against the winter cold. On the coastal mountain tracks they made easy targets for fighter planes, bombers and naval vessels. A group of 80 children evacuated from an orphanage was struck by machine guns and incendiary bombs – only ten survived. The refugees took to travelling by night, and spending their days in hiding or foraging for wild plants to eat. At least 5000 died on the journey, an average of one corpse for every 50 metres of the route.

Another party of foreign medical workers had made the hazardous trip towards Málaga some days in advance of Sir George Young's unit. A Canadian doctor and devout socialist, Norman Bethune, had designed a highly innovative mobile blood transfusion service that he was determined to provide to Republican troops fighting on the civil war's southern front. In Barcelona he bought a van and installed a generator, refrigerator and all necessary clinical equipment, and with two assistants drove westward from Almería towards Málaga. After mounting a rise in the road they were confronted by a seemingly endless stream of ragged and footsore fugitives, some of them critically injured and all thirsty and terrified. Bethune and his team turned their vehicle around, unloaded its precious contents onto the roadside, and crammed it with up to 40 people at a time, initially taking only those aged under ten who had a chance of survival. For the next three days and nights, almost without a pause, the men took turns driving back and forth to Almería, "working hard to evacuate the remaining population of an entire city".[25]

When Dorothy and her companions arrived in Almería several days later, they found the city overwhelmed with hungry, traumatised and desperate evacuees. "We arrived . . . in the evening," she wrote, "to find it in darkness, as it had been bombed either from the air or from the sea every day. The enemy is held at Motril, about 70 miles down the road, but Almeria is the next big town on the way". Sir George, she said, hoped, "to prevent this place from being sold to the rebels as Malaga was, whereby about 8000 people were shot."[26]

By a fortunate coincidence, on the same day as their arrival the British naval ship *Boadicea* had put into Almería with several tons of food supplies dispatched from London by Lady Young. The ambulance unit immediately used these to establish an emergency feeding depot in front of the central railway station. Every morning fresh milk was supplied to children and invalids, with soup in the afternoon for all who wanted it. "If the kind people who sent the stores could see the toddlers with their whole faces buried in a bowl of milk, small boys tearing wolfishly at the bread . . . women crying for joy when they saw the hot meals provided, they would feel rewarded", wrote one team member.[27]

Dorothy described the accommodation provided for her team as, "a most charming villa . . . about four miles out of the town. It is a lovely place, and its owners apparently left in a hurry at the beginning of the trouble here, and it was shut up. It is comfortably furnished, tiled all through like all Spanish houses."[28] This building, surrounded by its own gardens and grounds, was the Villa Maria, requisitioned earlier by Violetta Thurstan for conversion to a hospital. The need for the team's services was so acute that they were given just three days to rest before dividing into two groups. One remained at the villa to begin treating the civilian population of Almería. The other, in which Dorothy was included, moved towards the battlefront a short distance to the west to establish a field hospital for combatants. It was the first of a string of undoubtedly tiresome transfers from one newly established medical service to another, forced on the team by the rapidly shifting lines of battle.

In the civil war's first six months, Nationalist forces had greatly expanded the area of western Spain under their control and pushed the front eastward in a sweeping, irregular curve as they sought to capture their ultimate prize, the capital city of Madrid. By February 1937 the war's southern front ran from the coastal town of Motríl northwest towards the Portuguese border, through mountainous terrain that, in those winter months, was often barely accessible. It was an ill-defined and rapidly shifting front. In the week before the unit's arrival the Nationalists had advanced further eastward towards the Sierra Nevada range, the highest point in mainland Spain and named for the snow that then blanketed its mountains down to the foothills. The Republican side of this fluid and indeterminate battle-front could provide almost no medical services beyond a crude and minimal system for retrieving and evacuating the many hundreds of troops wounded in a series of desperate holding actions. The more fortunate of these were given rudimentary first aid and then trans-ported by mule for up to six hours to an ambulance. They then faced a further journey of at least 80 kilometres behind the lines to the nearest hospitals, in Republican-held territory around Almería.

The death rate suffered under this system, especially for patients with abdominal or head wounds, was predictably appalling. The Republican Army's embryonic medical service was fully aware that field hospitals capable of treating patients much closer to the front lines were needed desperately, and Sir George's ambulance unit was assigned to create one of these 'advance clearing stations' in the hill-side village of Albuñol. This village, wrote Dorothy, lay, "about ten miles behind the front, between the Sierra Nevada and the sea. There we were given a house to organise into a relief hospital to the big military base hospital nearer Almeria. The Spaniards are rather lazy and need a fair amount of direction in hospital matters. It took a day to get the place and another to get it ready."[29] In a matter of weeks, and with minimal training or other preparation, she was required to adjust from the safely predictable nursing she had practised in surroundings such as the Grosvenor Court Hotel, to vastly different conditions that placed her alongside colleagues who had often been trained under entirely different regimes, and held quite different cultural expectations.

Establishing a new medical facility at this whirlwind pace, with meagre resources and an incessant workload, was far from ideal in terms of patient care. Yet both on this front and elsewhere in the Republican sector, the war stimulated substantial and lasting advances in medicine and surgery that later proved of immense value both in war and peacetime. This paradoxical outcome resulted from the Republican army's need to develop medical responses to entirely new types of military casualty such as those produced by air raids. Spain's civil war was probably the first in modern times in which total civilian casualties exceeded those of combatants. This posed unprecedented problems of medical organisation and treatment, and new solutions were found to address them.

These medical advances were, overwhelmingly, initiated by the Republican side, due mainly to the influx of new medical personnel to their forces, and a consequent break with traditional systems and lines of authority. At the outbreak of the civil war, most of the Republican Army's doctors joined the Nationalists. They were replaced by Spanish civilian doctors and a further 200 or so doctors from overseas. Frontline Republican military hospitals were also expected to treat sick and wounded civilians, while wounded soldiers were evacuated to civilian hospitals behind the lines. The traditional distinctions between military and civilian medicine thus became blurred. This combination of demand and opportunity for medical innovation proved immensely productive.[30]

Norman Bethune's new and strikingly effective system for supplying blood transfusions in the field was only one of a number of medical advances which Dorothy was required to incorporate into her nursing practice. Another was an entirely original, and eventually internationally admired, system of wartime medical organisation. Although she is not likely to have discovered this so soon after her arrival, by an extraordinary coincidence the system had been pioneered by a former neighbour of hers in the small New Zealand mining town of Cromwell. His and Dorothy's lives had followed parallel but separate courses until the chaotic Spanish conflict brought them together again.

One of the greatest military surgeons of his era, Doug Jolly was the son of a Cromwell storekeeper who had been killed in action in World War One. He was born in the same year as Dorothy, and graduated from Otago Medical School as she was completing her nursing training. Later, the two both left independently for London, although Jolly did so to study for specialist qualifications in surgery. He was an active Christian socialist and took part in the great East End anti-fascist marches of early 1936. When the Spanish Civil War erupted later that year, he was some months short of completing the demanding qualifications for admission to the Royal College of Surgeons. Nevertheless, he willingly abandoned his studies and volunteered to join a British medical unit organised separately from Sir George Young's ambulance teams. Jolly left for Spain in November 1936, several months before Dorothy, and unlike her, was immediately placed under military orders. With the rank of lieutenant in the Republican Army, he first headed a 12-person mobile surgical unit treating casualties of the battle of Madrid. By the time Dorothy's team arrived in the mountains of the southern front, he had been promoted to captain and was working far to the north, in the cluster of heavily bombed villages where the battle of Guadarrama was being fought.[31]

During those frenetic four months Jolly recognised the crucial importance of placing surgeons like himself, backed with assistants, nurses and support staff, as close to the front as practically possible. Their presence minimised the time needed to bring critically injured men to where they could be treated, and greatly increased their chances of survival. Jolly refined this realisation into a hierarchy of treatment facilities which he termed the "three points forward" system. The first point was a casualty first aid post right at the front lines, where the wounded were given emergency treatment. Then they were sent to a mobile surgical hospital as near to the front as safety permitted. It was this type of hospital that Jolly himself headed, and which Dorothy and her colleagues created at Albuñol. Finally, as soon as it was safe to do so, the wounded were evacuated to a base hospital, in a safe area but still as close to the front lines as possible. This system, simple and logical though it now sounds, represented a dramatic departure from older systems of military medicine in which surgeons held an exalted status and worked safely distant from bullets, bombs or shelling.[32]

The 'three points forward' system was developed under onerous and brutal circumstances. Jolly's mobile medical team was present at many of the most crucial battles of the civil war, and in a February 1937 letter to his friends in England, he explained that "We always arrive where the danger is greatest and depart when the front is stabilised."[33] The same general policy applied to other units serving with the International Brigades, including Dorothy's. After only a few weeks in Albuñol, the field hospital she had helped to set up was handed over to a Spanish medical unit, and her team moved further north to a more active section of the front.

"Now we are about 60 miles away [from Almería], she wrote, "in another remote hill village . . . it is just about two and half miles behind the front line, but there is not much fighting going on at present, though we can hear explosions from time to time." The village of Torviscón was situated just a few kilometres from the enemy-occupied town of Órgiva on the lower slopes of the Sierra Nevada.[34] The surrounding region, the Alpujarras, was one of the wildest in Spain, and could boast few formed roads. "This place is rather primitive and dirty," Dorothy discovered. "It has been hard work making a hospital here."[35]

The determined Sir George met first with the village *alcalde*, or local mayor, who conducted his visitors around "the vilest hovels in this poverty stricken pueblo". From those the team selected the least delapidated, "and had the miscellaneous population of old women, goats, dogs, chickens, and children evicted. I commandeered men to clear out the worst of the filth and settled in by the light of 'candillis', wicks floating in oil. The next day we took over another house as hospital and had it cleaned and furnished while the surgeon, the doctor, the orderlies, the 'practicantes' and the rest of the staff looked on and commented . . . in two days we had a hospital, except that there was no water, no light, the sanitary arrangements were malodorous."[36]

This aristocratic Hispanophile could "manage the talking, which in Spain seems to be an endless affair," wrote Dorothy with evident relief, since her own Spanish was then still minimal. "We have raised a dust in other ways, and now have decent accommodation for about 20 men, and even a small operating theatre."[37] Water was supplied by siphoning it from a nearby spring through Roman Empire-era earthenware pipes, and rubber tubing. Eventually, the little hospital had both hot and cold running water and toilets.

As soon as this makeshift facility could admit its first patients, they began to pour in. The majority had not been wounded in enemy action but were suffering from exposure and frostbite contracted during guerilla actions in fierce blizzards at altitudes of up to 2700 metres in the Sierra de Mulhacén. These men had to be brought down from the mountains on mule litters, a jolting trek of three or four hours. Before the Torviscón hospital opened, however, the same patients would have faced a further journey of 80 or more kilometres to the nearest permanent hospital.

"Last night they brought in 16 men, a few wounded and the rest frostbitten," wrote Dorothy, in a letter published in the Christchurch *Press.* "The front up the road is held by parts of the International Brigade – anti-Fascist volunteers from every country in Europe. They are a very fine type indeed. They have borne the brunt of the heaviest fighting anywhere, and are very well organised . . . I heard rumours of a New Zealand man somewhere, but have not seen him yet."[38] The inordinately cosmopolitan International Brigades did indeed include a handful of combatants, as well as several medical personnel, from New Zealand. Details of their identities and actions are contradictory and incomplete, but it seems likely that Dorothy was referring here to a somewhat mysterious young man named William MacDonald.

From a prominent Dunedin family, MacDonald had spent time in jail in New Zealand for a botched bank robbery before he arrived in Spain in January 1937 and enlisted with US volunteers in the Abraham Lincoln Brigade. (The brigades were initially organised by national origin and often named for national heroes.) MacDonald was soon wounded by a machine-gun but he remained a dedicated combatant, confident of the Republic's eventual victory even if not of his own survival. "If I have to die, I shall die happy knowing that I have died for a cause for which many thousands, better men than I, have gladly given their lives."[39] In the event, this troubled and erratic volunteer did not die in Spain, although he and Dorothy apparently never succeeded in meeting during the war.

In the absence of any reliable system of communications across the dispersed and mountainous Motríl front, it was necessary to travel to the many individual Republican fighting units in the area to inform them of the new field hospital's existence, and tell them they no longer needed to transport their wounded on the much longer journey to a hospital in one of the cities. As the Torviscón unit's leader and its most authoritative Spanish speaker, the elderly Sir George carried out this task in person, spending up to ten hours a day travelling on horseback across snowbound mountain ranges to reach small parties of troops at distant outposts. "They were all very glad of the new hospital and come tramping over the mountain for dressings etc."[40]

As the Republican forces strengthened their position and captured, or recaptured, some of the mountain villages, Sir George was able to establish small clearing stations where wounded and ill troops could be given emergency treatment before they faced the excruciating mule-litter journey down the mountains to Torviscón. These stations, and the hospital itself, undoubtedly saved a great many lives, including those of men who might otherwise have been executed by their own side to end their suffering. Without the ambulance unit, claimed Sir George, the wounded, "would have had to go as far as Almeria and that in certain cases is hopeless, they would have been pistolled."[41]

Down in Torviscón itself, Dorothy grew skilled at treating frostbite, bullet wounds, head injuries and a host of other traumas seldom addressed in her training, or encountered in her earlier career. She was also faced with managing local staff whose language she struggled to understand, and whose working methods were sometimes even more incomprehensible. Nursing in Spain had traditionally been in the hands of nuns, who had tended to see their role as palliative rather than curative, and whose attitudes towards hygiene were primitive by comparison with the rigorous measures imposed in New Zealand.

"I am afraid I do not think much of Spanish methods" she wrote, seeming to choose her words as tactfully as possible. "Perhaps I have hardly had time to test them properly. Nursing as we know it is practically unknown here".[42]

She worked amid the pounding of artillery from the hills overhead, and the clatter of machine-gun fire. Along the mountain road through the village roared lorries crammed with militia, and sometimes bands of "very irregular cavalry". A communal kitchen had been organised to combine the villagers' available food supplies, and this served each resident a daily meal and bread, sometimes supplemented with wine or oranges. Sir George found that flu, dysentery and lice were rife in the villages he visited but somewhat surprisingly, his own staff avoided illness.

A more immediate concern was the prospect of being over-run by an enemy whose nearest town, Órgiva, was only five miles to the west. "If we hadn't got [the International Brigades] between us and Orgiva, I wouldn't stay here an hour," Sir George told his funders in Britain. In the months prior to the unit's arrival in Torviscón, the village had changed hands more than once under the tumultuous circumstances of the civil war. The previous summer the villagers had suffered a raid by the 'Pancho Villa' battalion of anarchist militia from Málaga, who contented themselves with "wrecking the waterclosets in the better class houses". They were followed by a gang of 'blue' (Nationalist) Requetés from Granada to the north, who "shot the more politically active of the villagers". When the Republicans retook the village, the widow of one of those shot, a woman named Emilia, was given "the honourable and comfortable post of hospital kitchenmaid".[43]

Torviscón was only one of several newly established medical facilities under Sir George's overall responsibility. He had by then recruited a staff of more than 50 foreign volunteers, including surgeons, doctors, nurses, drivers and secretaries, all unpaid apart from their daily expenses. The cost of this widely dispersed and altruistic relief operation was constantly rising, and finding the necessary funds formed a heavy part of Sir George's responsibilities. During April 1937 he returned to England to lecture and raise money for another ambulance and two more doctors. The shrewd former journalist clearly understood the importance of media publicity to the success of this work, and he gave vividly phrased interviews to the

British press. The civil war, he maintained, was nearing its final phase, and the Republican army would shortly overcome the rebels and restore the authority of the ousted government. He gave a specific incident that inspired this confidence – "A six-thousand foot pass over the Sierra Nevada and our overloaded ambulance crawling up against a howling blizzard. We find some young *milicianos* lying in the ditch half-dead from exhaustion and exposure: when got under shelter they revive and all, excepting one whose feet are frozen, start again on foot for the front."[44]

As the senior nurse at Torviscón, Dorothy presumably inherited extra responsibilities during Sir George's absence. By mid-April 1937, as spring reached the high-altitude villages and the snows retreated towards the mountain peaks, she could report that, "There are now two Spanish doctors, and their orderlies, and in a few days when things are running properly, I think we will leave them to it."[45] Continually escalating demands on the Republican Army's medical services decreed that once her team had built up an efficiently functioning centre, they were transferred yet again to a region of greater need, while their facility was handed over to less experienced personnel.

Before her next posting Dorothy was able to return, for a brief and no doubt welcome period, to the relative security of the children's hospital at Almería. The small hospital established at the Villa Maria was headed by her colleague Sinclair Cavell with the support of a number of Spanish staff, including a trained nurse and pediatrician and young local women who were trained to carry out the various other tasks required. Another foreign volunteer, the US relief worker Virginia Malbin, wrote that the hospital, "can accommodate only 25 children at a time and because it is frequently necessary to keep the children under medical supervision for from 2 to 6 months there is very little turnover and the hospital is unable to meet the needs of the area. In addition to hospital care, a morning clinic is run daily."[46]

This overcrowding had persisted despite the city officials' concerted efforts throughout February 1937 to evacuate as many Málaga refugees as possible to larger cities such as Barcelona. Some escaped evacuation by hiding in caves and other shelters, or were simply too ill to travel. A great many were malnourished, scantily clad and lacked resistance to the cold and damp conditions, while the medical supplies and trained staff needed to treat them remained in acutely short supply. Epidemics of flu and measles began to spread through the refugee population, and the risk grew of outbreaks of more serious illnesses such as typhus. Both the hospital staff and the municipal authorities, whose energy and efficiency greatly impressed Sir George, collaborated to introduce drinking water regulations, delousing stations and smallpox vaccinations. Even though obviously hopeless cases were refused, the death rate among the hospital patients remained stubbornly high. Only the arrival of warmer weather meant that fewer children and other critically ill patients died and the risk of devastating epidemics receded.

Over the same period the fighting to the west of Almería gradually succeeded in stabilising the Motríl front, and the bombing raids on the city ceased temporarily. This in turn enabled more empty villas to be converted for hospital use. The Villa Maria became a convalescent home, and the Villas San Juan and Elena were equipped with 20 and 40 beds respectively. Both were quickly filled to overflowing. The Australian nurse Elizabeth Burchill worked at the Villa Elena, and described it as "a two-storey brick building set high in an enclosed garden. It was protected by high brick walls, framed by tawny mountains and overlooked the old Moorish city of Almeria".[47]

From April to July 1937 the medical director of this hospital was another New Zealand volunteer, an exceptionally dedicated public health physician named Gladys Montgomery. The daughter of a Coromandel publican, she had gained a Diploma of Public Health in Glasgow in 1931, when large areas of that city were stricken with poverty and unemployment. She was on holiday in Europe in March 1937 but after hearing reports of the civil war in Spain she changed her plans and offered her services to Sir George Young's ambulance unit. She arrived at Almería soon after the city had been swamped by Málagan refugees.

> The children were suffering greatly from inanition [debilitation resulting from malnutrition], having been fed chiefly on half-boiled rice, and, of course, in their weakened condition, they became susceptible to pneumonia, broncho-pneumonia, diarrhoea, multiple abscesses, and so on. They were miserably thin, and one of them, the famous Bernardo, we seemed unable to satisfy, for at any hour of the day we would hear him calling,

'Pan, pan, pan' ('bread, bread, bread'). He had an aching void that we could not fill . . . The Spaniards are very kind to their children, though we found parental affection had its drawbacks. The close of visiting hour reminded one of the sounds emanating from the Wailing Wall in Jerusalem.[48]

The two New Zealand women had very little opportunity to work together. Soon after Dr. Montgomery's arrival, the Motríl front was consolidated along its entire length and many of its Republican troops were ordered to move to a new offensive further north that had begun facing heavy Nationalist assaults. In the forefront of the mobilisation were sections of the International Brigades, customarily regarded by the Republican Army commanders as its shock troops, even though few of them had any prior military experience. According to Sir George,

> the heaviest casualties always occurred where the shock troops went, and as our hospital was mobile and could follow an offensive, and the Spanish hospitals could not well do so, it was arranged that it should go with the Brigade. The movement to the next front but one to the north was effected with the greatest secrecy . . . This front is moving westward through the high rough plateaux of the Sierra Morena to the north of Cordova [more accurately, Córdoba] towards the Portuguese border. The conditions are those encountered at Torviscon in the first week, with heat substituted for cold.[49]

In Almería, Dorothy received instructions to follow the new offensive as soon as she could be spared. The arrival at Villa Elena of two more foreign volunteers, possibly the Australian Elizabeth Burchill and the Irishwoman Mary Elmes, was the signal for her departure. Before the end of April the unit's ambulance was loaded for a long trip, and it headed northwards behind the lines through the high and arid La Mancha plain, the land of Don Quixote, to join the Brigade in the impoverished province of Extremadura.

"It was a beautiful drive for two days," wrote Dorothy, "mostly through hilly olive country." The ambulance arrived at a field hospital about three miles from the new front at 10 o'clock at night. This small hospital had a staff of 30 men, "of all possible nationalities, even to a Chinese, who was their cook."[50] It was headed by Dr

Fritz Jensen, the Viennese commander of the 13th International Brigade's medical service, who was already known to Dorothy from a meeting soon after her arrival in Almería. Despite the lateness of the hour, she may have been relieved to learn that she was not allowed to remain at the field hospital, since it was the target of frequent aerial bombing and the latest attack had ended just an hour earlier.

> Although it was so late, (10.30 p.m.) Dr Jensen had my belongings trans-
> ferred to his car and, with our driver, we went about 30 miles. It was bright
> moonlight – good bombing light – and once we had to stop and put out
> our lights as a Fascist aeroplane flew over. They usually come swooping
> down with guns firing at cars, especially ambulances. Finally we arrived at
> a town among the hills about 12.30pm. Here there is a hospital of about
> 100 beds in a former convent. I was immediately shown over and saw the
> staff in action. There were three Spanish doctors and two Spanish nurses.
> Some wounded men had just come down by train from the front line. The
> Spanish girls are good, although some of the things they do make my blood
> run cold. Dr Jensen had an idea that I might teach them something of real
> nursing. However, you just can't teach a Spaniard anything . . . That was
> nine days ago. Five days and nights have been very busy as there have been
> several big actions. We deal with the wounded and evacuate them to a large
> hospital at Cuidad Real or to Valencia. Today was quiet. Dr Jensen came
> to see how I was getting on and to prepare me for more wounded. They
> expect an attack tonight.[51]

This "wild, desolate area," said Dorothy, was then perhaps the poorest region in the country.[52] By May 1937 it had become a crucial Nationalist stronghold, as Franco's troops fought to maintain a strategic corridor between the territories they held in the north and south of the country. The area contained highly productive mines and the Nationalists hoped to take the town of Almadén, which contained the most valuable mercury mine in Europe. They were also fighting to hold the lead mines at Peñarroya and Pueblo Nuevo del Terrible, which they had earlier captured from the Republicans.

They were opposed by the 13th International Brigade, whose members were drawn mainly from eastern European countries, espe-cially Slavs, Hungarians, Poles, Serbians and Austrian Jews. Many of them had been drawn into the conflict to escape savage repression in their homelands. Although their welter of languages must have made communication with her medical team exceptionally difficult, Dorothy formed the impression that "They are very fine types."[53] She was to spend the next four months with this brigade, and for much of that time worked alongside its medical captain, a Catalan surgeon named Josep Maria Massons, as his head nurse.

Massons, a handsome, sturdy and cheerful man, was nine years younger than Dorothy but already one of the most respected surgeons in the International Brigades. In his memoir he recalled that after qualifying in surgery in 1935 he hoped for a career that would combine surgical practice and teaching. However, the following year, while working at a Barcelona hospital, he heard the sounds of gunfire in the streets, signalling the outbreak of civil war. "I got dressed and ran to the Emergency Department. I didn't leave the hospital for a week."[54] Under the direction of Dr. Joaquín Trias, who had gained experience of military medicine while serving in Morocco in the 1920s, Massons rapidly learned to treat the deep and uneven wounds caused by bullets and shells, and to reduce the patient's risk of gangrene by scrupulously cleaning wounds and leaving them open to drain.

Only a small number of Spain's surgeons had offered their services to the Republican side after the outbreak of the war and when Massons did so, they were gratefully accepted. At the International Brigades headquarters in Albacete, Oskar Telge, the Brigades' Bulgarian chief medical officer, provided him with two assistants, one to help with the surgery and another to deal with internal medical problems.[55] Since he spoke excellent German and French, Massons was assigned to the polyglot 13th International Brigade and posted to Cabeza del Buey ('Ox's Head') in Extremadura, where Dorothy Morris later arrived to assist him.

This small town ringed by barren hills, with a population of 18,000, had served the surrounding rural villages, where activities were dominated by olive groves and tiny herds of sheep and pigs, for nearly two millennia. Its residents had voted overwhelmingly for the Republic in the 1936 election, and after the military uprising the town council formed a local militia with responsibility for guarding strategic sites. This, and the presence in mid-1937 of the International Brigade, meant that the town was not taken by Franco's forces until the summer of 1938.[56] Throughout the war, however, residents lived in danger of aerial bombardment or artillery attack, and also with the cruel consequences of political division, since rightist factions were also present and Cabeza del Buey had seen waves of internecine killings since the military uprising began a year earlier. The first victims were priests and well-known right-wing figures, killed by excitable local militias. When Republican army officers appeared some months later, they ordered the town's council to agree to the enlistment of its young men. The councillors refused, saying that Cabeza del Buey had already played its part for the Republic by carrying out the earlier killings. The officers responded by shooting several of the councillors, and any right-wingers who had survived the first round of executions. Perhaps 500 people were killed in this small town in the early months of the war. Its *alcalde,* or mayor, told Massons that the sight of the three-pointed star on his left arm, indicating that he was a captain in the International Brigades, could still strike terror into the hearts of the locals.[57]

Massons found that the town's local hospital was headed by an eminent Madrid neurosurgeon who was too old to cope with the unrelenting demands of front-line surgical work. He was transferred instead to a rearguard military hospital in the southern garrison town of Murcia, and Massons was left in complete control. "I taught two young lads from Cabeza de Buey, Blas and Pepe, how to use the autoclaves [for sterilizing equipment], how to cut the dressings for the compresses, etc., and I asked the mayor of the town for some girls for the cleaning, cooking and the washing." His nursing staff included a Madrid woman named Pepita Sicilia whom he recalled as "selfless and very loyal", a "disciplined and affectionate" German nurse, Käthe Forgasc, married to one of the battalion doctors, and his highly trained New Zealand head nurse.[58]

Dorothy's primary duty was to maintain the health of the International Brigaders stationed in the town. According to a US volunteer ambulance driver, when not in action, "hacking night coughs, jaundice, sores, itches, diarrhea and constipation are the occupational diseases of war in Spain . . . All cuts and scratches seem to infect."[59] The very inadequate food was shared by locals, troops and medical staff alike. It consisted mainly of unleavened bread, dried chickpeas and occasional supplies of meat such as boiled mule-ribs. Patients received the same, plus a small amount of condensed milk, eggs and other precious dietary supplements. "There is no officers' mess. Our officials eat with us. Dishes, cups and utensils are of tin. There are no tablecloths or napkins. Second servings are not given."[60]

Massons' description of Dorothy's appearance indicates the toll that her work over the previous winter had taken on her. She had lost weight, her parchment-like skin indicated the lack of fats in her diet, and she could have been mistaken for a much older woman. However, she had evidently lost none of her energy for her work, or her good nature. She insisted on high standards of cleanliness for the hospital facilities, its equipment and the patients themselves, and became known to the Spanish cleaning staff as Zanquiú, their imitation of 'thank you', "because she was a well-mannered woman who always thanked them in English."[61]

In his memoir Massons, grouped his patients, somewhat light-heartedly, into three categories – the aristocracy, the bourgeoisie and the proletariat. This latter group made up the bulk of the 13th Brigade. The English-speakers, particularly the Americans, generally belonged to the first group.

> They complained about everything, from the food to the nurses, even about the sheets, but they had their own hospital in Villa Paz and I used to send them there as fast as I could. They also caused trouble because one of the American political commissars used to bring them sweets and tobacco behind my back, and the other patients would get angry because they didn't get anything. The English were similar, but not as bad thanks to their humor and good manners.
>
> The French, Germans and central Europeans were the bourgeoisie: they understood that being in a war meant you could not expect anything luxurious, so they only asked for what they knew was possible. The proletarians, finally, were the Slavs and other east Europeans, who bore pain and death stoically and almost never complained about anything. The proletarians were from the Balkans, accustomed to working hard in the mines, and the bravest in the face of suffering and death.[62]

Within these categories Massons found a wide range of motives for entering the civil war, and his clear-eyed, non-ideological analysis provides a valuable counter to the high-minded self-justification that colours the wartime anecdotes of many International Brigaders.

> Some of them were professional soldiers who had been in earlier wars, and were talking about going to other wars afterwards. Others were idealists who had come to free Spain of fascism. Among the officials, there were many who had come to Spain only to gain credit for their political careers. It was clear that whoever returned to France or Holland with some braid [i.e. with an officer's commission] was more likely to be nominated to work for the Communist Party. There were also many Germans and Italians who had been exiled from their own countries. Finally, there was a group of English and North Americans working as ambulance drivers who had . . . come to Spain looking for adventure. They used to dream of winning a prize by writing a short story, or just to show off when they went back home.[63]

Just weeks after Dorothy's arrival, intense fighting to the west of Cabeza del Buey drove the battlefront closer to the town, and at short notice the hospital was forced to transfer some miles south to the neighbouring city of Belalcázar. There, Massons' team re-established their surgical service in the vacated buildings of local schools. The move was surprisingly straightforward (although Massons complained about the standard of the local cooking), and they were able to remain in Belalcázar until the end of June. The worst casualties in that time resulted from an air-raid on the nearby town of Hinojosa del Duque. "We had to spend all night operating on women, kids and old people with wounds from shell splinters", recalled Massons.[64]

This terse and dispassionate comment does not reveal the depth of emotional distress that often resulted from carrying out emergency operations of this type. For battlefield nurses as well as surgeons, operating on critically injured civilian patients could be an agonisingly traumatic experience that challenged the strongest political commitment. Dorothy Morris's own accounts of this period avoid any mention of operations of this kind, and this may be due to wartime censorship, the loss of her letters or, most likely, the desire to avoid distressing her family. Other foreign medical volunteers, however, have recorded their impressions of treating civilian victims of

Nationalist air-raids. They include the Cromwell surgeon Doug Jolly who wrote from Guadalajara in March 1937 that, "When 20 or 30 big Caproni [Italian] bombers come over one of these small towns . . . and drop a hundred or so large bombs on the streets where women and children go about their daily work – I can't describe the terrible horrors. When a dozen or so kids are brought in ripped to pieces, legs blown off, bellies and heads ripped open, it's almost the end of everything for me."[65]

Where these injuries resulted in fractured limbs, the patients were treated by a technique newly developed by the Republican medical services. Dorothy was shocked when she first saw it applied. "I was horrified because they put the wounded limbs in plaster of Paris and wouldn't let me dress them. They said that rest was what mattered. [It was] a new method, evolved by Dr Trueta".[66] Dr Josep Trueta i Raspall, a former colleague of Massons in Barcelona, was one of the most influential surgeons working for the Republic. His 'closed plaster' fracture treatment consisted of encasing the broken limb in plaster and then transporting the patient to a base hospital, which might be some hours distant. At that hospital, if the position of the fracture was found to be satisfactory, the plaster remained in place without further treatment for days or even weeks. During intense fighting in 1938, over 20,000 cases were treated by this method, with a death rate of less than one per cent. Trueta said later, "I sincerely believe that no other treatment could have enabled us to alleviate for so many victims the horrors of war and air raids."[67] From her own observations of this novel technique, Dorothy soon overcame her initial adverse reaction. "I must say it was very successful."[68]

Near the end of June 1937 Franco's Nationalist forces launched a massive new offensive on the city of Brunete to the west of Madrid, and Dorothy's team was brought forward to treat the defending Republican forces. By now highly proficient at short-notice evacuations, the team abandoned their facilities at Belalcázar, loaded their equipment onto a military train and then, at the rail junction of Tembleque, transferred it again onto trucks for the dangerous journey north to the far side of the battlefront. "The trucks took us along unsealed roads," recalled Massons, "travelling only at night and with the lights turned off, to avoid Nationalist artillery bombardments."

His team spent four days in this way, hiding by daylight in the cover of forests, before they reached the small village of Hoyo de Manzanares. There they were fortunate to find an existing tuberculosis sanatorium which was, "perfect for our hospital since it already had a theatre and wards."

"We were stationed on the high hills of the Sierra Morena," Dorothy wrote.[69] "We could see the smoke, flashes and movement of the battle below. One of only a few Western nurses, I worked with Spanish doctors. The wounded came directly from the forward dressing stations and were operated on in makeshift conditions."[70] Again, she gives no details, in these dispatches for a general readership, of the psychologically fraying conditions in which she worked. Massons, however, was unable to forget his experiences at Brunete for the rest of his life. "We had to rearrange our surgical teams to create three out of two. The theatre was working day and night, and the three teams swapped on 24-hour shifts. I suffered a lot in those days, not only physically, but also psychologically." This battle-hardened surgeon found that he was unable to sleep after finishing his shift and walking past "the wards of severely wounded men pleading for help, and to be the next ones going in to surgery. I saw many 17-year-old boys crying and asking for their mothers, and many men died while lying on bunks on the corridor waiting to be treated."[71] In an interview near the end of his life, Massons could still vividly recall hearing lines of wounded men pleading for emergency treatment, "saying things like, 'Me first – I have four sons'."[72]

Another account, from the Battle of the Ebro in the following year, describes the type of improvised operating theatre in which Massons and Dorothy were working.

> On the stretchers lie the worst of the mutilated, groaning in voices that don't seem to belong to human beings. . . . The floor becomes covered with cotton and gauze, soon soaked with pus and blood. The sharp smell of sweat, human filth, burnt oil and tobacco fills the dense, cold, atmosphere. The oil lamps only illuminate about a square meter and in this dark, suffocating, gloomy environment, people move laboriously, like ghosts.[73]

Medical supplies, and especially anaesthetics, were in very short supply by the time of the Brunete battle, in part because of a blockade of the Spanish coast by German and Italian submarines. Under the Non-Proliferation Agreement, which had become utterly discredited yet was still upheld by its principal signatories, France refused to allow cross-border traffic of medical equipment, and the Republican Army's main source for this had become the Soviet Union.[74]

Once their condition was stabilised, Dorothy's patients were evacuated by back roads from Hoyo de Manzanares to the large institutional hospitals in Madrid. The Nationalists' ultimate goal of capturing the capital was once again thwarted. "The famous Republican slogan 'They shall not pass' held true on this occasion", she wrote, "and Franco's attack failed."[75] However, the cost of the battle was shockingly high and resulted in the near-annihilation of the 13th International Brigade, which lost more than a thousand men. Its surviving members then refused orders to return to the front and their Brigade was disbanded amid scenes of great recrimination and violence.

A major reorganisation of the entire Republican ranks followed, and this affected Dorothy's surgical team. They returned to the International Brigades base at Albacete where Massons presented his personal papers, which bore a photograph of him taken a year earlier. The contrast with his current appearance was alarming. "I looked as if I was wasted away, like a living corpse, and Dr. Telge told me I needed a holiday and sent me back to Barcelona."[76] Dorothy also appeared very unlike the enthusiastic and healthy woman who had arrived in Spain in February. She had lost up to 10 kilograms in weight and was clearly no longer capable of remaining at work in the battlefield.[77] She was given a precious military pass permitting her to leave Spain, and a seat on a plane to Paris. These gifts came at a price. She was asked, and agreed, to carry highly secret documents to the French Communist Party headquarters, and concealed them in her vagina.[78] The papers were successfully delivered, and after several weeks of desperately needed rest, she returned to Spain by the same plane.[79]

Dorothy returned to the site of her first posting, the Almería hospital, to find that even this small, rearguard and entirely non-military facility was no longer a secure haven. A month earlier, in the early morning of 30 May 1937, five German battleships had anchored off Almería and shelled the city for half an hour. Sir George Young and four other members of his unit happened to be inside one of their hospitals, which received several shells during the bombardment. Sir George's personal assistant, Peter O'Donovan, was loading panic-stricken patients into an ambulance when he was cut above the right eye by flying glass. "The Germans sent in big shells with a time fuse," wrote Sir George, "which exploded some moments after contact and then scattered shrapnel laterally. The effect is to wound or kill all living creatures within many yards." Almería's civil governor reported that, "There is not one building in the whole town which has not been touched."[80]

Once again the rugged hill road that followed a famously beautiful stretch of Spain's Mediterranean coast was clogged with people fleeing on foot. Several thousand homeless and destitute escapees took to the road eastward from Almería in the hope of finding sanctuary in the next large town of Murcia. They included many who had already made the nightmarish journey from Málaga to Almería.

The departure of many of its refugees brought no relief to Almería's overworked hospitals, now faced with a fresh wave of patients from the naval attack. Sir George's staff remained at their posts, with all beds in the children's hospitals full and the out-patients' clinic working day and night. From Murcia came an urgent request to open a new hospital there to treat the sudden influx of exhausted humanity. The city officials reported that their own resources were already stretched beyond capacity. The only possible assistance for Murcia's surging refugee crisis, Sir George was told, was whatever his own volunteer staff might provide.

Chapter 3
Hospital Inglés de Niños

The dusty, provincial city of Murcia, lying in a valley 30 miles from the Mediterranean coast, had traditionally been regarded as a placid backwater. In August 1937, however, it was an 'abyss of misery' as thousands of traumatised and destitute refugees poured in from Málaga, Cadiz, Seville and other towns that had fallen to the Nationalists.[1] By some estimates, the population of 60,000 had almost doubled with the influx of desperately needy men, women and children.

These fugitives from coastal towns to Murcia's west were crammed alongside others from central Spain and Madrid, areas then still under Republican control but also threatened by the war. Murcia's civil authorities, including its cheerful and competent *alcalde,* had battled since the fall of Málaga in February to cope with their flood of war casualties and, with almost no outside support, had succeeded in housing more than 20,000 of them. About half of this number were placed with local families or in villages in the surrounding region. The remainder were crammed into five (eventually seven) *refugios,* refuges hastily constructed in available large buildings and named for heroes and heroines of the Republican movement. The largest and most chaotic of these was an unfinished concrete apartment block named for Pablo Iglesias, a revered labour leader who had died ten years earlier. Here several thousand refugees were living in conditions of utter degradation.

This nine-storied slum had no windows, doors or internal walls and was furnished only with a few straw mattresses. When the Quaker relief worker Francesca Wilson arrived in Murcia in April, she described it as a scene from a nightmare – "babies crying, boys rushing madly from floor to floor, sick people groaning, women shouting . . . They surged around us, telling us their stories, clinging to us like people drowning in a bog."[2]

The best efforts of Murcia's officials could not supply these refugees with food and clothing, let alone medical treatment. The dairying lands of Spain were almost all in the hands of Franco's forces, so the entire Republic suffered from a desperate shortage of milk. Swiftly and indomitably, Wilson arranged delivery of emergency food supplies from the Quaker relief depot in Valencia, and set up a breakfast canteen for refugee children and pregnant women.[3] By the following month, and with help from the nurses at Sir George Young's hospital in Almería, she was able to feed several thousand daily.

From her long experience of working with wartime refugees, Wilson was well aware that these emergency measures barely touched the surface of the crisis in Murcia. The neediest children were unable even to come to the canteens, and the infant death rate was estimated at 50%. Frida Stewart, an English leftist volunteer, wrote that many of the youngest refugees "arrived exhausted and fell ill in the 'refugios' which are not a fit place for any invalid . . . and quite a number were born and are now struggling for existence, tiny wizened things whom their underfed mothers can't adequately feed. There are a great many small children with huge bellies and scraggy arms and legs with skin diseases and diseased eyes, which would certainly get worse and spread among the others if not attended to soon."[4]

Murcia's provincial public hospital was already stretched to capacity. "The only solution," declared Francesca Wilson, "was to make a special hospital for these children."[5] In May 1937 she prevailed upon Sir George Young to extend his children's medical service to Murcia, and he agreed on the condition that she found and equipped a suitable building. This, with characteristic and seemingly irresistible charm and determination, she proceeded to do. The local headmistress and *alcalde* helped her to locate a suitable villa on the outskirts of the old town and near its 13th-century university, which itself had been converted into a large military hospital. In an article for the *Manchester Guardian* aimed at soliciting donations for her work, she described the premises as "the most perfect house in Murcia – a modern villa standing in its own grounds, beautifully fitted out with two bathrooms and two kitchens, cool tiled floors and marble stairs, balconies and a flat roof – an ideal place for a hospital".[6]

Wilson felt no qualms at seeing the villa's elderly and well-to-do owners turned out of their home, since they had another property to live in. It was ludicrous, she felt, "that such a place should be inhabited by a handful of people when it might be housing 30 sick children, some of whom would die if they did not come to it."[7] With similar brisk pragmatism, she welcomed gifts of crockery, cutlery and furniture for the new hospital, well aware that they had mostly been pilfered from the abandoned homes of other wealthy citizens.

Within two weeks the villa's garden was dug up and planted to provide fresh food. Cooks, nursing assistants and laundry staff (who had the most arduous task of all) were hired from the refugee population. Linen and hospital clothing was sewn by the refugees "at lightning speed", while Wilson bought up the town's entire available stock of medicines, beds, bowls and office equipment. Amid the excitement, it was "only when Don Alfonso, the excellent Spanish doctor who had been assigned to us, ordered a screen for the dying did I remember that it was not a convalescent home we were starting but something much more serious."[8]

The Hospital Inglés de Niños (English Children's Hospital) opened formally at the beginning of June 1937. Any doubts that refugee mothers would be willing to admit their children were immediately relieved. "The children began to pour in . . . We went round to the Refugios with a huge Hotel bus and collected all the sick children from their straw and flies and bought [sic] them along for examination . . . we found ourselves landed not only with babies but with mothers attached and for the first 8 days we looked rather like a Maternity Home. Then the typhoids began to pour in – typhoids in all stages of fever, delirium and sickness."[9] These 13 critically ill infants were treated by Nurse Shaw, an English nurse with recent experience of a typhoid epidemic in Bournemouth. She, together with Frida Stewart, had arrived in Murcia in an aging ambulance donated by Scottish miners.

They "were hard at it, day and night, during the first week," wrote Stewart later. "But the saving of those babies was the greatest challenge of all time, I felt, as I ran to and fro for the doctors with drugs and disinfectants and bedpans and bottles, and sterilised instruments and scrubbed clothing till I was blue in the face. And what pride and joy to know that every one of the thirteen was in fact saved".[10]

For the first fortnight the patients' relatives were permitted to visit
them at all hours, an indulgence to persuade mothers to leave their
children in the care of foreign-sounding strangers.[11] Providing suitable food for already undernourished and critically ill patients was a
problem from the outset, but supplies came from an unexpected
quarter.

Murcia was a garrison town, known as the 'town of the wounded'
since it housed four newly built military hospitals and a large and
revolving population of injured and convalescing troops. These
included a number of International Brigade veterans of the devastat-
ingly bloody battle of Jarama, who were treated at their own hospital,
named after the fiery Republican orator La Pasionaria and headed by
a Polish woman doctor, Suzanne Heck.[12] "There are a terrible number
of 'mutilados' [amputees] here from the I.B. [International
Brigades]" wrote Frida Stewart in a letter to her family. "Splendid
people and marvellously brave and of course, anti-fascist to the bone.
They are all champing to get back to the Front".[13] Some of these men
had been admitted to hospital so poorly clad that, when eventually
able to walk around the city, they were obliged to do so wearing
hospital pyjamas.[14] Yet they willingly volunteered to drive military
lorries to scour the countryside for fresh produce, and to travel to the
coast for fish.

The number of beds in the Children's Hospital soon rose to 50,
and every week hundreds more outpatients received medication from
its dispensary. Trained nurses were provided by Sir George Young's
two hospitals at Alméria and Alicante, and they were assisted by other
non-medical volunteers, such as Frida Stewart, who arrived directly
from Britain.

By the time a fulltime staff of three foreign-trained nurses was
engaged, the hospital's running expenses outstripped the combined
resources of Sir George and the English Quakers represented by
Francesca Wilson. This situation, she insisted, did not reflect poorly
on her impetuosity in establishing a hospital without securing the
funds to sustain it. "In relief work, prudence is not enough. When
needs are great, risks have to be taken."[15] A solution to the funding
crisis appeared through the growing presence of US Quakers among
the foreign agencies providing relief services in Spain. Francesca
Wilson negotiated with the American Friends Service Council, the

US equivalent of the British 'Friends', to assume responsibility for funding all three of the hospitals founded by Sir George Young.[16] This funding was maintained throughout and beyond the duration of the civil war. In July 1937, when Wilson had to return to her teaching job in England, her place was taken by Esther Farquhar, a capable social worker and fluent Spanish speaker from Ohio.

At this decisive stage Dorothy Morris, while still living in London, was recruited by the American Quakers to return to Murcia as head nurse of a hospital that had suddenly become 'English' in name only. She arrived in the teeming city in the searing heat and glare of midsummer 1937, but was given no time to adjust to the demands of her new position. On top of the needs of an unending stream of severely ill, undernourished and often traumatised children and mothers, she discovered that her staff had reached such a state of dysfunction that they were barely able to work together.

During the hospital's first few months, severe tensions had developed between its Spanish doctor, a devoted paediatrician named Don Amalio Fernandez, and his British nurses. Their disagreements were compounded by communication difficulties since neither party could speak the other's language well, but at the core of the dispute lay differences in attitude and medical procedures.

"The Spaniards believe in injections much more than we do," Dorothy explained to Francesca Wilson later. "Well, perhaps they are right. They say, 'plunk it in – then you're sure it gets there. If you give it by mouth, half the time the children will spit it out.' But injections frighten children, and our nurses rebelled. But I wouldn't have it. If you work in a foreign country, you've got to follow its system."[17]

According to Esther Farquhar, Don Amalio had never felt that the British nurses were prepared to obey his instructions. "The English nurses feel themselves far above the Spanish doctors in their knowledge of hygiene at least, and are very much opposed to the use of so many injections".[18] By the time Dorothy arrived, the doctor was threatening to resign unless the nurses showed confidence in him. "After a rather difficult session of the doctor with the nurses," Farquhar reported to her US office, "he decided that he would continue. Three of those four nurses have now gone home, and I am very happy to say that the administrator, Dorothy Morris, has worked with the Spanish doctors in the hospitals at the front enough to realise that even though their methods are different, they are good doctors and she thinks the English nurses should adapt themselves to the physician under whom they work."[19]

Dorothy's elementary but rapidly improving Spanish is likely to have helped repair the rift between the foreign and local medical professionals, and she confirmed Esther Farquhar's assessment that her recent front-line nursing experience gave her precious credibility in Spanish eyes. "My previous six months in the Brigade Hospitals and great friendship with my Spaniards was a priceless help."[20] Being thrust into the battlefield and forced to acquire the linguistic and other skills to practise in that environment (an ordeal, literally, by fire), Dorothy had acquired formidable authority in her new role, among both Spanish and non-Spanish staff. From being a novice member of a team she had suddenly become a leader and administrator, and thereafter she repeatedly demonstrated managerial as well as clinical skills.

The first intake of British nurses, she felt, comprised enthusiastic young women who, "hadn't had the least idea of what they were doing in Spain and had muddled a bit – nurses had come out from England for fun and adventure and hadn't attempted to see the Spanish point of view and had gone back ill or just dazed after a few months".[21] This naivety was compounded by the cultural obstacles presented by the locals recruited to work at the hospital. "The *chicas* (girls) from the refuges . . . had no idea of nursing at first because that had always been done by nuns". On the other hand the *practicantes* (medical students) "feel themselves halfway to doctors and too grand to do ordinary jobs." Despite this unpromising introduction, Dorothy appeared confident that she would turn the hospital around. The nurses sent most recently from Britain by the Quakers were, she thought, "very good and we are determined to teach the *chicas* properly. We must leave a legacy to Spain."[22]

After the constant uprooting of her previous six months, Dorothy was to remain at the Murcia children's hospital for over a year, practically a lifetime in the turbulent context of the war. A strict daily routine was established, governed by the deep-toned peals of the cathedral bell. Every morning, in time for the doctor's rounds at nine, the surgery was prepared and the villa's black-and-white marble tiled floors were swept and washed. Sometimes the older convalescent children were allowed to perform this task. "There is always a competition to get a job if one is going, and the most trustworthy child, temporarily appointed 'Responsable' (supervisor) of the convalescents, is asked to see to the work."[23] Overstressed city facilities meant that the hospital's water supply was regularly cut off, and enough water for two hours' use was always kept stored in great stone jars that were a traditional feature of Murcian homes. Hospital staff had the use of a car belonging to Murcia's Protestant pastor. His religion was regarded with some sympathy by the Republican movement and he was not subject to the violent reprisals carried out against priests, nuns and Catholic churches in the months preceding and following the outbreak of the war.[24]

Visiting hours were now limited to between four and five pm on Tuesdays and Fridays, when the hospital was filled with a 'tremendous hubbub', but at other times it appeared far more orderly than in the weeks after opening. "In July," said one English visitor, the refugee relatives of the young patients, "swept in a torrent into the wards; in September they went in as an orderly crowd."[25]

By comparison with her gruelling battlefield nursing for Dr Massons, Dorothy found the demands of managing this small hospital relatively pleasant. "I thoroughly enjoyed pulling in the various slacks I found," she told her family.[26] She was certainly proud of the hospital's record of treatment. "At one point we had measles, typhoid, meningitis and diphtheria all at the same moment, but no cross-infection and very few deaths."[27]

The nursing staff wore simple white cotton uniforms, without the cap that was traditionally the badge of their profession, or even stockings. Those articles of clothing had come to be seen by the local people as representing the wealthy classes and the dictatorial regime they had voted to reject. On their siesta, nurses would go up to the villa's flat roof overlooking the town, remove their uniforms and lie on airbeds in their underwear, basking in the Mediterranean sun and anticipating by several decades the tourism industry that would eventually transform the economy of the entire region.

A photograph taken in this period shows Dorothy sitting on the roof in her uniform and holding a shaven-headed patient in her lap. They are looking out beyond a fringe of palm trees at the city and the plain beyond, apparently in the early morning. It is a still and tranquil scene and the child, probably a boy, appears entirely at ease in the arms of his tall and commanding carer. Beneath their chair lies that small and vital item of children's rehabilitation equipment, a rubber ball.

This image, endearing as it is, belies the hospital's formidable workload. "After supper," wrote another English volunteer, "work is by no means over. Food for the morrow has to be discussed, accounts done, plans for any changes of routine made, reports on the condition of the patients to be made, visitors to see and enquiries to answer. Sometimes some of us are able to go out to the open air cinema, or we make a hurried visit to one of the hospitals for the wounded . . . We are rarely in bed before twelve".[28]

As she found time to explore beyond the hospital's walls, Dorothy learned that the recent crises of the civil war overlaid much older and entrenched social problems. Murcianos were among the poorest and most backward people in all of Spain, and long before the war they had been regarded with condescension, even contempt, by more sophisticated Spaniards. Many of the townspeople were landless farm-workers with no regular income over the winter months. Nearly all of them, even convent-trained nurses, were illiterate, since the church-based education system was inclined to regard literacy as the preserve of the elite. The Republican government had been elected on the promise of better schools and other social services, but had only begun to provide them when the civil war erupted.

Despite its entrenched poverty and dispiriting social structure, Murcia had its appeal for foreigners. It had been founded in the ninth century, like many of the towns of southern Spain, by Muslim colonisers from north Africa. Several centuries later the Muslims had been ejected, or converted, through a series of Christian crusades, but many signs of their influence remained. Murcia's two main thoroughfares, the Calle de la Platería and de la Traperia (the street of silversmiths, and of linen weavers), had once been Moorish marketplaces. The floridly baroque cathedral stood on the site of the town's mosque.

By the 20th century the most prominent surviving evidence of Moorish occupation was the great stone irrigation system which tamed the flood-prone Segura River and directed its waters across a huge cultivated area, the *huerta,* to the south of the city. When its Moorish builders were overthrown, this system was preserved and maintained by the Spanish, and after a millennium of steady use it continued to irrigate the Segura plain, forming an oasis of vegetation surrounded by treeless, barren hills. "This valley is one huge garden", Dorothy told her family in her first Murcian spring.[29]

A floodbank alongside the river, the Malecon, was the site for that most important Spanish spectacle, the evening promenade. "Even during the war it was crowded at sunset, the time of the Spanish *paseo*, mainly with girls walking arm-in-arm with each other and tossing their heads haughtily at the saucy remarks addressed them as homage by black-eyed Republican soldiers or blue-eyed International Brigaders. At one side of the Malecon are groves of date palms and orange trees, on the other the rushing brown river and the vast blue-green *huerta* ringed with tawny hills".[30]

Other features of the town were less attractive. It had no sewerage system and few proper toilets. People simply squatted among the crops or in the streets, and typhoid-laden dust blew over the produce on sale in the marketplace. The fierce white light of midsummer was searing, especially for unaccustomed foreigners, who learned to keep to the shade of the narrow, winding allies. Here a pedestrian might encounter a rumbling wooden water cart hauled by as many as five animals, often a mixture of donkeys, mules and horses hitched together in a single line with their carter walking behind them – the only arrangement that could negotiate the town's mediaeval passage-ways.[31]

Apart from the massive, squat cathedral which was kept locked up under guard, all of the town's many religious buildings had been converted to secular use, especially the production of war materials. With their pews pushed aside, the churches had become improvised factories and workshops, where workers feverishly sewed uniforms, packed munitions and repaired and converted vehicles. The town centre was "like an open-air public library," thought one recuperating English Brigader. " . . . everywhere there were posters".[32] The city's bullring still staged a few *corridas*, or bullfights, but their appeal was no longer simply as a spectacle but also as a potential food supply. "Occasionally, after a bullfight, there would be beef for sale and I would watch the butcher divide the carcase. Every one of his customers would leave his stall with only a pathetically thin strip of meat".[33]

Although the streets were thronged with troops, the Republican city officials and the imposition of military discipline made it safer, paradoxically, for a single woman to walk about than in the years before the outbreak of war.[34] In a letter to her family, Dorothy described a visit to the Thursday morning market.

> I went early this morning and bought young plants and rope alpagartas [canvas sandals with rope soles] and (nearly) a young pig. It is a fascinating sight – bright sunlight dappled by the shade of lacy gum trees in a big space where the animals are casually tied in groups: a river down below, and the sound of water rushing by in stone conduits, pouring into the old Moorish tanks where women come to do all the laundry. Then nearby in the cobbled narrow calles and on the plaza are the stalls with rough pottery and flowers and gimcracks. Spanish peasants are most amusing . . . there gathered a crowd of 11 and 8 donkeys. I was lucky in getting some apparently much coveted tomato plants and afterwards as we sat having a coffee in the sun on the plaza, odd people just kept drifting up and enquiring what I'd paid – the waiter said I'd done quite well.[35]

In September 1937 Francesca Wilson returned from England to inspect the hospital she had established four months earlier, finding it "enormously increased . . . the magnificent hall downstairs turned into a ward for a dozen children, more children (nearly fifty now), more nurses, more Spanish staff, more doctors: a tremendous hive of activity. In spite of being so much bigger it hadn't lost any of its kindliness, warmth of atmosphere and power of adapting itself to circumstances . . . at visiting times the place is full of picturesque, gipsy-like folk".[36] Inez McDonald, another British volunteer in this period, described the young patients as "unaffected, unselfconscious affectionate beings who were rarely naughty, considering their restricted life in the hospital; the people were almost every one of them passionately grateful for the little we were able to do for them."[37]

The young and energetic US Quaker Emily Parker found that the little hospital had given even the local medical personnel "an entirely new idea of how to treat sick children. Before, if they got sick, well, they did what they could but now an ambulance comes and gets the child, it is taken to the hospital where it receives good care and when it comes home again it is well and smiling. And they say 'we never saw such a thing before'".[38]

A photograph of a dozen convalescing children shows them ranged on the villa's front steps, from chubby toddlers at the bottom to solemn older boys standing in front of the door. They appear sturdy and cheerful, and evidently benefitting from the effects of the diet and rest provided at the hospital. Only the defiant stance and stern expressions of the oldest boys suggest the profound insecurity and recent trauma they had endured.

As the hospital's facilities and systems developed, it extended its services to address the longer-term needs of the refugee children. For the first week following their discharge, former patients could return for a daily meal.[39] They could also carry on attending a school set up within the hospital to teach convalescent children. Classes were given every afternoon by two young women teachers, members of the Republican student movement *Federación Universitaria Escolar*, after they had already worked a full day at a local school. One of the teachers, Pilar Barnés, recalled that the hospital paid them with food and other supplies, including "thread, needles, steel fountain pens that my sister exchanged in the vegetable garden for vegetables, bread, potatoes, flour".[40]

Towards the end of 1937 a second New Zealand nurse arrived at Murcia, not to work there but as a patient herself. Isobel Dodds had volunteered to nurse in the civil war less than a year after finishing her training at Wellington Hospital. She left New Zealand for Spain in May 1937 together with fellow nurses Renée Shadbolt and Millicent Sharples. She and Nurse Shadbolt were then based at an International Brigades hospital in a requisitioned convent in the town of Huete, in the arid and impoverished region of Castilla-La Mancha. After five months the harsh living conditions and overwork forced Dodds to take a break. "I wasn't exactly ill," she told an interviewer late in her life, "but I was suffering from what was almost like a gastric ulcer . . . The food was terribly poor where we were and it was at a period when winter had started, and it was very cold. And since there was a truck going down to Murcia to collect . . . some sort of hospital equipment, it was suggested I go down with the driver, and stay for a few days in Murcia, which was in the south, and warm."[41]

Nurse Dodds became one of very few women patients at the La Pasionaria International Brigades Hospital, housed in the ancient university building near the children's hospital. "How Dorothy Morris knew I was there I don't know, but she contacted me there and . . . suggested that I might find it more comfortable to come and stay with her. And I did that for about two weeks, I suppose." Dorothy was then living very frugally with another English nurse in a small apartment. The somewhat younger Isobel Dodds thought her to be, "quite good-looking, slim, brown-haired. She didn't wear a nurse's uniform or anything like that. . . . She was well-spoken and one would consider that she'd had a good education."[42]

Isobel was impressed by her quietly spoken host's dedication and work ethic. "She spoke good Spanish, and was taking lessons to improve her Spanish. Her reputation was very high amongst the people who knew her."[43] What particularly struck the younger nurse about her more experienced colleague was her open-minded spirit. She lacked the uncompromising sectarian zeal that impelled many of the overseas volunteers, both military and medical, who had arrived to support the embattled Republic. Nurse Dodds felt that Dorothy's attitude was primarily "humanitarian, she wasn't political."[44]

This impression, however, was gained from a two-week stay during Dodds' own convalescence, and was only partially accurate. Like the International Brigaders she had lately worked among, Dorothy was 'anti-fascist to the bone'. The six months she spent nursing at Guadalajara and the Brunete battlefront were always after-wards regarded as the most meaningful experience of her life. There is no evidence that she joined the Communist Party or any other political grouping during her civil war experience, but she was undoubtedly well informed about the international manoeuvres that were prolonging the war, and was critical of other volunteer nurses who made no attempt to fathom the circumstances that had precip-itated the crisis in Spain. Through BBC news broadcasts received by the hospital's radio, and occasional foreign newspapers, she kept in touch with the worsening political situation in Europe, and fumed with anger at vacillating politicians.

She also followed political developments in her own country, and rejoiced at the re-election in 1938 of New Zealand's first, and openly socialist, Labour government. Her parents, evidently, were much more ambivalent. "I don't quite know how you feel about the Labour success in NZ," she wrote. "Quite frankly I am very pleased they're back. It is easy to take an objective view when one is far from the scene of the struggle but if you look at what they are doing and understand why they're doing it their programme seems quite reasonable. I heard some queer things – quite true – when I was in England of the unsavoury attempts by the British Govt to undermine NZ credit and reputation – they were all however quite understandable to someone like myself who has seen and heard the course of events in Spain."[45]

By April 1938 Dorothy could reassure her family that she was faring "very well so far – possibly the calm in the centre of the storm!" She had evidently remained in touch with friends from the 13th Battalion after she left them to work behind the lines. When she met up with them in Murcia, "They all exclaimed at the difference in my looks".[46] Life as the head of the children's hospital, demanding though it was, had evidently enabled her to gain weight and generally appear healthier than when nursing on the battlefield. The staff divisions so evident when she arrived the previous August had also eased. "We are a very happy family . . . We continue to be very busy, as of course the number of refugees is increasing rather than diminishing, sad to say. We all love it here."[47] The letter provides a taste of her non-sectarian but fiercely held political convictions. "I was so thrilled to hear on our wireless that the only government which refused to back that old wicked devil of a Chamberlain up was New Zealand. This minute, we have here two children, most piteous little rascals of his 'Non Intervention'. They were bombed by huge ½ ton incendiary bombs dropped on them in Barcelona by his fellow fiends the Italians and Germans, and by 'Non Intervention', Spain can't buy the means to defend them. I don't want to rant but you can imagine how I feel."[48]

The news report she refers to is likely to have followed a speech at the League of Nations by the New Zealand delegate Bill Jordan, who broke with established colonial tradition by declining to vote with Britain to endorse an obviously ineffective policy of non-intervention. Instead, Jordan pressed for a more active stance on Spain. Apart from Mexico, New Zealand was the only member of the League, "prepared to openly criticize the restrictive action of the Non-Intervention Committee in regard to the role of the League of Nations".[49] Those two small voices, inevitably, had no effect on the League's policy, and Britain, France and other potentially powerful allies of Republican Spain scrupulously maintained their distance from the conflict, while Germany and Italy continued to pour advanced military equipment and trained troops into the Nationalist ranks.

Dorothy reserved her deepest contempt for Britain's Conservative prime minister Neville Chamberlain, whose later policy of appeasement towards Hitler and Mussolini was foreshadowed by his aloof disregard for the effects of the civil war on Spain's population. The Republican government was "prevented by 'Non Intervention' from buying anti aircraft guns to protect themselves, and this the direct work of the British who pride themselves on 'fair play.' I do so hope I live just long enough to be in at the day of retribution for all this" – hardly the words of an apolitical or non-partisan participant in the civil war.[50]

This undeniable anguish at the impacts of a token non-intervention pact can only have been strengthened by the course of the war. By early 1938 it was clear that the massive military support from its German and Italian allies gave the Nationalists a decisive advantage over the Republican army, whose international allies were, by comparison, amateurish, and pitifully trained and equipped. The fall of the city of Teruel and other Nationalist advances drove a fresh wave of refugees to Alicante, Murcia and Alméria, and disrupted communication and relief supplies. As Franco's forces advanced steadily southward, the children's hospital lost the support of the International Brigaders in the neighbouring hospital, who were urgently evacuated to new headquarters far to the north, in Barcelona. Dorothy told Francesca Wilson that the men "disappeared at twenty-four hours' notice in April – they got up to Barcelona just before the road was cut [by Nationalist troops], except for a few sick and wounded. I'll never forget that departure. It was tragic."[51]

This severe setback was compounded by Dorothy's declining health and morale. In a handwritten note to the Friends Service Council in London, Esther Farquhar refers to her "bad cold with other complications . . . Dorothy Morris should have a month's vacation – she is so nervous she drives the other nurses wild."[52] As she had done at a similarly low point the year before, Dorothy was able to leave her work and spend a week in Paris, this time in the company of her good friend Mary Elmes who was also urgently in need of respite. Although she had no nursing training (she had studied French and Spanish at Trinity College, Dublin), Mary ran the adjacent children's hospital at Alicante. Dorothy described her friend to her family as "very calm, collected and capable".[53] Both women returned somewhat refreshed in July.

The American Friends Service Committee in Philadelphia received a report in this period that "Murcia hospital is getting on fine under the capable supervision of Dorothy Morris. She has made some changes, such as having the telephone placed in her room, having locks put on several doors, and insisting upon knowing just what her staff is doing all the time they are on duty which has gained her the respect of the doctors and the hospital staff."[54]

"In many ways," wrote US volunteer Florence Conard, "Murcia seems to be an oasis of quiet. But certain things keep reminding us of what is happening outside. The soldiers, for instance, both wounded and well, the military trucks, the refuges and underground protections which have been built 'in case of accident' . . . so many of these terrible conditions here are not just war conditions, but are pre-war conditions." Near the hospital she encountered a gypsy family – "mother, grandmother and several wee, naked children" – living in the street without shelter of any kind.[55]

As the war entered its second full year, the routine food shortages were felt ever more acutely. The shrinking areas of the country still under Republican control included the largest population centres, while the main food-producing regions were firmly controlled by Franco's Nationalists. Murcia relied on supplies sent from distant Republican cities such as Valencia, and these were frequently delayed or pilfered, or failed to arrive altogether. "We used to have great crises when ships were delayed," remembered the US Friend Dorothy Davies, " but never actually had no food to give the children".[56]

With the threat of widespread starvation, the children's hospital and the town's other Quaker relief services faced growing pleas for help from the wider population of Murcia. In May 1938 the Quakers committed to providing a daily breakfast for an extra 4000 children. Each child received a piece of bread and a glass of milk, and if any bread was left over the older children received a second piece. Relief worker Emily Parker noticed that many of these ravenous children did not eat their extra bread but took it home for their mothers, or other family members too old to qualify for the free breakfast. The diet of foreign volunteers was only a little better. From 1938 they seldom ate meat apart from canned beef. Dorothy Davies "once saw and smelt something savoury frying on a little charcoal stove in the street. It looked like rabbit but was probably cat!"[57] The staple food was beans, served with dried cod from Denmark. A typical day's meal consisted of porridge for breakfast, served with Cadbury cocoa and milk powder. Lunch for the hospital staff was generally a plate of soup with beans and lettuce. Supper, served in Spanish style after 9pm, was much the same, together with oranges or nuts, "but the former very poor".[58]

As conditions worsened in the towns, medical and other services for the refugee children were progressively relocated to small villages in the surrounding region. The hospital at Alicante was moved in May 1938, when the town came under daily attack from German fighter-bombers. "The town is . . . half paralysed," wrote Francesca Wilson, "because almost every day there are air raids. These usually occur [in the late morning] and cause little loss of life. The sirens scream and the whole town disappears underground for an hour or two. . . . People wait patiently until it is over, but they look strained and anxious. Every crash they hear may mean their home in ruins. I was eager to get children away, and much as Spanish mothers hate to part with them they were eager, too."[59]

The personal background of the doctor at the Alicante hospital, Manuel Blanc Rodríguez, exemplified the complex, often contradictory loyalties which the ferociously ideological civil war forced on many dedicated Spaniards. Dr Rodríguez was Catholic and had been a member of a conservative party. For these affiliations, his brother, four cousins and a brother-in-law were murdered at the outbreak of the civil war. In order to continue working as a doctor, Rodríguez joined the powerful and fervently pro-Republican UGT trade union. In September 1937 he began working at the children's hospital in Alicante, and during the war he is thought to have saved many people from death or prison.[60]

The Alicante hospital's Irish director, Mary Elmes, took charge of transferring the children and hospital equipment about 40 miles north to the small mountain village of Polop.[61] Their new home was a wealthy merchant's *finca*, or farmhouse, which had stood empty since the war began two years earlier. Dorothy Davies, who worked alongside Mary Elmes, found it, "a joy to see the children improving day by day with sunshine and invigorating mountain air and freedom from anxiety. All had been through repeated air-raids and some had begun to look haggard and old. Some of the new cases who came to us were very, very ill, others were mainly in need of good food and normal healthy life".[62]

Dr Rodríguez now collected his young patients from refugee clinics along the coast and took them up to Polop by car. Stores were sent there each week from Murcia by *camioneta,* the small truck provided by the American Friends, and nursing staff were sometimes exchanged between the two hospitals as their workloads fluctuated. "Life passed fairly quietly at Polop. We used to hear the bombs falling on the coastal towns when the wind was in that direction and occasionally we saw the raiders on their way back to Majorca." Apart from those unpleasant signs of Nationalist activity, says Dorothy Davies, "There was little to remind us of war except that for weeks together we were without bread or flour or potatoes".[63]

Two months after its relocation to Polop, Dorothy Morris paid the new hospital a visit.

> One of our cars came through and picked me up and took me on for a few hours up into the hills to an old and picturesque pueblo where is now established our hospital. . . . It is rather remote but its doctor drives the 40-odd miles from outside Alicante twice a week bringing up sick children etc. They are in a nice house, roomy and cool with the most picturesque scenery in the world rolling all round them from the Sierras behind to the blue bay far below.[64]

The quietness and "clear sparkling air" of Polop made this village a favourite escape for Dorothy from the feverish atmosphere of Murcia. En route she was able to call at a coastal children's camp set up by the indefatigable Francesca Wilson. About 30 boys and girls were accommodated, at first in tents and later in a "spruce white villa" above the tiny fishing village of Benidorm whose name, at that time, had none of the connotations of package tourism it would later acquire.

1 The stalwart crew of the *Lucky Lady* gold dredge pose on board their vessel at Bannockburn Creek near Cromwell, 1901. Young engineer Geoffrey Morris is fourth from right.

2 Proud parents Rebecca and Geoffrey Morris with their first children – Dorothy (then aged about six) and Geoff junior.

3 A large crew and not a lifejacket in sight. The Morris children and friends set out for Quail Island in Lyttelton Harbour, c. 1914.

4 Rangi Ruru school prefects, 1920. Dorothy Morris third from right.

5 The Morris family in repose at Flackley Ash, c. 1925. From left Frank, Dorothy, their aunt Selena, Ruth, their mother Rebecca, Roger, and their father Geoffrey. The two boys wear the distinctive uniform of Christ's College, Christchurch.

6 A newly trained nurse, Dorothy relaxes at home in Lyttelton, c. 1930.

7 Dorothy Morris, studio portrait, c. 1926.

8 The Malecon, Murcia, southern Spain, c. 1937.

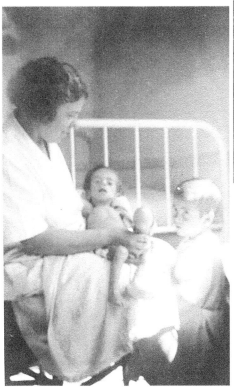

9 The villa that became the English Children's Hospital, Murcia, 1937. Several patients stand on the front steps.

10 Sylvia, a Spanish nurse aid whose surname is unknown, with two of her patients including a tiny 'starveling'.

12 These cheerful and sturdy convalescents are shown on the hospital's front steps.

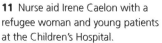

11 Nurse aid Irene Caelon with a refugee woman and young patients at the Children's Hospital.

13 Dorothy with an unidentified patient on the hospital roof, early morning, 1938.

14 Stylishly wrapped in winter coats, Mary Elmes (centre), Dorothy Morris and their driver Juan stand next to their delivery van, Perpignan, 1939.

15 La Coume, the French farmhouse that became a Quaker-owned refuge, c. 1940.

16 This small oil painting was one of Dorothy Morris's dearest possessions. It is likely to have been painted by a Spanish Civil War refugee in Perpignan, c. 1939, and shows a residential street in that region.

17 Dorothy in her last years in Christchurch, with her great-nephew Ben, 1981.

On her first visit to the camp in the spring of 1938, Dorothy Morris found it:

> a glorious spot about 20 miles up the coast beyond Alicante. There are about 30 children there safe away from the constant bombing and terrors in Alicante. A nice English girl is helping [Francesca Wilson] and a Spanish boy from here. We bathed in glorious sparkling blue sea from a heavenly beach – behind us the high yellow hills and in the foreground a medley of palms and pinos and old fig trees and cactus with the tents dotted here and there. Then all had a huge Spanish *ensalada* [salad] and grapes . . . This coast has never been known much to the outside world – why I can't imagine. To me it is the most glorious coast almost in the world – far, far more so than the Riviera – and with perfect bathing beaches. Then we drove back in the evening to Murcia – 5 hours but in sunset and then moonlight. This country is so superbly scenic that I never know when it looks more attractive. I've seen it in all its lights from dawn to late at night . . . The Alcalde [mayor] of Madrid is being brought down by our representative from Valencia to see us here in Murcia and the ex-Alicante hospital at Polop . . . They arrive any minute now, probably just for a short hour's visit, but I must away and see that everything looks smart. Also I will give them this letter – as the Valencia woman may be flying out next week and can post this in France or England.[65]

A year later she took another "heavenly restful holiday" at Polop, and described it to her family with the same fondness. The hospital itself, she said, was "a small square white country house, 'a finca', rather Moorish looking, has about 35 children mostly convalescent from their ills and running about in the lovely sun."

> The whole panorama is cut by deep ravines of mountain streams so that at all angles one can see the terraces with the neat rows of glossy green trees studded with the brilliant spots of oranges hanging in thousands – good crop I think and now in the last few days all the bare almond trees over the whole countryside have covered themselves with the most delicate blossom pink and white . . . Everywhere and there are little clusters of houses forming a pueblo making a tawny coloured huddle against the same coloured hillside though some of the houses are colour washed blue and pink or grey.[66]

These escapes from Murcia afforded Dorothy a brief respite from her deepening despair at the advance of fascism across Europe. She confessed to her family that she had been:

> in the depths of complete despair over the betrayal of Czeco-Slovakia [sic] to the Nazis by that inhuman old devil Chamberlain. By the papers that have arrived I gather that the desolation of spirit I felt was shared by millions – all those who had any conscience in fact in the civilised world. I should think it will be one of history's most dreadful crimes. It is good indeed, to be in a country which has fought and is fighting to the last inch to prevent itself suffering a similar fate.[67]

As that letter was written, in September 1938, the Republican forces were in disarray and the International Brigades were preparing to withdraw from Spain altogether. However, the children's hospital remained filled to capacity, and its work continued as efficiently as ever. "I am extraordinarily lucky," wrote Dorothy, "in having 2 splendid girls here with me – both English Quakers. . . . I think Quakers really are the salt of this earth – bar none. I never will be religious in the strict sense of the word and I doubt if I could be a Quaker – but they will always have my complete admiration for the 'sweet reasonableness' and 'selflessness' and humour".[68]

On her final visit to the hospital, Francesca Wilson found it "in wonderful shape". She described the New Zealand nurse, who had by then been in charge for over a year, as "tall and good-looking. She had the open, unself-conscious manner, the spontaneity and disregard of class distinction that made one realise at once that she had not been born in England." This impressive and direct figure left Wilson in no doubt that she and her fellow nurses found it extremely trying to cope with the unceasing flow of sick children amid wartime anxieties. Yet each time Francesca Wilson called in to the hospital, she wrote, it "looked a model – the marble floors scrubbed, the children neat and clean, with white bows in their hair, the convalescents in the garden, or having lessons with a Spanish teacher."[69]

Dorothy was particularly proud of the progress made in training the *chicas*, the young Spanish girls selected to work alongside the overseas nurses.

There is not a technique they do not know now. They have responsibility and take it in turns to go the round with [resident paediatrician] Don Alfonso and take his orders. They have come on very well. They love it. They put on their white coats and a bit of lipstick and are all set. I have had to insist on regular discipline. They have no idea of it – several of them can't read the clock. They are mostly illiterate, you see. But they adore children. Babies are kings and queens in Spain.[70]

Those achievements had been made in the face of unforeseen obstacles that underlay the very causes of the civil war. When Dorothy told her head doctor that it was a pity that the *señoritas*, the daughters of the town's wealthy citizens, did not also take up the opportunity to learn nursing, "he gave me an icy look and shrugged his shoulders. A pity – but so it was. A girl of good family wipe the behind of a refugee child? Of course, they think of these children as Reds."[71]

Dorothy was aware that many of the town's well-to-do, and probably others besides, were quietly concealing their active hostility towards the hospital and the town's Republican administration. "Murcia is full of Fifth Columnists, who are longing for Franco's entry." One of those covert Francoist supporters, she suspected, was working in a key role within the hospital itself. Don Ricardo Villalba, the assistant doctor, "is probably the head of their Falange [the openly fascist party within the Nationalist political alliance] – he has said some odd things to me sometimes."[72]

By October, air-raids by German bombers were near enough to be visible from Murcia. As waves of planes pounded Cartagena, on the coast to the south, US Quaker volunteer Ruth Cope, "could see the strings of red flares rising over the mountains that lie between us, and hear the detonations . . . We were up on the roof in the brilliant moonlight watching the southern sky while in the streets below the children were playing and laughing uproariously as children always do when allowed to play outside on a warm evening."[73]

Even in remote Polop, Dorothy found the local community consumed with anxiety over the course of the war. During one of her cherished breaks there, she wrote that, "Over it all hangs the sadness of quiet despair of war – the last of the youngish men have all been called up. . . . Today in a village to which we went for fish the women were all crying – their men had just left and what were they to do? they said."[74]

The approach of winter brought further anxieties, both major and petty. Dorothy had learned that the repressive heat of Murcia's summer could turn surprisingly cold when winter winds swept off the mountains, and "tiled floors are chilly in winter with no fires".[75] The hospital was equipped with a small heating system, and she hoped somehow to obtain enough coke to fuel it.

> This hospital goes on quite well though the difficulties of guiding it and keeping it in the right and proper path in these difficult days (which show no signs of changing for the better) occasionally make my hair stand up on end. However it's a great work and we all get enormous satisfaction out of it. The Spanish are a cheerful race. Their morale and order are both high and splendid . . . if Italy and Germany, aided by that Chamberlain horror, starve us out as at the moment they threaten to do, it will be the crime of the whole of civilization for standing by and permitting it.[76]

That year's Christmas celebrations were a determined attempt to overcome the gathering gloom and deprivation. "For days beforehand," wrote Dorothy:

> the little school under Doña Julia, a most charming woman and so clever, our teacher, had laboured at making the sweetest paper hats, nearly 100 – tied on with bright cheap ribbons. They were mostly quite Paris models – Spanish hands are so clever. Then a Swiss manager of a nearby jam factory had journeyed in his car up into the Sierras and got two fine little pine trees (tannenbaums), for us and in addition lent us all his own ornaments so that when decorated and lit up and sparkling on Christmas Eve they looked as I remembered like the tiny ones Grandad made for me long ago in Cromwell. The girls made bright paper flowers most artistically and we had flowers and greenery and balloons, American children had sent the Quakers heaps and heaps of toys so nothing lacked. Everyone here adores fiestas and was wildly excited.[77]

The local paper reported that the evening began with performances by the children, including works by Spain's greatest modern poets – Lorca, Machado, Alberti and others – and songs from "the rich folklore of the different Spanish provinces".[78]

"It really was quite a time of *emóción intima* (intimate emotion)", wrote US Quaker Ruth Cope.

> We all sat or stood or lay in cots about the little charcoal brazier with the lighted Christmas tree to one side, little chairs in front, cots on either side with the buxom Spanish nurses holding the silent wondering little babies . . . The porter, the cook, the charwomen, the gardener, the Mute (who is a grown man, but deaf since childhood, favoured of the children for he cannot scold) and by a miracle most of the children were able to be dressed, and only a few left in isolated wards . . . Everybody wore a paper cap of comical character. Even the leathern-faced gardener put on a cap, but the cook remained aloof in this particular.[79]

On two small kitchen stoves Dorothy and two colleagues "slaved madly" throughout Christmas Day to supply a succession of feasts.[80] First came the children's meal, served on a long table lined with coloured candles. It began with a huge dish of rice containing tinned fish, carefully hoarded for months beforehand. The highlight, however, was the first meat anyone had tasted in four months. The portions were meagre, but relished. A plucked turkey and two rabbits were chopped into unidentifiable morsels, and fried to provide, "a tiny piece of fresh meat for all who were well enough . . . and I think that was the biggest treat of all – the Christmas food."[81]

Next came the feast for the local staff, and finally the foreigners' meal, incorporating delicacies provided by invited guests. "Five of the Americanos working here came and ate with us – tomato soup, fried chicken (theirs) peas, potatoes, salad, tinned plum pudding (mine – from Selfridges), fruit salad and cream (tinned) and coffee and sweets etc. and a marvellous liqueur given us by our Spanish doctor, worth in these times a 'Kings ransom', which no one, being Quakers, drank but me." The evening ended, said, Dorothy, "with loud vivas" (toasts).[82]

Murcia's foreign volunteers gathered again on New Years Eve and by the light of the hospital's Christmas trees, heard the midnight chimes of Big Ben on the wireless. A few days later, Dorothy told her family, "Tomorrow [6 January] is the feast of the three Kings – the traditional children's feast day in Spain. The local committee of refugees has sent us nearly 100 fine toys to be given out tomorrow and that I hope will be the last fiesta for a while. My energy and the store cupboard are a bit lower than they were – but it was worth it."[83]

As the hospital expended all its resources to ensure that the seasonal festivities were observed as cheerfully as possible, a newly formed multinational body was preparing to address Spain's daunting humanitarian crisis. Influential British Quakers, including the former midwife Edith Pye, had convinced the governments of 24 European and other countries to create the new organisation to more effectively administer the various funds for Spanish relief supplied by governments, institutions and individuals, and coordinate their distribution through the main relief agencies.[84] New Zealand was the fifth country to promise its support to this plan, and was followed by 19 others. In December 1938 the new multinational organisation was named the International Commission for the Assistance of Child Refugees in Spain, although usually known by the less cumbersome title of the International Commission. (Confusingly, several other aid organisations also used that abbreviated name.)[85]

The International Commission planned to give one hot meal a day, scientifically planned for its nutritional value, to every Spanish child in need. From November 1938 the Commission employed Dorothy to run its feeding canteens in the Alicante region, and her place at the children's hospital was taken over by Mary Elmes. Setting up and running the Commission's canteens called for all of Dorothy's resources of energy and persuasion. Her colleague Francesca Wilson explained that the first step was to call on the local mayor to find a suitable locality and equipment, and to select the most needy children (often a whole school or age group). Then the local Women's Service was recruited to provide cooks and helpers. Only the head cook and overall supervisor received payment for their work. A lockable warehouse was vital to prevent pilfering of supplies, and even then supplies had to be audited frequently to prevent spoilage and black marketeering.[86]

Dorothy explained to her family that, "The International Commission . . . is using the Quakers organisation amongst others in Spain for the organisation and supervision of canteens for the distribution of chocolate and milk. In addition the American Govt has given an enormous quantity of flour – 75,000 tons or more – I'm not sure – which will be distributed as bread (if it isn't sunk at the ports – however the Americans have warned Mr Franco and so far USA ships are comparatively immune)."[87]

Her concern that the relief supply ships might be at risk from bombing raids proved well founded. Italian warplanes pounded the harbour several times in January 1939, as the US flour was unloaded.[88] Francesca Wilson was returning to the UK from this port, and her ship departed just minutes before the first air-raid. This experience deepened her growing conviction that the Republicans could not win the war and that the consequences of a Nationalist victory would reverberate throughout Europe and beyond.

The International Commission estimated the numbers of starving people in Spain as at least 10 million. As Nationalist forces advanced on several fronts, huge numbers of refugees began to converge on the country's northern borders and spill over into France. In far-off Murcia the situation was only a little less grim. US Quaker volunteer Emily Parker eventually saw babies being carried out of the children's hospital, "sometimes two and three a day in little coffins made from powdered milk boxes . . . children faint as they stand in line waiting for the bit we have to give!" The pacifist tenets of her religion, she felt, no longer provided adequate answers to "deaths by air raids on civilian villages or starvation by blockade."[89]

"Although people are wonderfully cheerful," Dorothy wrote in the first week of the new year:

they are suffering. As I told you we are being blockaded and starved out. We (i.e. the Quakers, Mennonites and the International Commission) are the only people with milk and eatables [in Murcia] other than what is grown – the Government has supplies and these are distributed as well as possible but owing to the pressing needs of the Army and the incredible difficulties of this war the rearguard comes second. Then too the enormous job of creating an efficient Army from nothing in these two years has absorbed most of the best brains (other than those killed) and some of the local administrators are new and raw. There are many other difficulties including the fact that the Government side is cut in two parts – so that all things considered we simply marvel that life goes on for people as well as it does.

With barely sufficient nourishment and always hungry they are –
mostly – gay. With no soap to speak of they are mostly fresh and beautifully groomed. I don't know how they manage. We here, in the hospitals,
have most of what we need but stocks are running low and we hope a ship
or so will get through the bombardments at one or other of the ports, soon.
We live frugally but our poor kids simply hate the time for home going,
much as they invariably adore their parents. We feed them for two weeks
afterwards if they come back to our little school or else draft them on to a
big canteen the International Commission has set up (chocolate and bread
breakfasts and teas for 1500). There is a network of canteens in neighbouring towns and also 5000 local school children get bread in the
mornings and the government runs a splendid Baby Clinic for 600 up-to-
2s – we supply most of the milk which they need so desperately and which
is so hard to get enough of. All this helps but not nearly sufficient, but it
is something in the right direction . . . now the Hospital functions very
well. 400 children passed through our hands in this year and 5000 through
an examination and milk clinic (run in conjunction by a Spanish doctor
and nurse in one of our rooms) . . . As you can imagine service in the
hospital is very eagerly sought after. We have a staff of 16, 11 bright pretty
Spanish nurses and the rest kitchen, cleaning and laundry staff.[90]

A weary, resigned and foreboding tone creeps in to Dorothy's last
letters from Murcia. "In all my time in Spain I have found good
friends who've looked after me and helped me marvellously. Then too
the Quakers who had assumed financial responsibility for the
Hospital (from Sir George Young) just before I came here . . . are
wonderful people to work for. Finally I felt I was helping Spain; and
in the doing I was fairly near the front line of the fight against the
forces of evil, which I have seen in all sorts of guises since I left you
4 years ago (this probably sounds melodramatic but I have lived
through so much melodrama in 2 years I know in these days fact has
left fiction far behind)". She contrived to find uplifting news to reassure her far-off family. "After some miserably cold weather we are
having a spell of most glorious clear sunny tranquil days – our dining
room has a glass bay that, during and after lunch, is a gorgeous
suntrap . . . Here spring is not so very marked, tho' further up the
coast among the almonds it is heavenly. The oranges and mandarins
are all ripe here – all the groves aglow, they are our main dessert."[91]

This brief and off-hand remark conceals the anxiety and uncertainty Dorothy must have felt as she considered the latest proposal from her Quaker sponsors. It would require her to leave the profession for which she been trained and embark on another, which she would follow intermittently over the next decade. For the immediate future, she had been asked to direct relief services:

> in La Mancha (Don Quixote's country) and going over to the remoter west near Cordoba where I was for 6 months last year with the International Brigade. Another American organisation affiliated to the Quakers is to take that [region] over and they want me to go up and help organize canteens. We have rations for 6000 breakfasts daily for at least 4 months with probably increase in numbers and time. Two new trucks and equipment and 2 Americans are on the sea from Marseilles and we hope they'll duly arrive. If someone can be found to carry on my job here I'll probably go up to Valdepeñas and Cuidad Real after Xmas. It will be a good deal of work as the Commission expect me to do all the inspection and weighing of children etc. At the moment I'm merely thinking it over and trying to plan it in.[92]

By February 1939 she appeared to have made up her mind. "I am handing over my job here to another girl as there is great need of someone to organise canteens over the Alicante province. Enormously greater stocks of milk and chocolate are being sent in and they want to get it out to the people with the greatest possible speed . . . I am going up today and am to work with Mary Elmes. A new car has just been landed and we will work with that."[93]

This confident tone was tempered by the knowledge that any plans made in the fast-changing circumstances created by the civil war, now entering its final stage, could only be provisional. Yet the starving Spanish people were in desperate need of humanitarian relief, and Dorothy was determined to act before an outright Nationalist victory, which she felt could only worsen their conditions. "We feel that we have very little time. God only knows what these people won't have to suffer inside a very few weeks."[94]

Neither at this point, nor in any of her other letters, did she hint to her family that she had a pressing personal reason to remain in Spain. By this time she had a lover, a Spanish doctor serving with the

Republican forces. Even late in her life, Dorothy preferred not to reveal his identity or how they came to meet. This may have been during her first months with the International Brigades, but it seems more likely that the romance developed in Murcia. A large medical staff worked in the town, and nurses from the children's hospital often went to dances and picnics with wounded troops from the nearby International Brigades hospital. The proximity of these damaged but admirable young men resulted in a number of liaisons with women volunteers.[95]

In late 1938 Dorothy's lover had been posted far to the north of Murcia, to a new battlefront on the River Ebro, and by the time of her departure for Alicante she had no further contact from him, or reliable news of his whereabouts or wellbeing.[96] In early 1939, as she prepared to leave Murcia for "Don Quixote's country", Dorothy could still hope to be reunited with the man she had fallen in love with in the middle of a war.

Chapter 4
With Horsebox and Lie-Low

*"This country and its people has for me such a fascination
that it will be a hard day when I have to leave it."* [1]

Dorothy sent this declaration to her family from Murcia in April
1938, when her work at the children's hospital was all-consuming yet
deeply satisfying, and when the outcome of the civil war remained
quite uncertain. The day she feared arrived less than a year later, in
February 1939. Her employers at Friends House in London sent terse
instructions to return to Britain within weeks, before the Republican
surrender that by then appeared imminent.

She opposed the order to evacuate with characteristic determination and vigor. "I left only because I had to! It was considered that
my life and liberty were in danger owing to the probable change of
regime. Franco and his fellow murderers hated the International
Brigade – because they were such fine soldiers and blocked him for
so long – so that anyone connected with them has been threatened
with much ferocity. And I of course 2 years ago did a lot of work for
the Brigade. As the German secret police – the Gestapo – are expected
to start work right away on Nazi models, the Quakers became
alarmed for my safety in case I should be arrested! Imagine – for
nursing sick men!" [2]

By her own account, Dorothy finally agreed to leave Spain to
ensure greater safety for colleagues who intended to remain working
there such as Mary Elmes. Elmes had worked only with children and
other non-combatants and so was less vulnerable to persecution, and
her services were likely to be needed even more desperately in the
aftermath of Franco's victory. "It was very bitter indeed to go" wrote
Dorothy, "to leave that country I love so much and all the people
who, I think, had liked and trusted me, and worked with me, just
in their worst hour: and knowing too, as I said goodbye, that death

or Africa or torture or a concentration camp lies before so many of my friends. Their blood will be on English hands always – that ruling section that prevented them defending themselves and their freedom."[3]

The firm instruction to leave the country arrived when Dorothy was in Alicante, a short distance along the coast from Murcia to the north. There, as she had agreed with the International Commission for Refugee Children, she had just begun working in a somewhat unfamiliar field. She was no longer a health professional but an aid worker, forming and running temporary canteens to distribute food and milk to communities faced with starvation.[4] This work had formed a central part of the Quaker relief effort in Spain since the outbreak of the civil war, but Dorothy had seldom taken part in it while her medical training remained in great demand. It appears that her high reputation among the Quaker administration, and an evident capacity for organisation and resourcefulness, meant she was selected to head the distribution of aid in Alicante.

Her hasty departure from Spain forced her to abandon this work at its outset, and she left the canteens in the care of the equally capable Mary Elmes. Travel plans were made with Air France, which ran a regular flight from Alicante, but to Dorothy's disgust, as soon as she had booked on this flight it ceased operating – "a result of that most infamous 'recognition' of Franco by England and France."[5]

She then had no choice but to make use of the British naval destroyer which called weekly at the nearby fishing port of Gandia. Other members of Quaker relief units had already called on Britain's token naval presence on the Spanish coast for the same purpose, but Dorothy was greatly reluctant to do so since she despised the navy's "desperate attempt to keep up some show of authority, having been completely outwitted in the Mediterranean by Italy and Germany". The ship that ultimately extracted her from the country where she had spent the previous two years was probably the small and newly built destroyer HMS *Escort*. Its voyage to Marseilles was swift and uneventful, although conversation in the wardroom evidently reached dangerously rancorous levels.

Dorothy already held the view that the British Navy was commanded by Blimpish bigots. The *Escort's* officers, "although amiable", said nothing to alter this impression. They were Franco supporters to a man, and she argued with them ferociously about the causes of the war and Spain's likely future. The debonair officers were confident that, following the total defeat of the Republican cause, Spain faced a bright future under Franco. Their lanky, vehement, deeply tanned New Zealand passenger, the only woman on board, poured scorn on this view. "In the next generation Spain will have a socialist government", she stormed.[6] Her prediction proved more accurate than theirs, although the *Escort*, sadly, did not survive to witness the restoration of Spanish democracy. Just a year after this voyage the destroyer was sunk by a torpedo from an Italian submarine, with the loss of two of its ratings.

Dorothy spent a week in Marseilles with friends from the aid worker community, then travelled to Paris, the headquarters for the International Commission which had employed her in Alicante, and which was anxious to debrief her on the prospects for Franco's takeover. Finally, deeply oppressed with the tragedy of the Republican defeat, she returned to London, finding cheap but comfortable accommodation near Euston Station, an area she chose because of its proximity to the venerable Quaker headquarters of Friends House, where she spent much of her time.

The embittered and tempestuous mood she had developed on the voyage from Spain was not improved by London's foul March weather. "The contrast between it and that heavenly Spring I had in Spain! . . . when I came [to London] I was quite brown, I'm now going mud colour like everyone else in this place."[7] For anyone with sustained and direct experience of warfare, making a sudden adjustment to peacetime society is typically problematic. For a zealous personality like Dorothy, fiercely dedicated to the people and values she had served in Spain, it was particularly galling to find herself so suddenly idle. However, this unsought inactivity provided an opportunity to correspond more readily with her family. From London she wrote to them much more frequently than in the past, at greater length and largely freed from censorship, although the tone of these letters is at first noticeably unlike the exhilaration and vigour of those from Spain. Writing in late winter, from a city that seemed to her blithely impervious to the approach of war in neighbouring countries, she sounds sour, censorious and outraged.

"Everyone here is still in a great way about Germany's snatching of Czechoslovakia and Memel [a disputed territory in Lithuania] and Romania. Well they may be. I do nothing to lighten the fears of the timorous when asked how it feels to be bombed. They have all been so amazingly philosophical about bombs – when they [the bombs] were in Spain."[8]

Arriving directly from a war-torn country that had survived repeated bombing raids on civilian and medical, as well as military, targets, Dorothy was appalled at London's unreadiness for similar attacks. "You should see the pitiful trenches grubbed in the parks that the 'authorities' are trying to pass off as shelter – or the tin sheds in the back yards. The ordinary Spanish child would know from experience that both are death traps." She placed the blame for this lack of adequate facilities to protect Britain's civilian population squarely on "these inhuman devils of Cabinet ministers" who, she claimed, had made provision for their own "funk holes in Wales or America or even in London" but were not prepared to allocate funds to provide for the population in general. "Hate is a small word, or loathing, or contempt, for the feelings one has for these people."[9]

Her vituperation was softened a little by acknowledging that Britain's population also comprised of "a great number of very fine people struggling hard to instil a little conscience into this vast selfish inert mass". Dorothy placed herself in the ranks of those people when the Quakers at Friends House prevailed upon her to lecture on her recent wartime experience. Although extremely nervous at the prospect, she agreed to speak about the effects of aerial bombing in cities, and the consequent need to care for large numbers of injured, traumatised and displaced casualties. Her eyewitness evidence gave her words immediacy and fire, and the talks proved less of an ordeal than she feared. "Fortunately my tongue seems able to wag on fairly intelligibly no matter what sort of sweat I'm in. It is rather a strain – but I agree with the 'Friends' on the great necessity of getting people here to understand Spanish matters."[10] She soon became a fairly accomplished public speaker, while admitting privately that, "I really need a metronome badly to keep check on my tongue because it appears I speak so fast. A bad habit but of course too late now to check it."[11]

Dorothy also indulged in the long-postponed pleasures of London's cinemas and theatres, "in intervals of thinking how lovely it would be to see Chamberlain and Co hanged, boiled and quartered". The overnight arrival, in early April, of the English spring was an even more welcome diversion. "All the trees came on with a rush and going down into the country the other day I saw the railway embankments simply yellow with primroses in some parts."[12] The weather had finally changed, and with it Dorothy's spirits, and her plans.

In Marseilles in February, while en route to London, she had heard patchy but deeply disturbing accounts of the evolving crisis in southern France triggered by the Nationalist victory in Spain. Tens of thousands of civilians and retreating Republican troops, fearing execution or imprisonment, were fleeing across their country's northern border and finding that the French local authorities were utterly unprepared, and often unwilling, to receive them. This mass exodus of impoverished, poorly clad and profoundly grief-stricken people had begun in earnest some months earlier, at the outbreak of winter, when refugees from Barcelona and other northern towns had escaped advancing Nationalist troops by struggling on foot across snowbound mountain passes in the eastern Pyrenees. Herding farm animals ahead of them, carrying babies, and supporting the elderly and crippled, they were described as "humanity reduced to the last stages of deprivation and misery".[13]

The fall of Barcelona in late January 1939 transformed this flow of struggling humanity into a torrent, and the French authorities closed their border posts in an attempt to deter the influx. The refugees simply banked up behind the control posts until they formed a solid mass "as one stands in the tube in rush-hours".[14] Some spent several winter days and nights in this state, enduring drenching rain and freezing temperatures with no shelter, until the troops manning the border posts relented and allowed the wretched civilians, and later also Republican troops, to enter France. In its entirety, this exodus became known as the Retirada, the Retreat, the greatest movement among Spain's population since the expulsion of the Moors in the early Middle Ages. In just three weeks during February 1939 over 450,000 refugees crossed the borders, a third of them women, children and the elderly.

France's cherished reputation for hospitality and *bonhomie* was not equal to the scale and pace of the human tide pouring across its mountain borders. Although individual French villagers offered food and comfort to the worst affected of the arrivals, their provincial governments were largely ill-prepared and reluctant to accommodate this great mass of grieving humanity, especially as much of it was made up of passionate Republicans, including some recent combatants. As a result the homeless Spaniards were held under conditions that added a further dimension to their sufferings. By the tens of thousands, they were herded into vast barbed-wire enclosures hastily erected along a bleak stretch of the Mediterranean coast swept, in that season, by an icy *tramontane* wind. Armed troops from France's African colonies guarded the gates, leading the inmates to conclude that they had escaped a war in their own country only to become prisoners in another.

Argelés, the first of these camps, was packed to capacity almost immediately, and other camps were constructed on the beaches of St Cyprien and Barcarés to the north. Most of the refugees were given no shelter beyond what they could improvise for themselves. Some of the women and children fared better, as school buildings and hospitals were roughly converted to house them, but for others the burrows they dug in the heavy, grey sand provided the only protection from daily sandstorms and freezing winds. A British aid worker saw "Bits of rushwood [reeds] gathered together to make a house. One hollow in the sand for all sanitary purposes. Four standpipes for water supply. Stand in line for hours for a small piece of bread and perhaps a scrap of meat."[15]

These atavistic conditions were recorded by the Hungarian-born photographer Robert Capa, who had earlier captured some of the most indelible images of the civil war. In January 1939 he joined the vast numbers crossing into France, and managed to reach Paris. Two months later he returned to the eastern Pyrenees to photograph within the internment camps. In frame after frame, he recorded the squalor and despair of huddled groups squatting like Neanderthal hunters in front of shelters roofed with oilskins and tree branches. The world-renowned cellist Pablo Casals came to Argelés, which held musicians who had played in his orchestra, and likened the camp to a scene from Dante's *Inferno*.[16] Other internees were well known to

Dorothy from her work in Murcia, including the German-born engineer Gerardo Ascher, known in Spain as Rubio ('the Blond'). With great energy and ingenuity, he had founded children's colonies in the villages of Crevillente and Benidorm, but as a Jew and anti-fascist, he was forced to abandon this work ahead of the Nationalist takeover, and was then held at Argelés because of irregularities with his travel permit.[17]

Infectious diseases, especially dysentery, pneumonia and TB, spread freely among this overcrowded population, already weakened by malnutrition and exhaustion. Inadequate sanitation supplied other infections, and the lack of facilities for washing clothes and bedding resulted in vast swarms of lice. The enormous Argelés camp's only medical facility was a sand-floored infirmary, so poorly equipped that its dressings had to be repeatedly reused.

For several weeks after the camps opened, no aid workers were permitted to enter them. One of the first to do so was the Quaker doctor Audrey Russell, who had worked with Dorothy in Murcia, and was afterwards sent to Argelés by British Friends. "There has never been anything as horrible as this since the Middle Ages," she informed them.[18] Francesca Wilson, whose tenacity had produced the first emergency medical facilities in Murcia, was similarly appalled. "I wanted to cover my eyes – it was a sight so wounding to human dignity. Men penned into cages like wild animals; exposed to the stare of the passer-by, like cattle in the market place."[19]

In response to accounts such as these, more Quakers and their staff arrived in the eastern Pyrenees, and in many cases discovered that they had worked together earlier, on aid and medical projects in Spain. Their funding and supplies were now provided primarily through the vastly experienced Quaker relief organiser Edith Pye, who had helped to create the International Commission for just such a purpose. By the end of February the Commission had an office in Perpignan with a staff recruited mainly from British and US Quakers. Equipped with a fleet of two cars and two small trucks, they began to distribute the first supplies of clothing and bedding. The trucks were also used as mobile canteens, supplying milk, bread, cheese and chocolate in the camps. Two tent hospitals were set up, and a number of orphaned children were transferred to suitable foster homes.

The problems the relief workers now faced were quite unlike those they had learned to deal with in Spain. The refugees were isolated from their local communities by language, custom and, in many cases, political allegiance. The Pyrenean French had seen their government remain aloof from the conflict across its southern border, and after that border was breached, regarded these battle-hardened immigrants with hostility and suspicion. As a result, the relief workers were obliged to call on the resourcefulness and skills of the refugees themselves. Among them were some of the best-educated and most gifted members of Spanish society, including senior Republican politicians and officials, and artists of international repute.

Francesca Wilson found that the Argelés camp, which had so horrified her when she first saw it in February, had become well organised from within two months later. Its occupants, she wrote, displayed "courage and energy and that resilience which is charac-teristic of Spaniards . . . even in the awful dead-end of the crowded camps. The stoicism and even gaiety with which they faced wounds, hunger and death during the war was startling, but now that that tension is over it is still more startling to find the same qualities when facing defeat."[20]

Although by April 1939 Argelés was nominally a male-only camp, it contained around 200 women who had utterly refused to be parted from their husbands, and threatened to kill themselves if forced to do so. They and the other inmates had formed themselves into groups of 40, each with a leader to receive rations and a cook, "who is busy a good part of the day stirring great pots over fires in the sand."[21]

Alongside such impressive resilience, the International Commission staff noted that a great many refugees displayed serious mental and nervous health conditions. For even the least affected, their dominant moods were anger, despair and depression. Francesca Wilson was told that "people are going mad in the camps because they have nothing to do but brood on the anguish of their situa-tion".[22] With no way of knowing how long they would be held behind the wire, people spent their days playing cards and dominoes, carving small objects from wood, or simply staring blankly at the sea.

In late April, wrote Francesca Wilson, "Men are still lying on improvised beds made of rough wood, on straw or on the damp sand, and covered with verminous blankets, for there are no sheets: and they

are still given lentils to eat for lack of invalid foods . . . Relief organisations have done what they can to supply needs, but there are
thousands of sick men, and funds are inadequate. It looks as if it will
be many months before a solution is found for most of these men . . .
To save abandoned men from madness something must be done for
their morale, for their cultural life."[23]

The best hope for such people, decided the Commission workers,
lay in organising workshops and educational initiatives similar to
those developed for civilian refugees in Murcia. A start had been made
by the most active and capable of the refugees themselves, who were
building barracks at Argelés to provide cultural activities. One was
reserved for visual artists, and another for the many excellent singers,
musicians and other performers. In a planned Centro de Cultura, the
camp's professors and schoolmasters would give lectures and
language classes. All of these projects, however, required books,
paintbrushes, writing materials and other supplies that were apparently unobtainable locally, and which the Commission staff
undertook to provide.

In late April 1939 Dorothy arrived in Perpignan to head the
International Commission's efforts there. Both her office and living
quarters were in the Hotel Regina in the centre of this compact and
easygoing city, the capital of the *Pyrénées-Orientales department* which
held the largest refugee camps. Once again she was employed through
the Quaker aid organisation, initially on a two-month contract, and
her somewhat wordy letterhead read – *Societe des Amis "Cuaquers" en
collaboration avec La Commission Internationale d'Aide aux Enfants espag-
nols refugies.*

Her immediate concern was for the women living in converted
schools and other public buildings, who had almost nothing to do all
day. Just as Francesca Wilson had found in Murcia, simply supplying
these women with fabric, needles and thread achieved several goals
simultaneously. The women could improve their wardrobes and
thereby their self-esteem, they could occupy themselves usefully, and
potentially earn money from the sale of their garments. Providing
books and other educational materials proved more difficult, but
Dorothy hoped to obtain these from Paris and other large centres.
Even postage stamps, she found, could lift spirits and generate
activity in men and women who otherwise appeared to have resigned

themselves to indefinite internment. The camp authorities permitted an allowance of only two stamps a week; a severe restriction, especially for the many refugees who were highly educated and longed to write and receive letters that could link them to the world beyond their present distress.

After just a few weeks in her new role, Dorothy welcomed the familiar, smiling and gentle presence of her closest acquaintance from the Murcia hospital. The slender and strongly principled Irishwoman Mary Elmes and her co-worker Jean Cottle arrived in Perpignan direct from Spain in mid-May 1939, bringing with them complete records of the various Quaker-supported hospitals, workshops, canteens and other relief projects.[24] The two women also brought the heartbreaking news that all of this hard-won activity had ceased under the Franco regime.

Dorothy was told that in the months after she left Murcia, food shortages had become so desperate that the hospital staff resorted to unpicking the cotton covers of beanbags sent out from the US as children's toys. The thoughtful volunteers who had sewn these bags had clearly anticipated this eventuality, and had filled the bags with beans that remained edible and even nutritious when boiled in a stew. The cloth coverings were then used to patch the trousers of the older boys.

When Franco's troops reached Murcia, they entered the children's hospital and Mary Elmes explained that she and the other staff wished to remain there, caring for their young patients under the new regime. This was not allowed. A Spanish woman, Miss Pedreno, was placed in charge of the hospital, and promptly insisted on closing it. The children, many of them very sick, were sent home to their families, apart from a few who were transferred to the less suitable Provincial Hospital to be nursed by nuns. All of the various convalescent homes in Polop and elsewhere were also shut down, and Dorothy learned that key figures in their establishment, such as Don Marcelino the school inspector and Manolo, chair of Murcia's refugee committee, had disappeared and were almost certainly shot by the new regime. Her former driver, Santiago Smilg, spent many years in prison in Murcia and Madrid.[25]

"All the Quaker work in Spain has been closed down, in spite of earnest efforts to cooperate with the Fascist regime," Dorothy lamented. "Food ships, hospitals, canteens, transport and supplies all ceased . . . the workers have all come out disgusted and angry. I am glad I did not see the end".[26]

The only valid response, it seemed, to the dismantling of the Quakers' work in Spain was to resurrect it among the Spanish in France. Towards the end of May Dorothy sent her family an update on her progress, incorporating untranslated Spanish terms that she apparently used unconsciously, and written in a triumphant tone that transformed her from the disheartened individual who had arrived in London three months before.

> "I have started 6 carpenters at work building cupboards for school, *taller* [workshop], etc. and the *taller* of 6 girls sewing and directing the small girls' activities who have already made themselves 100-odd *batas* (gowns) and are now outfitting themselves with underwear. The school is now equipped with stationary and blackboard etc. and there is a milk service going for children."[27]

For a group of vigorous young boys whose confinement in camp must have been a particular torment to them, an immediate and cheap form of recreation was provided. Dorothy expended a portion of her precious funds to buy them a football. "They swarmed around me with such complete delight that the 100-odd francs for the ball, I felt, was never better spent."[28] The boys instantly formed a camp team and were given permission by the commandant to go beyond the gates to play a local team in the village of Elne. The result was a draw and another game was scheduled against the much larger town of Perpignan. "Unfortunately their footwear doesn't match the new football, but perhaps we will be able to rectify that soon."[29]

Over the following year, the former nurse from New Zealand extended activities of this kind across much of the southern border region of France, as well as frequent longer trips to Paris and other centres to obtain supplies and negotiate with partner agencies. She was now the regional representative of a large and pioneering international aid agency, and her constant field trips were interspersed with long hours of paperwork in French, Spanish, English and occasionally Catalan, the native language of her team's chauffeur and storekeeper, and also of many of the Spanish refugees and their French neighbours. A typewriter was as vital a tool of this work as their three-ton Bedford truck, and from June 1939 Dorothy's letters to her family in Lyttelton appear in typescript for the first time. The Friends supplied a young American secretary, Ruth Cope, yet another former colleague in Murcia, to handle the never-ending correspondence with camp officials, local politicians, other aid workers and anguished refugees seeking to reunite with their families. However Dorothy, and especially Mary Elmes (who had "beautiful Spanish and French"), still needed to translate for her.[30]

A typical query arrived in July 1939 from the London-based 'Artists Refugee Committee, Spanish Section'. This voluntary collective of artists, architects and sculptors wished to donate art supplies to the camps, and Dorothy agreed to receive and distribute them.[31] A few weeks later she was able to inform the committee that a wide range of artworks had already been executed using their materials, and some of it – "small, sell-able stuff with not too grim a subject" – could be sent back to London to raise funds for their creators. She suggested that the committee charge "10s. or 1 Pound for the drawings and up to 5 pounds for bigger things".[32] A similar British organisation supported notable Spanish writers, but by July Dorothy could report that most of the eminent writers had already left the camps and that "it makes for great distress among the remainder . . . to single out individuals". She therefore allocated this organisation's funds to books and writing materials for the camp's general population.[33]

Other requests were on a much larger scale and less easily resolved. "I am at present extremely busy," she told her family, "procuring all kinds of text-books etc. to distribute to the Spanish Refugee Camps. In the 3 near Perpignan there are 100,000 men. Their physical condition is now fairly good but it is a wretched life, and they are too fine to be left to rot, and their minds must, we feel, be occupied. They long for books." Although Spanish literature was not easy to find in France, she had some success after a hurried trip to Paris in early summer, to deliver a refugee with appendicitis to the American Hospital there. In the many small bookshops on the Left Bank, "I came across much valuable new and 2nd hand stuff. I have a grant which I proceeded to spend – also ran riot in the lovely shops for artists' materials. I have also established a contact with S. America to get books published there. Returned here weighed down, taking 2 days over the return trip, which was glorious – France looking lovely."[34]

The seemingly obvious course of importing Spanish-language books from Spain itself was now out of the question, she explained. "There is horrible repression going on over the border – no modern or liberal works of any kind allowed. Most of the artists and writers in any case are here or in America, so we feel we are helping to save Spanish civilization in general, and that is one in the eye for Franco and Co. . . . As well as textbooks we hope to amass books for libraries in the camps – money is coming in and interest rising so I have high hopes of a good effort. I love Spanish literature so enjoy this work".[35] The following month she confessed to a colleague, "I wish I could fly over to South America and browse in Buenos Aires with my pocket book for one day. It would solve most of the book problems."[36]

Ameliorating conditions in the camps was a continuous preoccupation of Dorothy's International Commission team, but they also contributed to the ambitious project of finding new long-term destinations for the internees, both on an individual scale, by placing desperate men and women in touch with relatives and sponsors, and in June 1939, by assisting several thousand Spaniards to emigrate to Latin America. These efforts took place in the face of a prolonged campaign by officialdom in both France and Franco Spain to see the refugees returned to the country from which they had fled. In the weeks after the first camps opened, loudspeakers blared exhortations to volunteer for repatriation, and assurances that those who did so would not face retribution from the new government. A number of refugees took up this opportunity in the hope of returning to homes, families and occupations they had known before the civil war. Typically, after recrossing the border, they disappeared without trace.

Understandably, the great majority of refugees feared a return to Spain more than any other potential fate. Those in contact with relatives still living in their homeland were sent stories of persecution and repression, mass unemployment and terror, and Dorothy's office received daily letters, painstakingly printed on graph paper and other salvaged materials, pleading for help to avoid repatriation. The favoured alternative for most camp inmates was a passage to another Spanish-speaking country, preferably Mexico whose government had consistently and courageously supported the Spanish Republic.

Within weeks of taking up work with the International Commission, Dorothy was asked to temporarily abandon her relief actions in the Argelés camp to support another organisation, the National Joint Committee for Spanish Relief, which planned to send 2000 refugees to a new life in Mexico on board a chartered passenger ship, the *Sinaia*. This mammoth undertaking cost 17,000 pounds and was funded primarily from Britain, with large contributions from its trade union movement. Dorothy was given direct responsibility for about 560 women and children who had been dumped in the "appallingly inadequate" Haras camp, and were in a poor state of health.[37] She supervised their medical examinations, two sets of vaccinations, and a general outfitting before their departure.

The scale and symbolic value of the *Sinaia*'s voyage attracted attention from unexpected quarters and in the weeks before the ship's departure well-known figures from British high society arrived in Perpignan to support the venture. They included the aristocratic journalist Nancy Mitford, eldest of the sensation-loving siblings whose political affections spanned a spectrum from communism to Hitler. She herself was "pretty, frivolous, apolitical", yet apparently toiled for long hours with her husband Peter Rodd to ensure that the refugees were prepared to cope with the long sea voyage.[38] They had no experience of such work, and what Dorothy thought of their efforts is unknown, since neither woman apparently noted the presence of the other. However, the two forthright but otherwise entirely dissimilar women worked closely together as they raced to meet the *Sinaia*'s departure date.[39]

On 24 May the ship was given a grand send-off from the port of Séte, north of Perpignan. Dorothy had spent the previous 18 hours on feverish final preparations "as some passport arrangements had been held up in Paris".[40] Nancy Mitford also worked through the night, "as the embarkation went on until 6 a.m. and the people on the quay had to be fed and the babies given their bottle. There were 200 babies under 2 and 12 women are to have babies on board."[41] Some families were reunited on the quayside for the first time since the Retirada. At noon, as a "pathetic little" brass band successively played the national anthems of Britain, France and Spain, the *Sinaia* finally steamed away from the dock. Its passengers, exhausted yet relieved after years of war, their escape to France and ensuing months in overcrowded camps, gave three cheers for the homeland they never expected to see again. Nancy Mitford thought there were none who were not crying, while she had "never cried so much in my life."[42]

By August the long Mediterranean summer, although less fatiguing than in Spain and moderated by cool Pyrenean winds, was still hot enough to make Dorothy long for an afternoon siesta. She had by then fallen in love with the countryside surrounding Perpignan, and her letters give ecstatic descriptions of its beauty and fertility, which supplied her team with "masses of cherries, strawberries, peaches, asparagus, peas etc".[43] Yet her workload remained as demanding as ever and sightseeing could only be enjoyed during long and gruelling journeys between the various camps still being established around Perpignan.

The squalid Argelès camp was closed in August 1939 and its occupants relocated to St-Cyprien, where barracks had been provided so married men could stay with their wives and children. Smaller camps were created to house specific groups of refugees, such as Catalans, the elderly, International Brigades veterans, and women and children. They now received adequate supplies of food, and were housed under cover, but each camp still hoped for facilities such as schoolrooms, libraries and workshops so that its internees might have some form of occupation.

Dorothy's initial contract with the International Commission expired in July 1939 but she was re-engaged to continue working with women and children, and to expand the 'cultural work' of supplying books and other materials for intellectual activity. "The French military are not at all sympathetic but we put constant pressure on them, and have worn them down to a gratifying extent . . . we have just seen 2 libraries opened in the 2 largest camps, supplied by about 1000 Spanish books found and bought by me in Paris, and have supplied stationery and text-books for about 30,000 men, and completely equipped 2 children's schools for some 300 children".[44]

Perpignan remained the hub of the team's activities. As refugees were relocated to smaller and more distant sites, the International Commission lorries pushed further into the surrounding countryside to reach them. Their efforts seemed never to keep pace with the rising numbers of refugees who, throughout the year, continued to straggle across the mountains bringing stories of fresh horrors from the cleansing operations carried out by the Nationalists. The total number of Spanish refugees was estimated at 150,000 in August, when Dorothy negotiated an extension of funds from the Commission's Paris directorate to provide several new relief schemes.

At the village of Cerbere, right on the Spanish frontier, a school and *cantina* (canteen) were provided for 200 children, while a total of 2000 received a weekly provision of food. "If we had not done this, all these refugees would have had to go back to the horrors of Spain, or into the slightly less horrors of the French camps . . . the local people were being blackmailed by Fascist influences from Spain, to bring one or another alternative about, and the Mayor [of Cerbere] appealed to us for help, which we were glad to give."[45]

In late August Audrey Russell wrote from London to express her admiration for Dorothy's "passion for neat jigsaw organisation . . . while hell breaks loose all round". The work in France was likely to continue for some time yet, Dr Russell advised, "for nobody [in Britain] has much heart for a war . . . Franco is making friendly gestures towards England and declaring for neutrality . . . but at the same time he is massing troops near Gibraltar".[46] Just five days after this letter was written, its cautiously optimistic reading of the European situation was proven terribly misguided. German tanks rolled across Poland's borders and Britain, followed immediately by France, declared war on Germany.

Dorothy, less sanguine by temperament than many of her British colleagues, may not have been greatly surprised by this dismal turn of events. As early as June she had warned her family that "Europe is a tinder box at the moment and will be so for several years", at the same time insisting that she had no intention of returning home no matter how inflammatory the situation became.[47] Days after the invasion of Poland she wrote again, in light-hearted language evidently intended to reassure her family, "to apologise for getting into another war". Again she stressed that she had no plans to abandon her work in France. "I am glad to be here anyway – thoughts of England, full of hearty girls striding about in khaki, shouting orders, make my blood run cold . . . I don't feel worried about you because I think you are in one of the safest of places in the world, and I hope it will always remain so . . . I beg that you don't waste good energy worrying about my safety – whatever star I was born under has looked after me very well so far . . . Do keep calm and don't worry – this may all be over very soon."[48]

These soothing words were belied somewhat by actions not revealed to her family at that time. Even before the invasion of Poland, Dorothy instructed Ruth Cope, the American secretary whose efforts behind the typewriter had greatly benefited the team since the previous May, to return to her home country. The younger woman was baffled by the order since she fully expected to remain for the European summer, but Dorothy was adamant. A few months later she received "a gushing note from [Ruth's] parents, to whom it appears she has been snatched from the jaws of death".[49]

With France now openly on a war footing and preparing to repel a German invasion from the north, able-bodied male refugees were given the choice of either enlisting in the French forces or going out to work locally in agriculture and industry, or on military installations. The women and children, war amputees and thousands of elderly and incapable men remained dependent on the services provided by the International Commission and other relief agencies. A few people fell into particularly vulnerable indeterminate categories, requiring skilled and diplomatic action by their advocates.

One warm morning in early September Dorothy and her Catalan driver travelled for two hours inland from Perpignan and up into the foothills of the eastern Pyrenees. They stopped at the hillside village of Mosset, whose winding cobbled streets, whitewashed houses and red-tiled roofs had barely changed in appearance since the Middle Ages, and which remains today one of the most famously beautiful villages in France. From there they had to leave the car and walk several more kilometres up a steep and muddy trail to a centuries-old farmhouse, its windows protected by heavy wooden shutters. The house, with its barn and other outbuildings, lay in a sheltered hollow under the mountains and had therefore been named La Coume, the French equivalent of the English 'combe'.

For the past six years La Coume had served as a school and sanctuary for victims of war and repression. It had been founded by the distinguished Quaker nurse and midwife Edith Pye, whose work with women and children during World War One paralleled Dorothy's in Spain. Her companion and fellow Quaker Hilda Clark had leased, and later bought, the old farm as a place of refuge for Germans forced to leave their own country by the rise of Nazism. Its first residents were two young socialist intellectuals named Pitt and Yves Kruger. Pitt was German and Yves Swiss, and both were skilled teachers whose work in German secondary schools was inspired by liberal educationalists such as Montessori. When stormtroopers began imposing Hitler's ideology on schools and other institutions, they fled to France. Their Quaker friends led them to the abandoned and semi-derelict farmhouse high in the mountains, and the highly urbanised and cultured Krugers decided to acquire the rural skills needed to survive there.[50] The villagers of Mosset proved welcoming to these unusual strangers and one in particular, an illiterate Spanish shepherd named Santos, became a vital member of their household. They found that he knew more about animals than any vet, and could teach them to grow food crops and preserve them through the snowbound months of winter.[51]

The property had no electricity and only a mountain stream for washing and irrigation, but the Krugers, soon joined by other refugees from Nazism, slowly planted it in fruit trees and hosted a succession of convalescent refugees sent by the Quakers. By 1939 La Coume was permanently filled with as many as 20 children at a time. All of them received daily lessons from the Krugers while helping in the hard, self-sufficient life of the farm. Yves and Pitt taught their own two children to call them by their first names, so that the other children would not feel estranged.

At the time of Dorothy's visit in September that year, she found that La Coume provided a secure and healthy environment for its young residents, who spanned at least eight nationalities and languages and were sometimes deeply traumatised by their earlier experiences. Thanks to the work of the shepherd Santos, who slept in the hayloft, and to a young Spanish refugee who had been badly wounded in the civil war, they were producing enough food, including a large stock of rabbits, to survive the coming winter. However, the Krugers told Dorothy that they were greatly concerned that the hard work of the previous six years could be wasted if wartime mobilisation requirements forced them to leave. She promised to do all she could to help, and to return in a few days, wartime travel restrictions permitting.[52]

Two weeks later Dorothy accompanied Pitt to an interview with the *sub prefet*, or administrator, of the provincial centre of Prades. This man had earlier said, "rather brusquely that Pitt being a German, he would probably have to go into the Foreign Legion", and La Coume's neighbours in Mosset were also pressing for Pitt's enlistment. After an explanation of the couple's work with orphaned and other refugee children, the *sub prefet* became more sympathetic, and the Krugers were permitted to remain for the immediate future.[53] To secure their position, and win more support from their French neighbours, Dorothy began negotiating to have "a dozen or so delicate Alsatian refugee children" sent to the farm. "We do not think it would be wise to send German children there, but there are masses of poor little German-speaking French refugees who are terribly fish-out-of-water in ordinary French villages."[54]

This doubly compassionate proposal reflected a significant development in the nature of France's refugee population. While Spaniards continued to arrive in the country from the south – they totalled over 180,000 by October 1939, more than half of them women and children – they were now joined by growing numbers of bewildered, anxious and frequently destitute arrivals from France's other neighbouring countries that now also faced military takeover. From Holland, Belgium, Luxembourg, the French-speaking region of Germany and elsewhere, migrants arrived in France seeking safety from persecution. Internment camps, including the original and particularly despised Argelés camp that through hard work had been almost completely vacated by the Spanish, began to fill again with refugees speaking a mélange of tongues.

This fresh influx of newcomers further hardened French attitudes towards the Spanish refugees. They came under increased pressure from civic authorities in the Perpignan region to return to Spain, and some of the less capable succumbed to this coercion. Employers took advantage of others by paying them extremely low wages for long hours of work. The vineyards that surrounded Perpignan benefitted, in that autumn, from the labour of large numbers of Spanish pickers who had no other means of leaving the camps. According to one Quaker fieldworker, "any farmer or employer could ask for two or ten or twenty Spaniards, who were then bound over to him and would have to work for whatever wages he chose to pay, under whatever

living conditions he saw fit to provide. . . . A well-known Barcelona
surgeon worked as a wood-cutter for four years at twelve cents a day.
He is sixty-two and there is nothing unusual about his case."[55]

"By the grace of god, & myriad Permissions," wrote Dorothy, the
International Commission was able to carry on with its work under
these demanding and fast-changing circumstances. "It would have
been desolating to have had to cease just now, when we are needed as
much & more than ever." For some months in late 1939 restrictions
on travel confined her team to the immediate vicinity of Perpignan,
but in October she reported that, "we are completely fixed up, and
whiz about in the car & camion as hard as ever. Next month when
petrol-rationing comes in will confront us with some problems. Mary
[Elmes] has just returned from a trip to Paris, buying Spanish books
. . . she finds that we have almost cleaned up the entire town, and had
difficulty in getting enough for the various libraries, schools etc
which we have started, and hope to enlarge."[56]

The quietly dedicated Mary Elmes became a familiar figure in the
camps, where thousands knew her as 'Miss Mary' and turned to her
for solutions to their problems. She was frustrated by her inability to
solve one of those – how to provide Spanish translations of the author
who was more popular in the refugee camps than any other. "I can
obtain translations of all the great Latin, French and Greek classical
authors, but the edition of Shakespeare is now exhausted here in
France."[57]

Not far from Argelés stood the historic castle of Valmy, and its
compound included a magnificent country house called Mas de
l'Abat. The French authorities had granted permission for this beautiful building to be occupied by a community of 12 refugee artists
who organised exhibitions of their paintings, drawings and sculpture,
and performances of theatre and poetry. In September 1939 Dorothy
and Mary visited Mas de l'Abat and were inspired to leave in the 'livre
d'or', the castle visitors' book, the message "Spirit and enthusiasm are
the most important things in life, and these the Spaniards will have
for ever." They signed themselves, "Dorothy A. Morris & Mary
Elmes, Los Amigos Quakeros (the Quaker Friends)".[58]

By November 1939 the near-derelict Argelés camp again held
5,000 women and children and 30,000 men. As many as possible
were provided with warm accommodation and bedding, although

French armed forces now had priority for supplies of bedstraw. As the damp littoral winter approached, Dorothy thought nostalgically of the large and historic woollen mills at Kaiapoi, just to the north of her home town, and wished she could order a thousand of their heavy blankets for her camp inmates.

The range of her activities had now broadened to include providing tools and rehabilitation training for war amputees, clothing for members of compulsory work gangs, and exhaustive assistance to refugees hoping to be reunited with their families. A man with the very Catalan name of Angel Canut wrote movingly from St Cyprien camp, asking for any information about his children Angel and Montserrat, aged ten and eight. Dorothy's enquiries prompted a response from another aid agency advising that those names appeared on the list of residents of the _Colonie des Enfants Espagnola_ in the Dordogne region. However, the following month she was obliged to tell Señor Canut that his children were no longer in that colony and that she could find no other trace of their where-abouts.

For the tumult of children living in the camps themselves, Mary Elmes had founded three schools, at St Cyprien, Argelés and Cerbere. Argelés camp posed a further problem since it held 600 boys aged 14 to 17 who were too old to attend the school and "at present live as they can without any special attention or education among the grown-ups in the Men's camp". Dorothy, drawing on her Murcia experience, paid special attention to the health needs of the women and children. She persuaded the colonel who commanded the Argelés camp to allow her to install a _Gota de leche_ or crèche, which gave expec-tant mothers comfortable conditions and extra food for a month before and after their birth. "It is a great triumph", she informed Edith Pye some months later.[59] However, babies needed further help to thrive under the "primitive conditions of camp life", and Dorothy worked with a Swiss aid agency to open a maternity home in the quiet town of Elne, where mothers and babies could stay for several more weeks, "properly warmed and fed".[60]

By the end of the year both Dorothy and Mary had moved from the Hotel Regina to their own upstairs apartment in the nearby Avenue des Baleares. It was not only more spacious, but cheaper and more convenient, especially after "much concentrated pressure on the electrical company produced in turn the heating, the bath heater (a superb affair) and the cooking unit, all involving separate meters! . . . Therese our maid is a pleasant and obliging creature – and most important, a true jewel of a cook, in both French and Spanish."[61] A terrace overlooking the street was filled with flowers, growing in boxes along the edge and in two large blue tubs, and there the two women sat and rested whenever their arduous workload permitted.[62]

From this attractive base Dorothy strove to repeat, on a much large scale than in Murcia, efforts to provide a Christmas celebration for as many of the refugees as possible. This time ten large Christmas trees were decorated and distributed to various schools, camps and hospitals and over 6,000 children received parcels of sweets, oranges and nuts, "besides a great many small parcels to teachers, nurses and doctors etc all of whom, poor things! work very hard and do not get much, if anything".[63] She and Mary were invited to parties organised in both the St Cyprien and Argelés camps, where they were entertained with songs and dances by young and old. Dorothy spent Christmas Day itself with the Krugers at La Coume, and saw in the new year with her aid worker colleagues,

> high up in the mountains in an old Catalan village inn – thick stone walls and a huge fireplace, with logs piled high. We had a splendid and ample dinner in front of this, plenty to drink, and wireless to dance to: a most amiable and interesting crowd of locals helped us to pass the time. More from a sense of duty than anything else we toasted 1940 at midnight in champagne . . . knowing perfectly well that no amount of toasting will do it the slightest bit of good.[64]

Indeed, a fortnight later she found herself working harder than ever to protect camp inmates from the rigours of exceptionally harsh weather.

> Oldest inhabitants round here are busy comparing notes on our present winter, and all are unanimous on its uniquely awful qualities . . . I have never experienced anything quite so severe, I am sure, hard as iron and cold as ice. My poor refugees have been having a hell of a time, but they are bearing up in a pathetically marvellous way.[65]

The political climate was also growing ever more inclement, and decrees from Paris announced that all refugees who did not have steady work in France would soon be repatriated to Spain regardless of their wishes.[66] This draconian policy was prompted in part by the fast-growing numbers of refugees from other European countries. The International Commission, although formed to fund aid to Spanish refugees specifically, revised its remit to deal with refugees from all countries engaged in war, and established sub-offices in Toulouse and Bordeaux. Dorothy was instructed to divide her time between Perpignan and Toulouse, well to the northwest; "the idea does not attract me greatly, but presumably one can get used to anything."[67]

A reliable vehicle fleet, and the fuel and travel permits required to reach all corners of her enlarged field of activity, occupied ever more of Dorothy's time and energy.[68] Her team found that wherever they went, although officially known as the International Commission, they were welcomed by the refugees as 'Amigos Cuaqueros' ('Quaker Friends'). "This is the name so well known and respected in the camps", wrote one of them in February 1940.[69] The US Quakers' annual report recorded that "Workers from the Perpignan office moved up from the south to help in Montpellier, Narbonne and Sete. In great canteens they fed thousands daily, in public halls where straw mattresses were spread in long rows on the floor, they gave shelter."[70]

The liberal British daily the *Manchester Guardian* was still delivered fairly regularly to Perpignan and both women at the apartment in the Rue de Baleares were devoted readers of this reliable source of international news. Dorothy would have liked to send her family more details of the grim European situation, she told them, "but what with wars and censors and the like it isn't possible."[71] She was able to advise them that she was working harder than ever before, but with a great deal of satisfaction. She now owned a secondhand bicycle, with which she toured the surrounding countryside for much-needed exercise. "I have to spend more time than I like riding about in the car or the camion, and don't get nearly enough leg-stretching. Yesterday, for example, I made a trip of 300 miles; tomorrow I will have to do another 200 or more, and next week go to Toulouse and later to Marseilles."[72]

Just a month after that letter was mailed, German troops swept through Poland, Belgium and Holland, and refugees from those countries flooded into France as far as its southernmost *departments*. The Pyrenees-Orientales already held 40,000 Belgian refugees, with many more expected. The *department* of Aude prepared to receive 60,000 of them, Herault 100,000. Dorothy was allocated a thousand pounds, mainly from American Red Cross funds, and "spent it in an hour – mostly on bedding". She flatly refused, however, to loan one of her team's *camions*, or light trucks, to transport the refugees, saying, "We have at this point a very urgent situation here. . . . If you take our camion, we have no hope whatever of it being returned to us, and our work will be irrevocably held up."[73]

As their former homeland prepared to invade France itself, the gentle German-speaking Quakers at La Coume found their position within their adopted community barely sustainable. Dorothy wrote to Edith Pye in late May to say that both Yves and Pitt might soon be forced to leave the farm. "The local state of feeling after recent events in the north is disturbed, and the peculiar position of the 'Coume' has no doubt aggravated this."[74] The plan to billet Alsatian children with the Krugers had come to nothing, and Dorothy held several anguished meetings with them to find other solutions. Eventually, she said, Pitt was obliged to move to a refugee hostel near the Spanish border. Although his wife, as a Swiss national, was not subject to deportation, she could only visit her local village of Mosset after nightfall, "but I think will not be persecuted further".[75]

Dorothy now spent almost all her time on the road, making trips to Paris at least monthly and otherwise touring all of the numerous and far-flung refugee projects. Her transport fleet had been expanded by the addition of a motorised double horse-box, and with this versatile vehicle and a blow-up rubber air mattress (which she referred to as a 'lie-low', her version of the tradename LiLo) she was able to spend three or four days at a time away from Perpignan, sleeping in the horse-box wherever her driver paused for the night.[76]

Each of these expeditions was afterwards documented in a meticulous four- or six-page report to her London office, advising on the state of preparedness in each centre for handling anticipated numbers of Dutch, northern French, Belgian and Luxembourgoise refugees. Divisions within these nationalities caused endless anxieties for their host villages. "The Belgians themselves are sometimes bitterly divided into Belgians and Flemings, neither of whom get on nor can be placed in the same village with the Luxembourgoise."[77] In Montpellier she found "200 necessitous Luxembourg babies" and in Carcassonne "a small Pouponnerie [nursery] where the babies and small children are clothed, cleaned, fed and generally comforted. The local ladies in charge of this are efficient and very devoted, but were in great distress because they had come to the end of the resources."[78] The local newspaper *Petit Méridional* reported Dorothy's arrival in the district, misidentifying her as the regional delegate for the US Red Cross. "I suppose they thought it sounded better".[79]

The original purpose of Dorothy's assignment, to provide aid to Spanish refugees, had become almost entirely superseded by the more urgent requirements of the newer arrivals. She acknowledged this to her London-based colleague Sir Richard Rees in early June, saying that the great majority of Spaniards in her district had either been placed in employment, drafted into various branches of the French armed forces, or repatriated. She stressed that a considerable number still required support, and faced gross overcrowding in the camps since they were forced to make room for the new refugees. Her response to these chaotic and contentious circumstances was as constructive as possible – organising the existing Spanish sewing workshops to make clothes for Belgians in dire need of them, and re-equipping the camp schools to provide for new nationalities and languages. "I cannot expect, I think, to finish before mid-July. I would then like to have a holiday, which I would probably take here [in Perpignan]."[80]

This undoubtedly well-deserved summer holiday was forestalled by the unprecedented speed of the German blitzkrieg into France. Just three days after the above letter was written, Wehrmacht forces entered Paris and, in a near-repeat of the evacuation order that she received in Alicante the previous year, Dorothy and most other Quaker and International Commission staff were given urgent instructions to return immediately to Britain via the port of Bordeaux. The International Commission office there was headed by an exceptionally able American administrator named Margaret Frawley, and she saw a chance to evacuate her colleagues on what were likely to be the last British vessels to leave the port, a pair of cargo ships homeward-bound from South Africa.

In the last letter she sent her parents from France, Dorothy had sought to allay fears provoked by deeply disturbing reports in the New Zealand press of the worsening military action in Europe. As she had done before, she aimed to convince them that she was in no immediate danger, and was prepared for whatever might eventuate. "I have had such a marvellous experience these last 3 or 4 years, but what I have seen has essentially been one stage after another of an enormous tragedy of which perhaps the finale may be averted. I do so hope that it will never reach you. Don't ever worry about me. I assure you I don't worry about myself."[81]

As a final action before leaving Perpignan, she gave emergency funds to her Spanish co-workers, since they were not permitted to accompany her to Britain. Both office secretaries and the driver were given generous sums that might enable them to migrate elsewhere.[82] The Irish national Mary Elmes once again elected to remain in her job, but first she drove Dorothy and others across a country in utter chaos, in a desperate all-night bid to reach the departing ships.

Their car reached Bordeaux in the early dawn of mid-summer, finding it a wretched city, over-run with fugitives from throughout western Europe, many of them sleeping in the streets and all seemingly frantic to obtain travel permits, fares and tickets to a safe destination. At the International Commission office in the rue Vergniaud, these documents were provided by the anxious and assiduous Margaret Frawley, who told the carload of tousled and weary evacuees that they immediately needed to drive on to the coastal port of Le Verdon, where their ship was waiting to leave. The scream of a dive-bomber, defending ack-ack fire and the boom of explosives accompanied them on this final stage of the journey, through miles of vineyards bearing the names of famous vintages.

The road followed the course of the River Garonne to a wide estuary where it discharged into the Atlantic. Some distance offshore a muddy-yellow liner lay at anchor, and her launch shuttled to and fro throughout the morning to ferry passengers aboard. On a quay littered with cars abandoned by their departing owners, Dorothy and Mary bid each other a tearful farewell. They had worked closely and harmoniously together for more than three years, sometimes in conditions of great hardship and personal risk, but also in circumstances that both of them were afterwards happy to recall.

Dorothy had now become a refugee herself, and one who was better prepared psychologically and practically for the experience than most of the frightened people around her. Her luggage consisted of the single suitcase with which she had first arrived in Spain, and her blow-up mattress which she guessed, rightly, might prove useful on the voyage. As the launch brought her to the liner's side, Dorothy could see that its decks were entirely packed with people of all ages. The sight was not unlike the *Sinaia*'s departure for Mexico the previous year, although it lacked that ship's air of excited optimism. The *SS Madura* was an aging British tramp steamer battered by more than 15 years' service on Far Eastern routes. Her usual function was hauling cargo, and she had cabin accommodation for just 170 passengers and crew. As she climbed aboard clutching her rubber mattress, Dorothy found that the ship was equipped with four lifeboats. On this voyage she would carry around 1500 people across a sea filled with unknown dangers.

After delivering her colleagues aboard the *Madura*, Mary Elmes made the hazardous return journey across a shocked and reeling France to the first-floor apartment in the Rue de Baleares, and resumed the work that she and Dorothy had begun a year earlier. Working for the International Commission, and later directly for the US Quakers, she was to remain in her post until the total German occupation of France in November 1942. In that time another refugee camp opened in her region, at Rivesaltes, and many Spanish refugees were transferred there. In the months after Dorothy's departure, many thousands of Jewish refugees also poured into the Rivesaltes camp, and Mary's official correspondence from this period includes long lists of names of Jewish children newly orphaned or unable to rejoin their parents. These children became Mary's primary concern and on several occasions, to save them from deportation, she is known to have hidden children in the boot of her car and driven high into the Pyrenees to deliver them to safe houses such as La Coume. In January 1943 these activities caused her to be arrested by the Nazi occupation forces. She was held for six months at a prison near Paris before being released without charge. In later life she dismissed this incident as unexceptional. "Well, we all experienced inconveniences in those days, didn't we?"[83]

Unassuming, courageous and entirely selfless, Mary refused to

accept the medal of the *Legion d'Honneur* which the French government wished to bestow on her after the war. She married a
Frenchman, had two children and died in 2002, aged 92. Twelve
years later, as this book was in preparation, her name was added to
the list of the 'Righteous among the nations' – non-Jewish people
who risked their lives to save Jews during the Holocaust. The list
includes such names as Oskar Schindler, Queen Elisabeth of the
Belgians and Raoul Wallenberg. Mary Elmes is, at the time of
writing, the only Irish citizen so honoured.

Chapter 5

Wearing the Snood

Like a miniature and multinational version of the *Retirada*, the strange array of refugees crammed aboard the *Madura* featured some of the Continent's most distinguished citizens. Eve Curie, the daughter and biographer of the discoverer of radium, was one of them. Baron Rothschild and his family had managed to comfortably exceed the per-person luggage quota.[1] Senior figures in the French, Czech and Belgian governments hoped to form governments-in-exile in Britain. Several of those owed thanks to a remarkable diplomat, the Portuguese consul Aristides de Sousa Mendes. As the German advance was closing on Bordeaux, Portugal's dictator Salazar, an admirer of Hitler, instructed his diplomatic representatives to deny entry to their country to all Jews and dissidents. De Sousa Mendes agonised over this order for several days, and decided to disobey it. Instead he set up a production line of desks outside his consulate and on 17 June, as Dorothy was driving towards Bordeaux, he issued some 30,000 visas and other travel documents to the stateless and desperate. Almost half went to Jews. Other grateful recipients included the entire Belgian Cabinet. While their Portuguese documentation will have assisted their entry to a new country, it was not a requirement for a passage on the 'last boat from Bordeaux', as this voyage became known. None of those who boarded the ship was asked to pay a fare, or even to provide personal identification. This was an emergency evacuation, carried out under imminent threat of a German air attack.

The *Madura* was loaded past its Plimsoll line, with people sleeping on deck, in corridors and under dining tables. The few cabins, even the captain's, were reserved for invalids and elderly women, while the rest of the ship accommodated everyone from businessmen and "specimens of the retired-Colonel class from the Riviera", to frightened children and family pets.[2] In these desperately cramped conditions, anyone with medical knowledge is likely to have identified themselves to the crew in case of injury or illness among the passengers. Dr Thomas Kelly, an elderly Irish former army surgeon, later received a letter of thanks from the chairman of the *Madura*'s shipping line "for all that you, in conjunction with your colleagues on board, did under such difficult and harassing circumstances."[3]

Journalists made merry on the ship's middle deck, compensating for the shortage of food with a surplus of drink. In a ring of deck chairs sat the cream of Britain's European press corps – Sefton Delmer, who had covered the Spanish Civil War for the *Daily Express*, Hugh Greene, brother of the novelist Graham Greene and later head of the BBC, and at least 20 others. The young, dark and dashing Geoffrey Cox had made his reputation reporting from Madrid for the *News Chronicle* at the outbreak of the civil war. Like Dorothy, he was a New Zealander from Canterbury, and like her, he had been forced by the speed of the blitzkrieg to abandon his post in France and flee from the only port now offering a chance of returning to Britain and safety.

It was a warm, clear day with a miraculously flat sea. Late in the morning a German bomber flew low towards the ship, and her crew raced for the anti-aircraft guns. A French fighter plane appeared and chased the bomber inland, but nerves remained taut. Most of the passengers had arrived with little food of their own and the ship carried only its usual stores, so hunger contributed to the tension. The galley staff made heroic efforts and succeeded in supplying two meals a day in an unending succession of sittings – tea and bread in the morning, and Spam (tinned ham), potatoes and rice later in the day.[4] To the vast relief of those already on board, the *Madura* boarded her final passengers and hauled anchor at six in the evening. That night, wrote Hugh Greene, "The decks were a tangled mass of uneasily sleeping men and women, with their bodies twisted into the strangest shapes as they lay in their bed-chairs, on mattresses, suitcases or simply on the hard deck boards."[5] Dorothy's Quaker colleague Edith Pye recalled that, "One night four of us together, taking our shift at sleeping on the deck, were lying very close together to keep warm. A ship's officer came out of his cubby-hole and said he thought he could find us another blanket. He brought it out, tucked it very carefully round us, surveyed his work and remarked, 'Now I am the proud father of quads.'"[6]

The weather promised a perfect sea voyage, but increased the risk of enemy attack. Two British destroyers shadowed the ship and she took a time-consuming zigzag course to avoid submarines until, after 36 hours, she reached the Cornish port of Falmouth, where the entire town was assembled on the docks to welcome the now-famous shipload of refugees.[7]

All of the public buildings in the little town, from the churches to the cinema, were pressed into use as reception and catering areas. Many of them lacked sufficient sanitation, and buckets were supplied at the cinema. The Pavilion, an entertainment venue and garden, served meals provided by local well-wishers. The government appeared to have been taken by surprise by the arrival, in the remote west of the country, of so many diverse immigrants. Eventually immigration officials arrived with bundles of forms and after several uncomfortable days everyone was processed and permitted to leave.[8]

Although Dorothy cannot have realised it, she was part of a giant wartime rescue effort named Operation Aerial. In the three weeks between the evacuation of Dunkirk and the signing of the French-German armistice, about 180 merchant ships and twenty warships uplifted almost a quarter of a million people from French ports. This remarkable achievement could not, however, expunge the crushing humiliation of the retreat from Dunkirk, or counter the imminent threat of a German invasion of mainland Britain. On 18 June, as Dorothy was leaving Bordeaux, Churchill had made his 'finest hour' speech in the House of Commons, acknowledging that "the Battle of Britain is about to begin" but asserting that the British people would withstand a sustained Luftwaffe attack, "like the brave men of Barcelona."[9] His comparison with Republican resilience during the Spanish Civil War was not quite deserved. For all of Churchill's eloquence and booming certitude, the woeful state of civic unpreparedness that Dorothy had observed and publicly warned against during her brief residence in London in 1939 had not greatly improved by early September 1940, when the Blitz began in earnest.

The government had not built enough deep air-raid shelters in London to meet the public need, and lethally inadequate above-ground shelters were provided instead. East Enders who experienced the first waves of bombing sensibly refused to use them and forced their way into Underground stations, which proved largely effective for this purpose. The 'rest centres' provided for the tens of thousands rendered homeless by the bombing were overcrowded and pitifully ill-equipped by comparison with the Republican *refugios* that had housed refugees of the civil war.[10]

"The first few weeks of the Blitz were real Front Line stuff," wrote Dorothy some months afterwards, with more *sangfroid* than she could possibly have felt at the time. "It was not possible to sleep upstairs, with major battles going on just above the chimney pots, and the house rocking about occasionally when something landed near by." She avoided mentioning, in her letters home, that one air-raid flattened an entire row of houses on the opposite side of her street, killing numbers of her neighbours.[11]

During the night bombing raids, she says, "I had . . . the right to bunk in a sort of bear's den in the garden". This derisive description referred to the corrugated iron 'Anderson shelter' supplied to householders who chose not to enter public air-raid shelters. Dorothy scorned the use of her bear's den as well. "Early to bed in the basement with earplugs and a book was my lot for about 2 months . . . In that time no one went out at night at all unless on duty. It was terrific to watch and worse to listen to. We were high up with A.A. [ack-ack – anti-aircraft batteries] not far off to increase the din."[12] This blithe attitude saw her endure the Blitz unharmed, and she spent the war working in a variety of posts connected with the domestic war effort.

The first of these roles disregarded all of her earlier training and experience except, perhaps, from childhood memories of her father's profession. In August 1940 Dorothy enrolled for a two-month course run by the Society of Women Engineers to prepare women for technical positions left vacant by men who had enlisted, and whose work was rendered especially vital by the demands of the armaments factories. The training was provided at the elegant brick Beaufoy Institute in Lambeth, founded in the 19th century as a boy's vocational school. "It is just off the Thames," she wrote, "opposite the Houses of Parliament." In her first month the Queen paid a visit to the Beaufoy to boost morale, but as a devout republican Dorothy did not mention this event in her letters home. And as a confirmed democrat from the colonies, she observed disapprovingly that, "lots of Ladys & Honourables took [the training course] & had their photos in the

Tatler etc leering at the lathes, and smirking at the handiwork (often largely the handiwork of the charming & patient instructors)."[13]

She found her training "very leisurely and pleasant – 9.30 to 5, and the War seemed such a long way off", despite the nightly air-raids that began during her second month at the Beaufoy. "Well, there I happily pottered," she wrote, "often thinking – this is dreamland, it just isn't the same world that I've been living in these last few years. Everybody else seemed quite happy in dreamland in England though".[14]

In taking the training course, Dorothy anticipated by up to a year the influx of large numbers of women into the nation's engineering workshops and factories. By late 1940 official steps to address a chronic shortfall in military and other industrial production remained token and embryonic, and Dorothy vented her exasperation in her letters home. "I get impatient with English slowness often . . . so stupid they seem in comparison with Spaniards; and then of course this war is not the burning personal affair that the Spanish War was – that was a most glorious Crusade . . . where I encountered some of the finest people I feel sure, in the world – some of the craziest as well. This affair is a loathsome bore that has to be endured to the finish, which I fear will probably be a horrid sticky one . . . It is good to be doing something definite & worthwhile tho', & I'm quite content".[15]

Her recent experience of centralised planning in Republican-held areas of Spain made Dorothy sharply critical of Britain's languid, haphazard and tardy approach to total war. "Life is much more normal than you would think possible, under the circumstances. I think it's too darn normal. There should, for instance, be far stricter rationing than there is . . . the waste and muddling that goes on is truly appalling. In Spain I saw much more really intelligent planning, with vision & imagination. Here they are trying to bring themselves to State planning in a big way . . . but oh HOW it hurts, & what messes they make."[16]

These firmly leftwing views on the state of British military preparedness were put into practice immediately after Dorothy completed her engineering course, when she moved directly into war production. She "finished with [her] lathes and files quite regretfully," she told her family, and went to work in a large aircraft

factory in west London. This job proved tiring but "intensely interesting . . . we had to work immensely clever machines and assist the
tool setters – it was hoped that eventually we would be able to
replace them."[17] Before that stage was reached, in late 1940,
Dorothy was co-opted, at the urging of former colleagues from the
aid sector, into a more influential position that recognised her
exceptional capabilities at working with displaced communities,
and especially with women and children. She was initially reluctant
to give up working on the factory floor but changed her mind after
realising that "I find human beings more interesting than
machines". Accordingly, she became a welfare and personnel supervisor for a military equipment manufacturer needing to rapidly
expand its workforce to match the pace of the government's re-
armament programme. By the end of the year she could claim to
hold, "one of the most sought-after jobs for women that are to be
had in wartime England", and she would retain that post, apart
from one unsought intermission, for the following three years.[18]

The wholesale recruitment of untrained women, both to replace
and to extend the work of men recruited into the armed forces, was
an ambitious and contentious project, fraught with risk. Women
were needed not simply for repetitive work in munitions factories, as
they had been in the First World War, but also to operate heavy
machinery, turn lathes, stoke boilers and perform many other tasks
for which they had never previously been considered capable. Factory
work paid well, and there was no shortage of applicants, but the pace
and scale of workforce mobilisation raised problems faster than solutions could be found to meet them. Women working long hours –
and 80-hour weeks were soon commonplace – would, it was feared,
neglect their children and skimp their other domestic duties. Family
harmony would deteriorate if husbands working in reserved occupations came home to scanty meals and cold beds.

Despite such well-founded anxieties, the war allowed no alternative to the mass conscription of women into the industrial workforce,
along with rigorous and practical training schemes to prepare them
for their new activities. To Dorothy's satisfaction, the engineering
course she had taken at the Beaufoy was taken over by the Ministry
of Labour, which cut the training period to six weeks, introduced
night classes, and was soon training large numbers of women from all

levels of society. A similar process of streamlining and pragmatism was applied to training the welfare supervisors who were employed within large factories to oversee the health and wellbeing of their workforces of newly industrialised women. The Institute of Labour Management set up short courses at Cambridge University and elsewhere to train women for these supervisory roles, which had suddenly assumed greatly increased importance, "in view of the great necessity for watching the health of the enormous numbers of people now working at such extreme pressure at war work (and in the blitz)".[19]

While still working in the aircraft factory, Dorothy was urged to undertake one of these training courses, but she refused on the grounds that she had recently completed one course and could not justify leaving the workforce to gain yet another qualification. She was then told that a large London firm was prepared to overlook her lack of formal qualifications as a welfare supervisor, on the grounds of her prior experience and evident suitability for the role. A meeting was arranged with its manager, and the outcome was an offer of employment which she accepted modestly but with typical determination.

"I agreed to go in under a 'probationary' trial with one of their existing Welfare Supervisors to teach me the rudiments and I'm still in this stage", she wrote on Christmas Day 1940. "It's all very complex and interesting and it is very necessary to fit in perfectly with a very complex organisation working at pressure and under difficulties – they recently lost a splendid main factory [due to a German bombing raid]. My work in Spain and France where I was almost completely boss of my own job and many other people and disposed of large quantities of money may be not the best training for this. The management seem to think I'll do, tho' I have qualms".[20]

In fact Dorothy proved highly competent in this role, and was repeatedly promoted within the company to supervise successively larger workforces. Her employer was the Mills Equipment Company, a long-established firm whose main product was webbing for military uniforms, but which also made other woven cloth materials such as machine-gun ammunition belts, rifle slings, haversacks and carrying bags for tools and weapons. The company had been founded in the 19th century by an iconclastic US Army officer, Anson Mills, who believed that cotton webbing was superior to the standard leather equipment then supplied to his troops. He developed his own sample products which were eventually adopted as standard by US armed forces. In 1899 a factory was set up in the UK to supply cartridge bandoliers and belts for the Boer War. This became an independent company which eventually supplied not only the British armed forces but those of some 50 other countries including, Dorothy noted, her own. During the Second World War the Mills Equipment Company employed some 7000 staff, almost all women, in a number of hastily equipped and uncomfortable factories scattered across north London.

The Mills workers generally wore a standard uniform of wraparound or bib-and-dungaree overalls (the former were preferred because they made it easier to undress to use the toilet). Hair was covered in either a headscarf or a 'snood' (a large hairnet) to protect it from dirt and moving machinery. Their welfare supervisor was expected to help them find accommodation and childcare facilities handy to the workplace, and might also be asked to intervene when angry husbands and boyfriends arrived unexpectedly to complain about neglect of domestic commitments. "I have to watch over about 1600 people's comfort & wellbeing during their working hours," wrote Dorothy. "I find my experience in Spain of enormous help. Identical problems arise every day. I have also a clinic with 2 nurses always busy, so my nursing has come in handy again, tho' it is a long while since I have done any, and I am distinctly rusty."[21]

Her nursing training is likely to have been called upon to treat women suffering the cumulative effects of long working hours and a diet limited by food rationing. Some women supplemented their food ration by rearing chickens or rabbits at home, and Dorothy could give practical advice on this activity since her family had kept both when she was a child in Lyttelton. Clothing was also rationed, and both ingenuity and hours of queuing were required to keep a family decently dressed. Dorothy herself, perhaps with more disposable income than many of her workmates, commissioned a practical but stylish outfit from a dress shop which bought its own supplies of woolen cloth direct from handweavers in the Scottish isles. "I have had a very satisfactory suit tailored – Harris tweed (handwoven, spun-&-dyed!) – brown with faint yellow squares and blue line. It is very warm and I just never wear anything else."[22]

Working mothers were encouraged to send their young children to safe havens in the countryside but many refused, and local authorities developed day nurseries to care for their children near at hand.[23] The lively camaraderie between the women compensated for many of the difficulties of wartime work, but even the most stoutly patriotic could break down under the strain and loss of sleep caused by nightly air-raids. The Mills company's factories were in densely populated working class districts, and many of the employees lived in the surrounding streets. For night after night in early 1941 they woke to the ululating howl of air-raid sirens, and spent sleepless hours packed alongside terrified family members and neighbours, waiting and hoping for the all-clear.

As a 36-year-old single woman who had spent the previous four years living among victims of war, Dorothy's own physical and emotional health must inevitably have become strained while working in a city under constant nightly bombardment. Her route to work from her north London apartment might require sudden detours to avoid cratered streets and charred terraces. She assured her parents during the harsh winter of 1940-41 that she continued "to be well and hearty except for the intermittent colds that this nasty climate engenders", but could not conceal her regret at leaving southern Europe.[24] "I'm haunted all the time by visions and remembrances of Mediterranean Springs – ever since January, when I knew there would be great masses of almond blossom on the bare hills & they would be picking oranges in heavenly sunshine in Spain, and in Perpignan there would be piles of strawberries and asparagus in the Market. I had never thought or intended to endure another English winter."[25]

These nostalgic reveries were tempered by the grim news emerging from Spain and France. Francesca Wilson met frequently with Dorothy while she worked as a welfare supervisor, and passed on news of the Quakers' efforts to sustain their refugee work under German occupation.[26] " . . . the American Quakers are in charge of all the Relief Work in France now & they have incorporated all the work we, in the Int. Commission, were doing, as well as all those neutral workers who were able to stay in Europe after the fall of most of it. The reports are intensely interesting – & appalling in their implications. Nothing is now being done at all in Spain, where things are frightful, owing to the hostile attitude of the Fascist regime, which has behaved with even more beastliness than even we feared."[27]

In March 1941 Dorothy was based in the large Mills sewing plant, housing 900 industrial sewing machines, in Angel Road (now the North Circular A406) in Enfield. This north London borough had a long tradition of arms manufacture, and had given its name to the army's standard-issue Lee-Enfield rifle. The Mills factory stood on a strategically important and exposed site near a railway yard, and had suffered several minor bombing attacks. On the night of 19 March 1941 it became a primary target. From 11pm, a succession of flares and incendiary bombs were dropped directly over the sprawling, single-storey building, turning it into a fireball which other bombers then used as a sighting aid. The local press reported that the raid, "presented a spectacle of a colossal firework display as the sky was lit up first by a greenish blue which turned to a red glare, amid the dropping of H. E. [high explosive] bombs . . . Using the big fire as the target, enemy planes circled for some hours around the area scattering their bombs indiscriminately . . . Widespread damage was done to a number of working-class homes".[28]

By simple good fortune, no nightshift was working in the factory that night. Human casualties from the raid amounted to seven killed and about 50 wounded, but the goal of destroying this significant element of British war production was entirely achieved. Air raid wardens assessed the damage and reported, "Mills Equipment Factory gutted. No production possible."[29] "Hitler – blast him – has destroyed my work for the third time in four years", Dorothy fumed. Her employers thought sufficiently highly of her services to offer to retain her on the payroll while a new factory was located and production was rebuilt. She declined this offer since, "they are being so long about it . . . that I was in no mood to play about waiting even tho' they were amiable enough to pay me for so doing."[30]

As often in the past, a new professional responsibility supplied a distraction from immediate personal concerns. The International Commission, the Quaker-based refugee aid agency which had employed Dorothy in both Spain and France, had been renamed the Commission for War Refugees in Britain. Senior members of its administration remembered the tall New Zealand nurse with the calm demeanour and reputation for reliability, and were eager to reengage her. She was asked to run a large hostel in north Devon housing women and children refugees from France and Belgium, and decided that, "It will be pleasant to have some country air after the long winter in London."[31] The hostel, she found, was in a fine country house called Miramar, surrounded by a beautiful garden and standing above a quiet and remote bay. The work was light and the conditions luxurious after factory work in heavily bombed London. As well as offering rest, fresh air and security, living in Devon meant a better diet than severely rationed Londoners received. Dorothy took advantage of the availability of fresh farm produce to supply a cake to one of her brothers, Roger, then serving with New Zealand forces in the Middle East. "I managed to amass 7 eggs and enough margarine, sugar, and fruit and had a cake made by a champion cake baker in the village of Lee, which I carefully packed and dispatched".[32]

This relatively idyllic existence lasted only a few months, by Dorothy's own choice. "I have had a lovely summer there," she wrote on her return to London in November 1941. "I quite liked the French and Belgians too, but didn't want to spend the winter with them. The [International] Commission were pleased and grateful for what I had done for them there, and of course, did not want me to relinquish the job. But frankly I felt I should. It was all too remote and peaceful."[33]

Even though the Blitz had at last ended, presumably few residents of the shattered city of London would have opted to live there in this period, in preference to a sleepy seaside combe. Yet Dorothy enthusiastically returned to work for Mills Equipment, which was expanding its facilities to meet the endless demand for war materials. She now had substantial experience as a welfare supervisor and became known to some of the most senior officials in the world of industrial production and labour resources. These included the large and shambling figure of Ernest Bevin, the Minister of Labour and of National Service, whose extraordinary powers to direct the country's workforce made him, in the judgement of many, the most powerful figure in Britain in this period, commanding greater authority than even his prime minister, Winston Churchill.[34]

Bevin's unlikely political ascendence could only have occurred under the desperate conditions facing Britain at the outbreak of the war. The son of a farm labourer, his formal education had ended at age eleven. He went on to establish the immensely powerful Transport and General Workers Union, Britain's largest union, and as its general secretary, regularly crossed swords with Churchill in the years before the war. Yet, early in 1940 Churchill was sufficiently impressed by Bevin to offer him a highly ranked place in his War Cabinet. Bevin, who was not then an MP and had never held any other political office, accepted on condition that the many lines of responsibility for manpower allocation and industrial production should all be centralised in his hands.[35]

In spite of this almost unlimited authority to direct where Britons would work, and their wages, hours and conditions, Bevin disliked using his legislative powers of compulsion and preferred to encourage voluntary compliance where possible. He also introduced ambitious mechanisms for tripartite consultation between employers, unions and the government, and insisted that his drive for greater industrial production would take account not only of workplace health and safety but of workers' welfare and living conditions, including their accommodation and transport needs.[36] He had a high regard for the work of the welfare supervisors, and set up a Factory and Welfare Division within his Ministry. This introduced an industrial medical service and vastly expanded the works canteens which provided hot meals at low rates.[37] Bevin, the veteran unionist, also arranged for lunchtime concerts to be performed in factories, and for uplifting programmes – 'Music while you work', 'Worker's Playtime' – to be broadcast by the BBC and piped into factory floors through their loudspeaker systems.[38]

As the domestic war effort accelerated, Bevin stumped the country visiting factories, mines, docks and shipyards to expound his plans to their staff, and endeavour to unblock obstacles to meeting his production targets. On several occasions this booming bear of a man arrived at Mills Equipment Company factories and talked with Dorothy. She was encouraged to communicate directly with his office if she encountered any difficulties requiring his intervention.[39] The two evidently felt a mutual respect, and Dorothy firmly backed Bevin's sweeping powers to command the nation's labour relations, as a practical means to shorten the war. She had little patience with vacuous appeals to patriotism or national sentiment. "My opinion is that this 'honour' that gets so much talked about can better be saved by whipping up production rather than recklessly chucking away brave lives. The country isn't <u>nearly</u> at full speed yet and its machine production side is utterly disgraceful after nearly two years of war".[40]

Until 1943 Dorothy remained with the Mills Equipment Co., monitoring the health of the factory staff, listening to their concerns and intervening with higher authorities on their behalf. She then took up an entirely different position that recalled her work in Murcia. Why she changed direction in this way is not clear. The reason may be as straightforward as simple restlessness, coupled with her consistent urge to apply her skills where they were most urgently needed. She had once revealed to her family that "My hero is, I think, Roosevelt. He's got what it takes not only to beat Hitler but also his own Big Industry Boys who are just about as dangerous. I hope he can get the Americans to do their stuff before it is too late though".[41] By 1943 Bevin's plans for industrial production were nearing fulfillment, and Roosevelt had indeed got the Americans to do their stuff. Perhaps Dorothy felt the need for a new challenge.

In April 1943 she became the matron of a residential nursery occupying a handsome manor house near Edinburgh. This was a charitable institution where children, some of whom had lost parents or homes during the war, could live until permanent accommodation was found for them. By choosing to work with child victims of war who had experienced bombing, the loss of family members, dislocation and other traumas, Dorothy was resuming a local version of her work in both Murcia and Perpignan, and also entering a system of charitable work for child refugees which had arisen in Spain during the civil war. The same system supported several nurseries in London, developed in parallel with hers in Edinburgh and possibly interacting with it, which were founded by the most famous surname in the history of psychoanalysis.

Six years earlier, in July 1937, just as Dorothy was beginning her work at the Murcia children's hospital, thousands of other needy children were adrift in the northern Spanish city of Santander after a Republican military defeat. More than 10,000 refugees passed though the city's railway station every day, some of them unaccompanied children. A British journalist, John Langdon-Davies, was covering the civil war for the *News Chronicle* when he noticed a boy of five clutching a handwritten note – "This is José. I am his father.

When Santander falls I shall be shot. Whoever finds my son, I beg of him to take care of him for my sake." This incident prompted Langdon-Davies, together with a young aid worker named Eric Muggeridge who had been delivering food supplies to Murcia and other refugee centres, to form Foster Parents Plan for Children in Spain. It funded several 'colonies' outside the embattled cities where 300 Spanish children could live safely and learn to cope with the trauma of the war. During the Second World War this organisation, renamed Foster Parents Plan for War Children, worked with displaced children throughout Europe.[42] At the height of the Blitz it provided shelter to some 4,000 children in Britain, of several nationalities.

Just as the gifted and progressive teachers Pitt and Yves Kruger had been driven by Nazi ideology to leave their own country and find refuge in France, Sigmund Freud fled Vienna in 1938 and came to London with his family. Anna Freud was the youngest of his six children, and the only one to follow their father's profession. With her lifelong companion Dorothy Burlingham, and with funding from the Foster Parents Plan, she opened the Children's Rest Centre in Hampstead in January 1941.[43] Most of its early residents, who slept in three tiers of bunks, were children from the East End whose homes had been badly damaged in bombing raids. "We . . . accept children," the two women wrote, "who have suffered through bombing, shelter sleeping, indiscriminate evacuation and billeting. We try to serve on the one hand as a convalescent home and on the other, where necessary, as a home for problem children."[44] Like most other parts of inner London, Hampstead was subject to bombing raids during the Blitz, and when air-raid sirens sounded the children were hurried down to an emergency shelter in the basement. After one massive raid the nursery staff ventured outside next morning to find an unexploded bomb in the garden of the neighbouring house. The children greatly resented losing access to their own garden for two weeks, until the bomb was removed by disposal experts.[45]

In mid-1941 two more centres were opened, including a large residential nursery for babies and young children whose mothers were employed in industrial production. Collectively these were known as the Hampstead War Nurseries, and although their original function was as a welfare service, they later became internationally known centres for research and training in the then-nascent field of child pyschology. Anna Freud adopted a policy, at that time uncommon and controversial, of involving the children's parents in their care as much as possible. Mothers and, where possible, fathers were given unlimited access to their children day and night. Mothers were encouraged to live in and contribute to the running of the nurseries, and many did so. To ensure that the emotional needs of all the children were met, they were eventually organised into 'artificial families' of four or five children and one 'mother', who was sometimes a regular staff member. Freud corresponded constantly with fathers serving overseas or working outside London, encouraging them to have ongoing contact with their children. To provide a regular male presence she invited six young conscientious objectors to work at the War Nurseries, carrying out maintenance and gardening tasks while playing and interacting with the children. Freud also encouraged her staff to closely observe and note the children's perceptions and fears, and later published these findings as *War and Children*, a pioneering study of the mental and emotional life of the traumatised child.[46]

In addition to individual donations through the Foster Parents Plan, Freud's War Nurseries received financial support from the International Commission, now primarily backed by US funds, and from the British War Relief Society which, despite its name, was a US organisation formed to distribute aid to Britain. Like the Commission, the Society served as the umbrella body and administrative arm for a range of more specific charities. Some of its efforts, such as the supply of children's scarlet skull-caps bearing a 'V for victory' symbol, were alarmingly gung-ho. However, it also funded nursery homes throughout England, both day nurseries where working women could leave their children during working hours, and residential nurseries.

One of those was Dorothy's nursery in Edinburgh. She worked there as matron, with responsibility for the staff and overall administration, until late 1944, as V1 and V2 rockets rained down on London in Germany's lethal last-gasp revival of the Blitz. None of her letters from this period have survived, so the extent to which her nursery interacted with those formed by Anna Freud is not known. However, both charitable institutions shared a common source of funding, and the practices Dorothy employed earlier in the Murcia children's hospital suggest that she is likely to have approved of and perhaps emulated Freud's in Hampstead.

Throughout the latter part of the war, Dorothy's concerns for the children under her care were compounded by anxiety at the circumstances of two of her brothers, Frank and Roger. Both had enlisted with the New Zealand army at an early opportunity, in opposition to her own expressed wishes. Writing to their parents in early 1939, when Britain's, and therefore New Zealand's, active participation in the war was still hypothetical, she said, "I do beg the boys never to leave New Zealand to fight abroad. . . . I, having seen something of modern war, can only say that the individual soldier is worth far less than the ground of the burrow he has to cower in. Better far to stay in their own place and defend that."[47] Later that year, on the day after both countries declared war on Germany, she asked somewhat rhetorically, "Is it too late to hope that the boys aren't going overseas? Once again I beg them to realise that NZ is the place to defend now, if they want to live in it . . . of course, I know, I had a really marvellous fling in my first experience of war; but . . . that was really fought for an idea, and was utterly romantic, and fantastic and glorious – even in defeat."[48]

The two young men were evidently unmoved by their elder sister's entreaties and both enlisted in the first days of the war. After cursory infantry training, they left New Zealand with the first echelon in January 1940 and were stationed in tents at Maadi Camp, near Cairo.[49] She was deeply relieved to hear from them there in May, when they had yet to see action. "They were in good health and spirits but marvelling at the Oriental dirt around them," she told their parents. At the end of that year, as Dorothy shivered in a London wracked by bombing, Frank sent her "an ecstatic description of bathing" in the Mediterranean, "so blue and buoyant it is that just to read his few words took me far from cold suet pudding England."[50] However, news arrived from Maadi only intermittently. "I do so wish I knew how things are with them at this moment and what part of the present scrap they are in," she told her parents as the year ended. "I've sent each of them a khaki cashmere cardigan for Xmas which I hope will have arrived." These expensive gifts, from the venerable West End menswear firm of Austin Reed, might seem an unusual choice to send to the Middle East but Dorothy was distantly familiar with that region from having lived on the opposite coast, and was confident that warm clothing would be appreciated in Egypt. "Mediterranean winds can be bitter at this time of year."[51]

In the following year Dorothy and her parents struggled to make sense of heavily censored news reports of military engagements in the the Middle East, and occasional pre-printed army postcards.[52] "I'm wondering very anxiously if you have news of the boys," she wrote in May 1941. "I gathered they had gone to Greece so my heart has been in my mouth . . . So one can only pray to whatever gods may be (and there used to be lots in Greece I believe) that the boys have come through."[53] In fact, only one of her brothers – Frank, the elder of the two, with the rank of corporal – had been transferred by ship to Greece, while Roger remained in the Maadi training camp.

The Allied campaign in Greece and Crete was a disaster in which New Zealand troops were heavily outnumbered and outgunned. Along with many others, Frank was wounded in the thigh and became a prisoner of war in German Sudetenland. Dorothy received no word from him until some months after the Battle of Crete, when a cryptic letter arrived which her sources at the New Zealand High Commision in London told her had been sent from a military hospital in Athens. She urged her parents not to feel unduly anxious, since the High Commision was compiling lists of all New Zealand POWs and expected soon to learn Frank's whereabouts in Germany. "As soon as they get his Prison Camp address through from the Geneva International Red Cross they will start sending monthly food parcels . . . Don't worry too much. He is apparently not too badly off. In addition I have invoked all the assistance I can from the International Commission. They are writing to one of the heads of the International Red Cross in Geneva making special enquiry for Frank and that may hasten matters."[54]

By the end of 1941 it was known that Frank was held at Stalag VIIIB camp in south Germany, and Dorothy received a reassuring postcard from him. "He reports that he is fit and suffering no after effects from the 'smack in the leg.' He asked for a cap, mittens, golf sox, sweets and a pair of braces. I was at Miramar [the refugee hostel in Devon], where luckily, there was some wool (which is couponed [i.e. rationed] here these days). I immediately got a knitting party going hard . . . Parcels of clothes may only be sent every three months, so unfortunately my really fine stuff will now have to wait until February. Nonetheless I was shown a standard [Red Cross] parcel, and I thought it very good indeed. It included sweater, pyjamas, sox, muffler, gloves (I think), dental and shaving tackle, chocolate, 1 lb. They can no longer send shirts or blankets – the Germans pinch them en route".[55]

The Morris family's concern for Frank's wellbeing was compounded early in 1942 by the news that Roger had finally gone into action against Rommel's troops in the desert, and had also been wounded and captured. With a large group of other POWs, he was taken by ship to Naples, and then to a military hospital near the Swiss border, where he was treated for an abdominal injury. He was held in a succession of concentration camps in Italy and Germany, eventually at Stalag VIIIA, on the Polish border, at the opposite end of Germany from his brother.[56]

By mid-1945 both Morris brothers had been imprisoned for at least three years, while Dorothy had endured four years on the home front. At that late stage of the war, however, she could take comfort from the ever-growing number of Allied victories in several countries, indicating that the end was in sight. As an experienced refugee worker, she would have known that the next great challenge would be to handle the hundreds of thousands, perhaps millions, of displaced refugees whose needs would constitute a humanitarian crisis greater than any seen before. As this situation became daily more evident, Dorothy decided to leave her senior and innovative role at the Edinburgh nursery and resume working with displaced refugees and other civilian casualties of war. She applied for a position with the central international body responsible for war refugees, the newly created United Nations Relief and Rehabilitation Agency, and was accepted in July 1944, apparently the first New Zealand nurse to work for this agency.[57] The international community's response to the unfolding refugee crisis would, Dorothy believed, be the ultimate test of the victory won over fascism.

Chapter 6
The Conscience of the World

Rows of rectangular, buff-coloured tents in precise grid formation stretched across the desert sands east of Cairo until their lines disappeared into the heat haze. Each one housed a single family transferred from the Balkan coast of the Mediterranean, far to the north. Throughout 1944 Yugoslav, Dalmatian and Greek refugees had been progressively relocated to this blistering desert beside the Red Sea, the headquarters for British military forces in the Mediterranean. When Dorothy Morris arrived at the El Shatt displaced persons camp in mid-1944 it housed more than 20,000 people, and would eventually hold twice that number, mainly women and children but also the elderly and partisans injured in the war still being fought in their homeland.

Any comparisons between this camp and those flung up for Spanish civil war refugees five years earlier on the opposite coast of the Mediterranean must have been striking, and encouraging. The population of this vast tent city had not been hastily crammed together by a deeply reluctant host country, but instead transferred steadily and efficiently by military authorities so that families and even entire villages remained intact in their strange new surroundings. The first ten thousand had arrived just six months earlier. They were mainly Dalmatians, evacuated from their homes when fighting between local partisans and German troops destroyed their crops and threatened them with starvation. In El Shatt they were provided with British army-surplus tents whose double roofs proved comfortable even in the searing heat. The water and sanitation facilities were makeshift but adequate, and meals were prepared in enormous army kitchens.

This sprawling yet tightly managed refugee centre had grown, seemingly overnight, out of an empty desert with equipment and manpower supplied by British forces. In May 1944, control of El

Shatt was transferred to the United Nations Relief and Rehabilitation Administration (UNRRA), a new and untested international agency formed to manage the transition from war to peace. It represented the culmination of the hopes of longtime relief workers such as Francesca Wilson and Edith Pye, whose experience since World War One had convinced them that only a coordinated effort by the governments of all Allied countries could adequately meet the needs of the millions of civilians whose lives had been upturned by the current war. A multinational body for this purpose had been envisaged before the first signs of an Allied victory and, wrote Francesca Wilson optimistically, "opens the way to the first experiment in worldwide economic co-operation".[1] The scale of the task confronting the new agency was barely imaginable. Tens of millions of Latvians, Poles, Ukrainians, Yugoslavs and others had been displaced from their national territories, either by the need to flee to safety from battle zones, because they had been forcibly relocated to concentration camps, or as slave labour for Germany's factories, farms and households. Others, like the Krugers of La Coume, were anti-Nazi exiles and victims of persecution. A large proportion were Jewish, but their fate in the concentration camps was still little known by 1944, and the term 'holocaust' had not yet been coined to describe it.

It was US President Roosevelt, the wartime leader most admired by Dorothy Morris, who took the central role in forming the UNRRA. He proposed the agency in 1943 after obtaining support from the UK, the Soviet Union and China. Later 40 other nations, including Dorothy's, agreed to join the first organisation to carry the official title 'United Nations'. At that point the UN itself was still a remote ideal, and the term was used only to refer to those countries opposed to the Axis powers of Germany and Japan – Italy having already surrendered. At a ceremony in the White House in November 1943, Roosevelt described the new organisation's purpose as the repatriation and support of refugees who would come under Allied control by the end of the war. In terms sounding quaintly pompous today, he said, "The sufferings of the little men and women who have been ground under the Axis heel can be relieved only if we utilize the production of *all* the world to balance the want of *all* the world. In UNRRA we have devised a mechanism, based on the processes of true democracy, which can go far toward accomplishment of such an objective in the days and months of desperate emergency which will follow the overthrow of the Axis."[2] Representatives of each of the 44 member nations signed the UNRRA's founding document. New Zealand's signatory was the former war correspondent Geoffrey Cox, last seen with Dorothy on board the *Madura* and now First Secretary at New Zealand's embassy in Washington.[3]

Besides the sheer numbers of displaced persons eventually entitled to UNRRA's support, the scope of its responsibilities towards them was dauntingly broad. It extended to providing food and shelter to the populations of newly liberated areas, providing health services and preventing disease, and preparing them for repatriation, a role that included rebuilding agricultural and industrial production and restoring essential services in their home countries.[4] The amount of financial and other resources needed to implement these obligations across an entire continent was far beyond any prior reckoning, and the 44 contributing nations debated hotly over how each of them would contribute. At the first session of the UNRRA Council in December 1943, the US delegate proposed that each member country not then occupied by the enemy should contribute one percent of its annual income. New Zealand's representative challenged this calculation on the grounds that a flat-rate contribution, like a flat tax on income, favoured wealthier nations. This argument won support from other minor partners, and a variation to the one-percent basic rate was introduced.[5] Ultimately, the US provided the bulk of UNRRA funds although smaller countries made valuable specific contributions, New Zealand's mainly in the form of woollen cloth and readymade clothing.

The core of UNRRA's personnel was its civilian relief teams, who carried out the primary work of coordinating relief efforts and managing displaced persons' camps. Recruiting sufficient numbers of suitably trained and experienced staff was a chronic problem for the organisation's first year, and Dorothy's application, endorsed by distinguished Quaker aid workers such as Dr Audrey Russell, Francesca Wilson and Edith Pye, must have been accepted with alacrity when she submitted it in July 1944. She offered her services for "as long as required", specifying a preference for working either in the Balkans or in western Europe more generally.[6] However, like almost all UNRRA staff in this early period, she was posted initially

to El Shatt in the Middle East, since that was the only region where
fieldwork, and not just training or administration, was carried out
during 1944. Such a limited field of activity was an early sign of problems that would grow and eventually overwhelm the pioneering
organisation. It had assumed a vast and urgent role without the
opportunity to develop the infrastructure to adequately carry it out.
This acute lack of preparedness earned it the mocking nickname
'UNRRA the Unready', and other aid organisations later read its
initials as 'You Never Really Relieved Anybody'.

In the high summer of 1944, however, as Allied forces forced back
German troops in both Russia and France, the prospect of providing
substantial and coordinated support to the millions of wartime
refugees was at once challenging and inspiring. Dorothy arrived at El
Shatt wearing the first military-type uniform of her career – khaki
with scarlet shoulder flashes and cap badge.[7] As a nursing officer, she
worked alongside her team's doctor but also with welfare officers
charged with developing recreational and training facilities inside the
great sea of neatly aligned tents. She quickly discovered that El Shatt
comprised three (eventually six) sub-camps, based on geographical
regions in their occupants' home countries, so that different ethnic
and language groups lived alongside each other and pre-war connections were retained. Serbo-Croat, a language related to Russian, was
the common tongue of almost all the refugees, although some spoke
a little French or German and at least one, a tall young lawyer and
former partisan named Durshan Curcia, was fluent in English and
therefore a valued spokesperson.[8]

UNRAA had assumed formal control of El Shatt from the military authorities just months before Dorothy's arrival, but well before
that the refugees themselves had created their own internal administration, as the Spanish had done in the camps around Perpignan. This
elected structure of refugee representatives was modelled on the
councils in Croatian villages, and helped to mitigate the disruption
resulting from the rapid turnover of aid administrators. John
Corsellis, a British Quaker who worked as an ambulance driver at the
camp, noted that the refugees had collectively taken the initiative of
tiling the floors of their tents and setting up small schools and clinics.
By late 1944 they had formed a theatre group, courts and a police
force, and produced a camp newspaper, *Nas List (Our Paper)*. "There

is a sizeable hospital, apart from three independent camp 'outpatient departments' and dispensaries, all of which keep seven or eight ambulances busy. Everything is under canvas except the shower and laundry rooms, hospital and officers' mess . . . Of our colleagues, one is a pharmacist helping in the dispensary, one a trained nurse supervising a ward, one does clerical and one administrative work, and one is engaged on other transport work. We live in a comfortable tent, feed and sit around in the officers' mess where the food is good and well served, and have access to showers that work well".[9] A constant priority of the medical staff was the care of the newborn and their mothers. During the 18-month life of the camp, 650 babies were born there, and UNRRA archives hold photographs showing its nurses caring for them in tented clinics equipped with rudimentary but functional bathing and laundry tubs made from canvas.

Francesca Wilson, having recommended Dorothy to the UNRRA, later joined the organisation herself and became chief welfare officer for the British section. Based on her experience in Spain and elsewhere, she insisted that her staff should not limit their efforts to short-term emergency relief, but also work towards the refugees' long-term rehabilitation by providing workshops where they could practise productive skills and, not least, through educational and cultural projects. Here again, the Slavic communities which had reformed at El Shatt had anticipated these ideas and established a number of workshops to provide badly needed equipment, and to train their young people for peacetime employment.

John Corsellis toured the workshops soon after Dorothy's arrival, finding that, "The work that is being done there is extremely impressive and increased my admiration for the Yugoslavs: some eight months ago these refugees arrived with virtually nothing except the clothes they were in . . . They now have flourishing carpentry, shoemaking, tin-smiths', tailors', blacksmiths' and painters' shops." The carpenters, with the help of the blacksmith, first had to provide most of their own tools, but Corsellis found them turning out "an incredible variety of things including marionettes, blackboards, easels and guitars." The greatest benefit gained from the workshops, he believed, came not from the articles they produced, "but in the fact that a large number of youths who would otherwise be kicking their heels in idleness are getting excellent training in useful jobs: especially those working in the carpenters', tinsmiths' and blacksmiths' shops will be able to help in the enormous reconstruction job that awaits them in Yugoslavia, and disabled soldiers are being taught tailoring and shoemaking."[10] These achievements were made in a desolate landscape and in the face of great practical difficulties. "I must not give the impression that these people created a little paradise here on the desert with their resourcefulness," wrote Corsellis. "Their extreme lack of everything only makes what they do more impressive, standing as it does against such a background."[11]

The camp schools lacked any textbooks, and pupils were taught to read from old copies of the camp's own newsletter. More serious still was the lack of medical supplies. El Shatt's population was disproportionately weighted to the very young and very old, and both groups required a level of medical attention and supplies that the UNRRA teams were rarely able to provide. More than 800 residents of El Shatt died during the camps' short lifespan. In early 1945, its New Zealand nurse appeared likely to add to that number.

Although her normally robust health had enabled Dorothy to survive the rigours of a decade of trauma nursing and relief work with no serious illness, at El Shatt she contracted a high fever which her own colleagues were unable to diagnose or treat effectively. She was transferred to the British military hospital at Alexandria, whose staff also failed to control her fever. She had become too weak to be moved elsewhere and, she later told her family, was "put into a corner of the hospital to die".[12] As a very experienced nurse who had seen numbers of patients die under her care, she was quite convinced that her own death was imminent, and maintained that her life was saved only by an extraordinary coincidence. Doug Jolly, the New Zealand doctor whose skills as a front-line surgeon during the Spanish Civil War had earned him the reputation of "the most important volunteer to come from the British Commonwealth", had subsequently joined Britain's Royal Army Medical Corps, and was stationed in Tobruk.[13] He happened to arrive at the port of Alexandria on a hospital ship and discovered that she was a critically ill patient there. The two were not only compatriots but had both been born in the tiny mining town of Cromwell, an important bond. According to Dorothy, Jolly "scoured the hospital for me and found me in a small corner. And he brought with him the new life-saving penicillin."[14]

This powerful new antibiotic, still scarce and in great demand throughout the Allied zones, proved effective against the fever, and Dorothy recovered sufficiently to be invalided back to London in early May. VE (Victory in Europe) Day had just been declared and the streets were crammed with wildly exuberant celebrants, including large numbers of demobbed servicemen. In the midst of this chaotic rejoicing, the still-convalescent Dorothy made a phone call to Broadstairs, the rest and rehabilitation centre for New Zealand troops in London, in the faint hope of locating her brothers, Frank and Roger. By a second remarkable coincidence, both men were in the building when she rang, and the three were reunited for the first time in an exceptionally eventful decade.

In a flurry of anecdotes, the three Morrises filled each other in on the previous few years. Both brothers had been repeatedly transferred between a succession of POW camps, where they had each worked in slave labour gangs for local industries. By late 1944 the daily pastime for Roger, from his camp in north Germany, was "watching the Allied Air forces fly overhead to bomb Bremen, Hamburg, Hanover and Berlin, for we saw them either coming or going and it was a very heartening sight."[15] The following April a convoy of British Army tanks trundled towards the camp, and before the end of that month Roger was flown back to Britain.

Frank was initially held in camps to the southeast, where he worked in industries such as a paper factory and a sawmill. He escaped, and was transferred to Theresienstadt (Terezin), a notorious labour camp in what is now the Czech Republic, and was later returned to the POW camp Stalag VIIIB. After a further escape he was sheltered by members of the Czech Resistance.[16] US troops liberated the area, and Frank arrived in London several weeks after his brother. The men could not expect to return to New Zealand for at least two months so a springtime holiday was arranged. Through contacts with a British officer, Frank bought a 1934 Standard 12 car, unused throughout the war, for a hundred pounds.[17] Immediately afterwards Dorothy made her fortuitous phone call, and she was promptly added to the expedition. Displaying the opportunistic circumvention of regulations that flourishes in wartime, the three siblings sold the car to each other in turn to claim the maximum possible petrol ration. The result was enough fuel to travel across much of southwest England and Wales, from Gloucester to Cornwall. This happy excursion ended in Brighton when a gasket blew out, and the trio took the train back to London. Frank returned to collect the car, had it repaired and sold it for a small profit, just before he and his brother were ordered to board a troopship for the journey home to New Zealand.[18] "We got into Lyttelton – everything was lit up and the band was playing. My family was there to meet me, and that was that."[19]

The Morris family was notably diminished since Geoff, Dorothy's father, had died during the war.[20] Her two brothers adjusted easily to civilian life in New Zealand but Dorothy, although her health was still delicate, chose to remain working in the continent where she had already spent much of her adult life. Her deep love for the landscape and culture of southern Europe was presumably a factor in this decision, but the over-riding reason was her exceptional dedication to duty. Dorothy's war, unlike her brothers', was not yet over. The work of UNRRA was rapidly expanding into Europe, and her training and experience were needed even more urgently than in El Shatt.

The release, together with many thousands of other prisoners of war, of Frank and Roger Morris was a clear indication that large areas of Europe were falling under Allied military control. UNRRA had no brief to care for POWs, but the newly liberated areas also proved to hold vast numbers of slave labourers and concentration camp inmates who had no military affiliation. Most of them were in poor health, and many not much more than walking cadavers. Without formal provision for their support, they were reduced to scavenging for food in the surrounding countryside. They were also vulnerable to epidemics of typhus and other highly infectious diseases. In an agreement signed in late 1944, UNRRA was authorised to rapidly expand its operations in Europe to relieve demands on military personnel.[21] Hundreds of new teams of fieldworkers were to be formed, each made up of specialists so that they could act independently within a displaced persons' (DP) centre. Although twelve-person teams were initially specified, it proved impossible to recruit and train enough people, especially in the area of health services, to make up this number and more versatile eight-member teams were formed to expedite operations in the camps.[22]

Two months after her brothers left London, Dorothy Morris was reappointed as a UNRRA nursing officer, this time as a member of a team working in northwest Germany, the sector allocated to the British, the rest of the country having been divided up between France, the US and Russia. The British sector contained more than five million displaced Hungarians, Rumanians, Poles, Yugoslavs and various other nationalities in about 100 camps whose populations changed continuously as the refugees were repatriated and replaced by others, often from different ethnic or language groups.

Before venturing into the field, UNRRA staff were given a crash training course at a bleak centre on the Normandy coast of France. The course was progressively reduced in length from eight to two weeks, as the pressure to deploy field workers became ever more intense, and the value of their training proved less important than real-world experience. At the Granville centre, instructors with little or no practical experience of UNRRA work themselves lectured seasoned veterans such as Dorothy, aiming to prepare them for the welter of cultures, geopolitical backgrounds and historical rivalries represented among the refugee population. Trainees were encouraged to build a system of self-government within the different national groups. They also learned about the UNRRA's mandate and structure, and were cautioned to act ethically and impartially while representing the organisation. The most practical component of the course warned against overcrowding, and advised on maintaining the standard of sanitation and water supplies. Every adult refugee was to be provided with at least 2000 calories daily, although most of this food, along with medications and other supplies, would have to be obtained from German stocks in the region of each camp and provisions might therefore be unpredictable. The UNRRA trainees themselves had often endured years of strict rationing, and any discussion of food supplies was of deep interest to them. The highlight of the course for many was the catering. US army rations included delights such as butter and real fruit jam which most had not tasted for years.[23]

The freshly trained field officer then faced an anxious period of waiting to learn the region and role to which they had been assigned. The UNRRA's exponential growth rate, problems of communicating across numerous countries and between civil and military hierarchies, and the sheer scale of the task ahead had resulted in a bureaucratic logjam that a fiercely pragmatic New Zealander must have found exasperating. However, a hero appeared in the form of a young Australian ex-army officer named Robert Jackson, who took over the 'chaotic and dysfunctional' organisation's administration, wrested control from the military, and revitalised the staff.[24]

Shortly before Dorothy was sent to Germany, the UNRRA was placed in unchallenged command of all the country's displaced persons' camps, and some of their directors banned troops of any nation from entering them except by permission. This increased autonomy sped up the work of obtaining supplies and planning for repatriation, although military personnel and equipment were still needed to provide transport and security.

The German camps were different in most respects from the huge, hot and orderly tent city of El Shatt. The best of them had been converted from well-established facilities only recently vacated by defeated German troops, and they included impressive stone buildings which could house hospitals and clinics, while the more able-bodied were accommodated in large barracks and dormitories. Other camps fell well short of this standard, at least when they first opened. The Quaker ambulance driver John Corsellis was transferred from El Shatt to the German town of Klagenfurt, which was ringed by makeshift camps housing 6,000 Slovenes. In June 1945 he reported that, "Most refugees live in the open – using for shelter what material they find – tents made from sacking, gas capes, overcoat and blankets, some have shacks made of wood and bark and some live in their carts with material stretched over the top."[25] By the following month, however, they had all been relocated to smaller camps where they were housed in huts, and could start developing the schools, workshops, concerts and other activities broadly termed 'cultural work' which had been found so essential to the process of rehabilitation.

Even for a practised polyglot like Dorothy, working with large numbers of refugees from across Europe posed severe language problems. UNRRA policy emphasised the development of a preliminary form of national sovereignty through the organisation of the camps themselves. Refugees with a common language or cultural origin were ideally grouped together following registration, and then elected or appointed their national representatives, with whom the relief workers would liaise over their needs, allocations and necessary tasks.[26] In practice, this goal was often difficult to implement, and capable interpreters were in constant demand. However, many of the camp occupants spoke more than one language, and the cosmopolitan make-up of the UNRRA staff themselves – Australian head nurse Muriel Doherty supervised nurses of ten different nationalities at one time – meant that some common language could usually be found among them.[27]

Incoming refugees tended to arrive at the nearest railway station after a long journey in over-crowded cattle cars, in batches of from 500 to several thousand. Careless or unlucky passengers might have been left behind during hasty toilet stops, and their numbers were made up by new babies born en route. It was common for a train to reach its destination some days after its passengers had exhausted their supplies of food or diapers for babies. Refugees would therefore disembark from the trains with haggard faces, the old ladies wrapped in shawls and cradling infants, the women guarding their few possessions. A UNRRA nurse's first encounter with a new intake typically included 'dusting' the entire group with DDT as a preventative against the louse-borne disease typhus. This meant blowing the powerful insecticide in powdered form under clothing using a simple hand bellows. It was an uncomfortable and, for many arrivals, an undignified procedure, but those who had experienced the ravages of typhus were happy to submit to it. Later, mass immunisations using military pharmaceutical supplies were carried out against diphtheria and typhoid, together with screenings for other infectious diseases such as VD.

Almost all prior training and public health experience seemed irrelevant when confronting the worst cases of starvation and untreated disease among concentration camp survivors. Some were no more than living skeletons covered in skin diseases and barely able to speak. Dorothy was fortunate not to be included in the group of British Zone nurses sent to the Bergen-Belsen death camp after it was liberated in April 1945. They found more than 40,000 people "in the most awful state of emaciation and neglect and suffering from practically every known disease . . . dying in thousands daily".[28] Many were so traumatised that any proposed treatment, such as a bath, haircut or injection, filled them with terror. Within a week, however, the daily death rate was halved, then halved again. The typhus-ridden huts where inmates had lived were vacated and burnt one after another, and patients were nursed in the spacious and luxurious buildings built for the camp's guards and officials. Eventually, as quarantine was lifted and the standard of equipment and treatment steadily increased, this former death camp, renamed Hohne to escape the associations of its original name, became the medical centre for the entire British Zone.

In the camps where Dorothy was based, conditions were far less extreme but still posed challenges rarely faced in more routine nursing assignments. The nursing teams' duties included supervising the sanitation of camp buildings and grounds, organising immunisation clinics, overseeing the care given to refugee patients in civilian hospitals, and giving basic instruction to trainee nurses and nurse aides from among the displaced-person communities.[29] UNRRA nurses were expected to raise the overall health of a camp population that may have faced years of overwork and semi-starvation, but they were provided with so little medical equipment that "heroic scrounging" in the surrounding countryside was needed to obtain thermometers, bedpans, syringes and penicillin, generally paid for not with cash but with highly prized trade goods such as silk stockings, cigarettes or coffee.[30]

The urgency of the work, and the hastily drawn-up protocols provided to the nurses, gave rise to internal disagreements over the most appropriate ways to deal with people whose cultural backgrounds were unfamiliar and whose recent experiences sometimes too painful to imagine. British-trained nurses disapproved of newborn babies sleeping with their mothers, but their mothers refused to be parted from them and would avoid giving birth in hospital for fear of this happening.[31] When a young Ukrainian woman picked up her crying baby and placed the child on her breast, she was reprimanded by an over-conscientious nurse who believed in imposing strict hours for infant feeding. A compromise was reached that avoided the rigid, and later discredited, by-the-clock breast-feeding advocated by the New Zealand paediatrician Truby King.[32]

A Canadian nurse working in a camp near Stuttgart in August 1945 found that "Nearly every night someone gets shot and of course they never can find the weapon or who did it."[33] The victim was very often a former collaborator with the German forces, who had been marked for revenge. Some camps even included outright war criminals who had worked in the Nazi death camps. Resourceful drinkers made illicit stills to produce crude alcohol, and cases of alcohol poisoning were common. Many medical conditions were either caused or compounded by the long period of hardship and terror the camp residents had endured. Suicides were not uncommon, and mealtimes were problematic because food was constantly spirited away to be cached under pillows or in other hiding places by people long accustomed to struggling against their own companions for survival. A child who was told he would be admitted to the camp hospital begged his nurses, "Please shoot me, don't put me in the gas chamber."[34] Other children had become mentally retarded after years of persecution and undernourishment, and required specialist nursing which was seldom available. Even the most able adults might suddenly display symptoms of a psychological condition named 'liberation complex', such as violent attacks on local Germans or anything belonging to or representing them.[35] This could be highly disruptive for health care in the camps since, to make up for the shortage of trained nurses, German nurses who had worked under the Nazi regime were employed in UNRRA hospitals.[36]

In a pamphlet titled *Advice to Relief Workers*, Dorothy's close friend and mentor Francesca Wilson, who became chief welfare officer to the British Zone, cautioned her colleagues against expecting a display of gratitude from the people they worked among. "Refugees are often accused of not being grateful. Why should they be? Their misfortune is none of their seeking."[37] Women, she said, were particularly effective at many areas of relief work and should be permitted to play a greater part in the task of refugee relief, especially as capable personnel were usually in short supply and teams were often found to include utterly unsuitable members. "It is difficult to choose the right people for relief work abroad," she acknowledged. "Upheavals attract the unbalanced as well as those with constructive powers," and since UNRRA paid US-scale salaries that were higher than other countries offered, its teams attracted the self-interested and unscrupulous. Some French nurses were discovered to be benefitting from their proximity to army bases by moonlighting as prostitutes.[38]

"All experts must be prepared to make compromises," thought Wilson, "and also to do the job on hand even if it is 'beneath them' or outside their sphere of special knowledge." [39] She identified New Zealand and Australian relief workers as particularly ready to demonstrate an all-purpose practicality and disregard for professional status, and Australasians were among the most productive and well-regarded UNRRA staff in this period.

An Australian nurse, Muriel Doherty, headed the team charged with saving the lives of the survivors of Belsen. The renowned New Zealand plastic surgeon Harold Gillies created special centres in Yugoslavia to treat the disfiguring injuries inflicted on its people during the war. The director of the entire British zone was the unassuming Australian lawyer and doctor Raphael Cilento, a vigorous innovator with world-leading expertise in epidemic control. Cilento had little patience with the tortuous UNRRA bureaucracy and he cheerfully commandeered military and civilian resources, and engaged nurses without formal authorisation, as he set up his headquarters in the small village of Senge, near Düsseldorf.[40] His head nurse, a Canadian named Lyle Creelman, then attempted to contact all of the UNRRA nurses within her zone. She was "occupied in visiting them in their camps, interviewing their team Directors and Medical Officers, trying to help solve some of the problems that confronted them." Her successor as chief nurse believed that through these efforts, the morale of all nurses in the zone "was considerably raised".[41]

By this time the worst medical conditions in the camps had begun to subside and attention turned towards activities that would make the refugees more self-reliant and optimistic, and therefore more willing and able to return to their own countries. As Dorothy had learned earlier in both Spain and southern France, cultural, recreational and vocational projects were an essential adjunct to health care in restoring the spirits of entire communities of displaced people, and some leading figures in the world of relief work, such as Francesca Wilson, rated these projects the most important element.

The bewildering variety of ethnic, religious, linguistic and national groups represented among several million displaced persons in the British Zone proved both an advantage and a minefield of difficulties for UNRRA welfare workers. The burning desire to use their native languages, perform their national dances, and educate their children in their traditions was a huge incentive to set up newspapers, theatre groups, bands and orchestras. The periodical *Laiks Latviesu Zurnals* (*News for Latvian DPs*), edited and produced in camps where Dorothy was based, was circulated among all displaced persons who shared the Latvian language, and its content was subject to less official vetting than when those camps had been under military control.[42] The Baltic camps were regarded as models of self-management, where the occupants grew quantities of flowers and vegetables, the women produced beautiful textiles, and choirs performed the folksongs and patriotic tunes of their region to a standard that astonished UNRRA visitors.[43] Schools and other teaching and training centres offered the possibility not only of improving camp life in the present, but of training leaders, intellectuals and artisans for the postwar future.[44] The camps proved to be full of trained teachers and specialists in certain subjects, and they held regular classes at every level from pre-school nurseries to tertiary institutions, such as the much-admired Baltic University formed in a bombed-out museum in Hamburg.

These impressive and mostly self-generated rehabilitation efforts took place against the backdrop of routine camp life – meetings of block and section committees and the need to arbitrate disputes between them, the growing and increasingly sophisticated output of the carpenters', blacksmiths' and cobblers' workshops, and endless searches for food, medicines and other necessities. By late 1945 this final task became more pressing as staff raced to prepare for the oncoming winter – installing stoves, obtaining warm and weatherproof clothing, stockpiling food and firewood – a process given the all-purpose term 'winterisation'.

From October 1945 the UNRRA also came under pressure to speed up repatriation of the displaced people under their care. This development was partly attributable to the progress made within the camps, where health standards, resourcefulness and confidence in the future had all been measurably advanced. Nurses could look forward to seeing large numbers of camp occupants returning to their homelands in the following spring, and in preparation for this goal they launched ambitious maternal and child health programmes and systematic nursing education.

Raphael Cilento's Christmas speech to his staff at the former Belsen concentration camp rang with encouragement and congratulation, but also sounded a note of warning at the uncertainties and obstacles ahead. "We have before us immediately the Winter and its difficulties, Spring with its new movements, especially the great mass movement of all that huge concourse of unhappy people that was turned loose from its homes as a by-product of Hitler's Europe . . . There are 470,000 people left [in the British Zone] and, with the Spring, it will be determined who can be repatriated, who can and will go home and those who cannot go . . . Somehow, somewhere, however, these people must be provided for, because they sit upon the conscience of the world."[45]

The repatriation programme began in a spirit of rejoicing, expectancy and resurgent patriotism. Instead of the crammed and unheated cattle wagons, lined with straw at best, that had brought many refugees into the DP camps, they were often able to depart from the camps for their own countries in specially equipped carriages, each with its own stove and supply of firewood, food, blankets and candles. Hospital carriages were provided for expectant mothers and other vulnerable passengers. The repatriating passengers were accompanied by a 'flight team' of a UNRRA nurse and two nurse aides, often nationals of their own countries.[46] The camps, and their nearest railway stations, took on an air of gaiety and pride whenever a full trainload departed. Hand-stitched national flags, patriotic banners and leafy tree branches and wildflowers adorned the sides of each loaded wagon. Chalk and paint was hoarded in advance so that carriages could be further decorated with images of national heroes and historic scenes, and the names of the towns and villages the passengers were destined for. Friends and relatives pressed *bon voyage* presents on them. Lined up on the platform, the camp band played sprightly tunes and, as the train pulled out, the refugees' national anthem, with all present joining in singing it. Such occasions must have reminded Dorothy of the departure of the emigrant ship *Sinaia* for Mexico seven years before, except that the repatriation trains continued to steam away for week after week, and their passengers were not departing from their homelands, but returning to them.

Behind these uplifting scenes, a more disturbing picture of the repatriation programme was forming, both within camp administrations and in the upper echelons of the UNRRA hierarchy. The organ-isation's finances were in chronic deficit as demands for its services consistently outstripped each new budget. At ground level, the best efforts of field workers and camp committees could not prevent rampant looting and black-market trafficking of supplies, which compounded financial problems, dampened morale and stained the UNRRA's reputation with other international bodies. The many years of bitter deprivation and ruthless efforts at self-preservation suffered by the camp inmates made it inevitable that the sudden appearance of seemingly endless quantities of equipment, medicines and foodstuffs proved irresistibly tempting to the dishonest. Even so, the scale of the misappropriations was mindboggling. Entire convoys of new vehicles would disappear between their port of arrival and intended destination.[47]

The swift evaporation of the strategic wartime entente between the Soviet Union and western Allies gave a political dimension to the looters' actions, and deepened divisions between the UNRRA's member nations. Since the organisation was founded the US had been its largest funder, and allegations that its donated tractors, industrial machinery and X-ray equipment were being sidetracked to countries within the new Soviet bloc enflamed Cold War atti-tudes and threatened the reputation and viability of the idealistic aid agency. These views were reinforced by the realisation that many thousands of displaced persons were being repatriated to their for-mer homes in what had since become Soviet territory. Russian authorities were adamant that all citizens of East European coun-tries should be returned there, against their will if necessary. This prospect was anathema to many of the displaced persons, including Jews who found anti-Semitism thriving under Soviet authority. There were no easy solutions to these difficulties. The UNRRA was under heavy pressure to empty all its camps during 1946 to cut expenses, yet a hard core of displaced persons flatly refused to leave.[48] In this period, nursing staff even had to cope with outbreaks of panic among their patients sparked by rumours of renewed Nazi activity.

The repatriation programme slowed and sometimes stalled alto-gether, as numbers of repatriated people reappeared in camps they had left, relating stories of repression and appalling living conditions in their homelands. When forced repatriation was attempted, some displaced persons committed suicide rather than return home against their will. Refugees whose term in the camps was intended to be as short as possible now looked likely to remain there for years, imposing an unforeseen financial burden on the UNRRA which its sponsor governments refused to accept.

These anxieties were highly distressing to the camp populations, especially the ill and infirm, and therefore added greatly to the workload of nursing staff in the British Zone. Yet the staff carried on with their duties, and even expanded their efforts to train displaced persons to work as nurses with their own people. The British Zone HQ at Hohne was the first of the four occupied zones to launch a nursing training programme, and its chief nurse considered this "one of the most worthwhile of all the nursing activities" carried out under UNRRA's brief.[49] The training included lectures on the psychology of displaced persons and the nurse's place in the medical team, as well as practical classes on child welfare and midwifery, and on the principles of public health.[50] Since no suitable nursing manuals were available, the training staff compiled their own in their spare time.[51] However the facilities and equipment in the complex of hospitals and clinics at the former death camp had grown so that they provided a near-ideal teaching environment. Head nurse Muriel Doherty believed that, "The kitchens with their vast and modern equipment would make many a Hospital matron envious".[52]

Although Dorothy Morris was apparently the first New Zealand fieldworker for the UNRRA, by late 1945 she had been joined by others such as the nurse Alice Reid, who was assigned specifically to the nurse training programme.[53] These developments made Dorothy's own role less crucial, and in early 1946 she prepared to resign from her UNRRA contract. The deciding factor was the prospect of being sent to work with the large numbers of children who had been newly released from concentration camps. The likely physical strain, health risks, and in particular the emotional demands of this work were, she told her employers, more than she was willing to face.[54] The nightmarish conditions in the concentration camps were by then indisputable through events such as the war crimes trial of senior officials at the Bergen-Belsen camp, held in September 1945 in the town of Luneberg, near Hamburg, and attended by members of the British zone's nursing staff.[55] In March 1946 Dorothy's resignation was accepted, with her personnel record stating that she had served "very satisfactorily" as a nursing officer.[56]

For perhaps the first time in her career, Dorothy had terminated her employment of her own volition, and not because of external circumstances or in order to take up a position elsewhere. Her decision was an acknowledgement of the exceptional demands made on UNRRA staff who worked directly with displaced persons. "I have never before encountered a life that requires such intestinal fortitude as this one," wrote Kay Hulme, deputy director of Wildflecken DP camp, and a former shipyard welder. "It takes a lusty, enduring nature to withstand this life".[57] Dorothy possessed such a nature, but after a decade of ministration in communities blighted by either current, recent or imminent warfare, she appeared to have reached the limit of her personal resources. The experience she had acquired in that decade, especially at working with deeply traumatised children, at merging both traditional nursing and welfare activities, and at implementing plans and expending funds on behalf of a range of agencies, had proved an ideal testing ground for working with the almost overwhelming numbers of people, and depths of human distress, found in the displaced persons' camps.

She left an organisation which had been founded with the highest ideals and a blazingly ambitious remit. The UNRRA has been described as "not simply an instrument for repairing the horrors of war but as the first of the United Nations agencies taking international action to tackle the problems of the world."[58] It is hardly surprising, given its position at the centre of a clash of global ideologies, that it failed to fulfil many of those expectations. The year after Dorothy's departure, with millions of refugees still refusing to return to countries that they felt had been transformed out of recognition since the war, the UNRRA was declared insolvent and its tasks were delegated to a successor agency which excluded the Soviet Union from membership.

In the 18 months in which she worked for the UNRRA, Dorothy contributed to a remarkable attempt to ameliorate some of the most destructive and intractable consequences of World War II. In the years since, few better solutions have emerged to lasting problems such as the effective distribution of humanitarian aid, the levels of immigration that societies can safely absorb, and the durable transition of power from an occupying force to a defeated enemy.

Chapter 7
'Brazen and Tyrannical'

Twelve highly eventful years had passed since an able, unconventional and adventurous nurse left New Zealand to find more challenging professional opportunities than her own country seemed likely to provide. In that time she had surely exceeded her most idealistic expectations for her nursing career, while also enduring bitter personal and political disappointment, physical hardship and severe illness. By the time she left Germany Dorothy's health had again collapsed, perhaps with a recurrence of the mysterious gastric infection that first struck her in Alexandria the year before. Appearing somewhat gaunt and exhausted, she returned to Lyttelton and her family to recuperate in late 1946.

The absence of the father she greatly admired, and in certain ways resembled, must have subdued the family reunion at Flackley Ash. Dorothy found that her mother Rebecca had also grown very deaf and withdrawn, and her sister Ruth was living in the family home and caring for her while working as one of New Zealand's first female air traffic controllers. As she recovered her strength and adjusted to her familiar yet permanently altered surroundings, Dorothy was able to contribute substantially to her mother's care, and also to come to terms with her own life and career, free of the dramatic outside forces and influences that had dominated it.

She re-established contact with old school friends who proudly presented their baby-boomer children, including a six-year-old named Jane who was Dorothy's god-daughter. Even at that early age, young Jane Hanna (later Taylor) was deeply struck by her tall and elegant godmother with her "well-groomed head of strong jet black hair".[1] During the summer of 1946-47, the little girl and her imposing 42-year-old companion would walk hand-in-hand down the hill from Flackley Ash to the bay where Dorothy would give her swimming lessons.

With no children of her own, Dorothy remained close to Jane and her sister Elisabeth Hanna (later Ogilvie) for the rest of her life. She sent them gifts regularly – a doll, nylon stockings before they were available in New Zealand, fashionable clothing. Although not instinctively affectionate or expressive, the older woman drew on her wide knowledge of ill and orphaned children to contribute thoughtfully towards their upbringing, particularly after both their parents died at a relatively early age. "I think she was mindful of returning good deeds and love," Jane believes. "There was a softer side that we were privileged to see. She understood the feelings and fears of children. I found her to be a magical, energetic, larger than life role model."[2]

Dorothy was determined to provide her young protégées with the cultural riches she had experienced during her years in Europe. When she learned that a touring company from Britain's Royal Ballet was giving a rare performance of *Swan Lake* in Christchurch, she made sure that Jane and her sister joined her in the audience. Neither of the girls had seen a production remotely like it, and the experience was unforgettable and formative.[3] As Jane grew older, Dorothy sent her books that had a similar impact. *The White Goddess*, Robert Graves' densely allegorical history of European goddess worship, was not common reading matter for a young New Zealander, but Jane treasured it.

Dorothy's own personality was as influential as her cultural prescriptions. "Her dark eyes were vital and flashed when she discussed matters that were close to her heart, usually political, like the Spanish Civil War, Royalists, Quakers . . . No statesman of the time escaped a strident comment from her. She had no need to persuade me of her views but only wished to nurture me."[4]

Within a year of returning home, Dorothy recovered her health and began to feel confined by the circumscribed social horizons that had led her to escape New Zealand in the previous decade. "She found New Zealand fairly insular," says Geoff Morris, one of her several nephews, and in 1947 she returned to England.[5] There she remained until old age, in an adopted homeland that her restless and cosmopolitan spirit could abide.

One of her first actions on returning to London was to make a covert and extremely risky trip to Franco-ruled Spain, in the hope of determining the fate of the doctor she had met and loved during the civil war years. As with many other recognized supporters of the Spanish Republic, the name of Dorothy Morris featured on a watch-list maintained by the new regime's large and active secret police force, which might arrest and detain her if she was identified on Spanish territory. Her old school friend Edna Jackson (Jane's mother) provided the funds to enable her to reach Perpignan. From there, posing as a tourist, Dorothy bicycled up the Tet Valley to the Spanish frontier at Bourg-Madame. Under conditions of great secrecy, she eventually made contact with former colleagues from the civil war who had managed to remain living in Spain after the Franco takeover. The information they could provide was scanty and inconclusive, and she was forced to return to London still uncertain of the fate of her mystery lover. She had left her address with her informants, and soon after returning home she received a final answer to the question she had carried with her for the previous eight years. While her lover was serving in the Republican Army's medical corps at the battle of the Ebro River, the ambulance in which he was travelling took a direct hit from Nationalist artillery. He did not survive.[6]

According to several of her friends, Dorothy's life could be sharply divided into the periods before and after she received this anguishing confirmation. "She had very definitely loved and lost," says Jane Taylor, and she remained steadfastly unmarried and unattached for the rest of her life.[7] She seems never to have revealed her lover's name to her friends and family, and later researchers have not succeeded in identifying him.[8]

As with many other foreign volunteers to Spain's civil war, Dorothy's commitment to the Spanish Republican cause had been so whole-hearted and life-changing that she found postwar life pallid and inconsequential by comparison. For some years she returned to casual, freelance nursing, and by the mid-1950s became matron of her own small, private institution, a nursing home and children's hospital in Enfield, the same north London suburb where she worked in arms factories during the war. She ran her hospital on the severe but efficient lines of the Karitane nursing homes developed in New Zealand at the beginning of the century, and preferred to employ visiting New Zealand nurses when possible.[9]

At this purpose-designed British version of the hospital she had headed in Murcia, Dorothy spent the final decade of her working life. She bought a spacious and comfortable house nearby and decorated it with mementoes she had acquired in Spain, and a few luxuries from her favourite West End stores – linen from Heals, cutlery from Mappin and Webb. She even became a member of a London club, possibly the Lyceum where she had originally met her one-time mentor, the journalist Evelyn Isitt.[10]

There is no evidence that Dorothy ever took part in postwar activities on behalf of the victims of the Spanish Civil War. Other British veterans and their supporters formed the International Brigades Association, which campaigned relentlessly for the release of prominent Brigaders from Franco's prisons. Dorothy is likely to have known several of those imprisoned, but she appears to have chosen to focus her concern on her new patients, and as far as possible to leave behind her civil war experience with its painfully disappointing outcome.

This somewhat eccentric and solitary figure remained a keen reader, and especially devoured studies of ancient and classical civilisations. As her hospital became established, she was able to consider visiting the places she read about, and foreign travel became a defining enthusiasm of her later years. Returning to Spain was out of the question during the deadening, censorious and seemingly interminable dictatorship of Franco, but other countries she had seen during the war years seemed increasingly attractive.

In May 1969, just two years after the Six-Day War between Israel and its Arab neighbours, Dorothy joined a guided tour to Jerusalem and other Holy Land sites, and in that intensely politically charged environment, she apparently made little attempt to temper her strong will and outspoken views.

> The tour was guided by a stentorian Jew called Meir, a *sabra* (i.e. Israeli born) but of German extraction, a type I particularly dislike ever since I encountered them in Spain in the International Brigades. They tried to be bullies, both in the German and Jewish way, and particularly as regards their attitude to women, whom they expect to bow down to them as their mothers, wives, sisters do. Not me![11]

This hapless guide was a veteran of Haganah, the Israeli paramilitary movement which had fought British Mandate forces in 1946. According to Dorothy, his hard-won experience of his country's recent history was no match for her own background reading and fleeting first-hand knowledge of the Middle East.

> Poor old Meir was worn out long before I was. I tended to challenge pretty well all his more controversial statements . . . on the grounds that I knew the country under the Mandate – i.e. in '45 when I came up from Egypt . . . When I mentioned that I was originally from New Zealand, I found that I was partially forgiven for my apparent 'Britishness' – Aussies and NZers apparently made a good impression on the Palestine Jews, partly because they used to visit the Kibbutzes and help knowledgeably with the farm work, harvesting etc. . . . The rest of the busload of mixed nationalities were completely mystified by the constant exchange of differences of opinion between Guide Meir and me.[12]

As on several later overseas excursions, Dorothy was dismayed at the changes to the landscape and the society that she had known many years before.

> I couldn't help remembering, and regretting, the quiet pastoral peace of the Holy Land, the Palestine I – and Frank and Roger – knew 24 years ago . . . I had visited Nazareth in '45 – a simple, quiet country town living mostly on its 'holy' tourist trade then. It has greatly changed – is noisy and dirty and the Arabs are very unhappy at all the change . . . as I considered all that I had seen, I simply sympathised more with the Arabs, and found the Jews just too intolerably brazen and tyrannical. Granted that the Arabs are tiresome, one can't see them just 'giving in' to the Jews.[13]

This irascible and opiniated tourist returned to the Middle East some years later for a winter cruise along the Nile, telling her god-daughter beforehand "after the revoltingly soggy summer we have endured, the thought of the sun on my back at Luxor and Assouan is something I can scarcely wait for".[14] This holiday appears to have provided less opportunity for Dorothy to exercise her talent for controversy.

By then she had retired from the hospital and moved to a smaller house in Chorleywood, in London's northwest outskirts. In those leafy surroundings she was able to indulge another enthusiasm. Despite her property's unpromising "thin and chalky" soil, she created a flourishing garden. Every spring, chestnuts, lilac, laburnum, azaleas and tulips surged into blossom, and she proudly reported that, "I set up a most successful vegetable garden, reaping an astonishingly good crop of beans, potatoes, marrows etc. There was once a cattle pasture here so I had the benefit of that perhaps."[15]

London's bleak climate ensured that occasions for spending time in this garden were strictly limited, and the weather was a perennial subject of complaint in Dorothy's letters to New Zealand. By the winter of 1977 she was at last able to realise her long-deferred dream of returning to the coastal villages of southern Spain that she had come to love during the civil war. Franco's death two years earlier, and his country's tentative return to democracy, permitted her to follow the example of the tens of thousands of Britons who were already accustomed to holidaying on the Costa del Sol. In Dorothy's case, it was a holiday steeped in nostalgia and dogged by the ghosts of people she had known 40 years before.

"Things seem to be improving [in Spain], with the first free elections promised," she told her family, somewhat defensively, as she prepared to depart.[16] Over the next several months she visited the southern cities of Andalucia – Córdoba, Granada, Seville, Ronda and Málaga, and relished the enormous changes she observed.

> What with the huge influx of tourists in search of sun n' sea and the special Spanish *ambient* – and American dollars for bases etc. – the whole country seems a busy beehive . . . In his last days, Franco had to yield so much of what the Republicans had fought for, and which the huge majority sullenly demanded over the years, that I was amazed at the comparative rise in well-being – and social welfare measures once scarcely hoped for. Even the Church seems tamed! Old Franco, before his departure, was heard to exclaim that never would he have thought he'd have to set up a special prison for refractory priests – mostly young – who had set themselves up against his sacred Fascist State! Remembering them in my day, I must say I was equally amazed.[17]

Much of this uplifting holiday was spent in a rented apartment on the Costa Blanca, the part of Spain that I knew many years ago when I was running a small children's hospital in Murcia, further south. In those days it was wild, strange and deserted – and lovely. Now I find it pullulating with thousands of every kind of villa.[18]

These holiday homes had been built, she reported,

in the boom of the last decade by thousands of Dutch, Germans and assorted Scandinavians for their retirement, mostly . . . also a few scattered English, but gone are their great days . . . That part of the Coast does not please me as when, 40 years ago, it was wild and deserted. Spain has its troubles – regional restlessness, inflation and plenty of social problems – and a very materialistic middleclass mad on money. The excessive new building has slowed down somewhat, but there does seem an endless supply of foreign money to invest.

The Mediterranean weather lived up to all expectations. "A fabulously sunny Spring. Never have I seen more splendid wildflowers." Dorothy was also treated to "a splendid spring show of almonds in thousands flowering all over the bare hills and in valleys with the citrus crop ripening among them". Her apartment was not far inland from the "overbuilt resort of Benidorm" which she found had experienced a sorry decline since she last saw its "two wild and splendid beaches". She avoided the crammed coastline altogether and instead spent her time in the hills "sunbathing and ozone-sniffing – very health-making"[19]

This poignant and satisfying journey was made when Dorothy was aged over 70 and growing increasingly deaf, a condition which can only have exacerbated her fiery temper. Three years later, in 1980, she returned permanently to New Zealand to be cared for by her family, and especially her much younger sister Ruth. Although increasingly frail, she remained determinedly independent and continued living alone in a flat in the well-to-do Christchurch suburb of Merivale. Speaking in the crisp accents of an educated Englishwoman accustomed to being obeyed, she entertained old acquaintances and a succession of much younger relatives who had only a faint understanding of the life their formidable aunt had led, but were left in no doubt about her exceptional personal qualities.

"The family were proud of her, but a bit in awe of her," thought her cousin Mary.[20]

One nephew, Roger Morris, remembers her as

> a fantastic woman. Tall. Fierce. She went to Spain on her own volition, which says much for her intuition and recognition of the forces at work in that country . . . She was stern, foreboding to me, but very forthcoming to my partner Marianne Muggeridge whom she admired and toward whom she extended a real goodwill. My great failing was in not knowing enough of the Spanish War and the importance of it before her death. We were her brothers' sons, all boys, and I had the distinct impression we were not quite 'up to it'. After her experiences on the front lines of anti-fascism, the men and women she had known alive and dead, I can see why . . . A truly remarkable woman. I am very proud of her.[21]

After half a lifetime of issuing instructions to others, this arch and outspoken woman could greatly embarrass her companions in public, especially once she became very deaf. One evening Jane Taylor returned the favour Dorothy had done her as a child by taking the old lady to a performance of the ballet.

> In an extremely quiet moment at the end of one of the acts she announced in a very loud, well-modulated English voice that the lead male dancer was every bit as good as Nureyev but the leading lady was not a patch on Fonteyn. And that she was the only person in the theatre who would know that the Basque dancing was original and authentic. My daughter and I longed to slip under the seats out of sight.[22]

Several years after her return home, Christchurch's daily paper published an admiring half-page feature written by Jane's sister Elisabeth Ogilvie, whose mother had been a friend of Dorothy's from school days. This article traced the entire course of the expatriate's life, from her childhood in Lyttelton to her nursing studies in the city's main hospital, to war in Spain, to refugee camps in France and munitions factories in London, and to her work with Second World War refugees in Egypt and Germany. Accompanying photographs of a Republican hospital train and of the shocked faces of Málagan women after a bombing raid left readers in no doubt about the pivotal episode in this remarkable career. "The commitment and the intensity of the years in Spain remain brightest in her memory," wrote Ogilvie. "She is one of many who, in every decade, work unstintingly for the innocent people caught in the crossfire and chaos of war."[23]

That article appears to be the longest single account of Dorothy's extraordinary career to be published in her lifetime. She was several times urged to record her own life story, especially by her sister, but persistently refused on the grounds that the events she had participated in and the individuals she had known were all "past history."[24] This book appears almost 20 years after her death, and therefore could not draw on the memories of surviving acquaintances who knew her as an active woman.

As she grew steadily more frail, the legacy of a lifetime spent issuing orders to teams of medical staff, combined with a naturally domineering personality, produced traits that strained the patience of her family and caregivers. A niece, Anne Morris, recalls that the imperious old lady was quite capable of ringing the local ambulance crew and instructing them to come and make her a cup of tea.[25]

In Dorothy's final years her god-daughter, Jane Taylor, grew closer to her than ever.

We had a strong rapport. In the few months before she died I would sit with her and she would sleep a bit, wake up a bit, and tell me she was going back over her life. Pieces would emerge. I was very privileged to be the one with her when she died. I arrived from Ashburton to relieve the night nurse. I sat with her, holding her hand, which was a bit uncharacteristic because she was definitely not a huggy, kissing, holding-hands person.[26]

On the evening of 23 January 1998, having seen almost the full span of the 20th century and participated in some of its most decisive moments, Dorothy Morris's fiercely independent spirit at last gave in to the demands of her great age.

Since the death of this dauntless and assured New Zealander, the events she witnessed, the medical techniques she practised and the ethical questions she confronted have not receded into historical oblivion, as she sometimes claimed to wish. Instead, the Spanish Civil War and the political and military circumstances surrounding it have assumed increased significance for a later generation. In the cynical and self-interested present day, the civil war, and especially the actions of the foreign volunteers who arrived to reinforce the Republican defence, have come to represent an affirmation of idealism and internationalism that remains profoundly inspirational and politically germane.

Dorothy's achievements as nurse and relief worker in Spain and elsewhere, especially among children and refugees, are categorically impressive and worthy of record. In addition to saving lives and mitigating suffering, often at the cost of her own health, she contributed to far-reaching medical and social advances. The career which compiled this distinguished professional legacy was guided by an ardently progressive standpoint on issues of social justice.

As Dorothy's letters make exuberantly clear, her dedication to a personal sense of duty cohabited easily with an appreciation of beauty and refinement. Even when facing the bullets of war and repression, she retained her sense of delight in the petals of wildflowers and spring blossoms that signified those qualities in humanity she cherished and upheld.

Notes

Introduction: A Life Devoted to Nursing

1 Shepherd, Ben *The Long Road Home – The aftermath of the Second World War*, London: The Bodley Head, 2010, p. 6.

2 Derby, Mark *Kiwi Compañeros – New Zealand and the Spanish Civil War*, Christchurch: Canterbury University Press 2009. Spanish translation by Cristina Gomez de la Torre Curt published as *Compañeros "Kiwis" – Nueva Zealanda y la Guerra Civil Española,* Colleción La Luz de la Memoria no. 9, Cuenca: Ediciones de la Universidad de Castilla La Mancha 2011.

3 DM letter, Alexander Turnbull Library (hereafter ATL), 2 December 1938.

4 DM letter, ATL, 26 December 1940.

5 DM letter, ATL, 2 December 1938.

6 DM letter, ATL, 2 September 1938.

7 Ruth Morris, personal communication with Michael O'Shaughnessy, 27 February 1998.

8 Geoffrey Cox, *Defence of Madrid* 1937; 2006.

9 DM letter, 20 August 1939.

10 DM letter, 22 April 1941.

1 The Morris Family Yacht

1 Welch, *The Lucifer*, p. 97.

2 *Sun*, 7 May 1932, p. 7.

3 E. Ogilvie, eulogy for funeral of Dorothy Morris; Ogilvie family collection.

4 Frank Morris, oral history interview, Tape 1, Side 1 (hereafter T1, S1).

5 Elizabeth Ogilvie, *Press*, 17 Dec. 1983, p. 21.

6 Chris Morris, personal communication, 26 July 2014.

7 Chris Morris, personal communication, 11 April 2014.

8 Scotter, *A History of Port Lyttelton*, p. 250.

9 *Press*, Christchurch, 3 May 1919, p. 3.

10 Frank Morris, oral history interview, T1, S2.

11 *Ibid.*, T1, S1.

12 Quoted in Jane Taylor, 'A significant older person', unpublished ms., Taylor collection, 2013.
13 Scotter, *A History of Port Lyttelton*, p. 179.
14 Parsons, 'The Christchurch community at war 1914–1918', p. 141.
15 Belcher, *A History of Rangi-Ruru School*, p. 37.
16 *Press*, 11 December 1920, p. 3.
17 *Christchurch Hospital Nursing School*, p. 20.
18 *Ibid.*, p. 12.
19 Christchurch Hospital records, Archives New Zealand.
20 *Christchurch Hospital Nursing School*, p. 12.
21 Wilson, *In the Margins of Chaos*, p. 217.
22 Rodgers 'Nursing education in New Zealand, 1883 to 1930', p. 56.
23 I. Dodds interview, T1, S1.
24 Wilson, *In the Margins of Chaos*, p. 217.
25 Wood, 'Nursing the patient, the room and the doctor', pp. 140–144.
26 Dunstan, 'The collective voice – where to now?', p. 130.
27 *Ibid.*, p. 142.
28 *Canterbury Times*, 22 August 1930, p. 12.
29 Dorothy Morris nursing file, Archives NZ.
30 Geoffrey Rice, personal communication, 9 March 2014.
31 *Press,* 17 April 1931, p. 4.
32 *Lyttelton Times*, 22 May 1931, p. 6.
33 *Canterbury Times*, 6 May 1930, p. 1.
34 *Canterbury Times*, 1 November 1933; 5 December 1933.
35 *Ibid.*, 24 April 1933.
36 *Ibid.*, 29 October 1930.
37 Quoted in Dunstan, 'The collective voice . . . ', p. 148.
38 Elizabeth Ogilvie, *Press*, 17 December 1983, p. 21.
39 Personal communication, Mary Stapylton-Smith, 27 November 2014.
40 Dorothy Morris nursing file, Archives NZ.

2 Good Bombing Light

1 DM letter, ATL, 29 November 1935.
2 I. Dodds interview, T4, S7.
3 Burchill, *The Paths I've Trod*, p. 38.
4 DM letter, ATL, 29 November 1935.
5 Quoted in Wilson, *In the Margins*, p. 217.
6 DM letter, ATL, 29 November 1935.
7 *Ibid.*, Underlining in original.
8 DM letter, ATL, 12 October 1939.

9 Veatch, 'The League of Nations and the Spanish Civil War, 1936–9', p. 183.
10 Ogilvie, *Press*, 17 December 1983, p. 21.
11 Willis, 'Medical responses to civil war and revolution in Spain, 1936–1939", p. 160.
12 Burchill, *The Paths I've Trod*, p. 49.
13 Patricia Whyte to Michael O'Shaughnessy, 18 August 1998; O'Shaughnessy collection.
14 Quoted in Jackson, *British Women and the Spanish Civil War*, p. 183 fn.
15 Burchill, *The Paths I've Trod*, p. 51.
16 Quoted in Palfreeman, *Aristocrats, Adventurers and Ambulances*, p. 130.
17 I. Ehrenburg, quoted in *ibid.*, p. 125.
18 G. Young, quoted in *ibid.*, p. 126.
19 Quoted in Preston, *The Spanish Holocaust*, p. 149.
20 Fyrth, *The Signal Was Spain*, p. 159.
21 Palfreeman, *Aristocrats*, p. 167.
22 Quoted in *ibid.*, p. 133.
23 *Press*, Christchurch, 17 December 1983, p. 21.
24 *Ibid.*, 7 May 1937, p. 14.
25 Quoted in Lethbridge, *Norman Bethune in Spain*, p. 135.
26 *Press*, Christchurch, 7 May 1937, p. 14.
27 Quoted in Palfreeman, *Aristocrats, Adventurer*, p. 147.
28 *Press*, Christchurch, 7 May 1937, p. 14.
29 *Ibid.*
30 Derby, 'Josep Trueta and Douglas Jolly', unpublished conference paper, 2010.
31 Derby, 'Doug Jolly: battlefield surgeon', in *Kiwi Compañeros*, pp. 123–133.
32 The outstanding effectiveness of Jolly's methods, and the evidently imminent need for their much wider application after the civil war, led him to write a detailed account of his system that was published in October 1940. *Field Surgery in Total War* was an immediate international success and became required reading in the US Army Medical Service during the Second World War. According to one US authority, Jolly's methods "undoubtedly contributed more to the saving of lives of patients with abdominal wounds than any other single factor".
33 D. Jolly, letter to family, 8 February 1937; Painter family collection.
34 *Press*, Christchurch, 7 May 1937, p. 14.
35 *Ibid.*
36 Quoted in Palfreeman, *Aristocrats*, p. 162.
37 *Press*, Christchurch, 7 May 1937, p. 14.

38 *Ibid.*
39 Letter published *Evening Post*, 26 May 1937, p. 10. After numerous later military actions, William MacDonald left Spain along with all other International Brigaders in late 1938. He resurfaced in the 1950s as British consul in Tripoli, and died in Portugal in 1968.
40 Quoted in Palfreeman, *Aristocrats*, p. 162.
41 Quoted in *ibid.*, p. 163.
42 *Press*, Christchurch, 7 May 1937, p. 14.
43 Quoted in Palfreeman, *Aristocrats,* pp. 164–5. The Requetés, whose name derives from a term for a hunting call, were an intensely religious right-wing militia who regarded the civil war as a holy crusade.
44 Quoted in *ibid.*, p. 171.
45 *Press,* Christchurch, 7 May 1937, p. 14.
46 Quoted in Palfreeman, *Aristocrats*, p. 152.
47 Burchill, *The Paths I've Trod*, p. 64.
48 'With the refugees', *Auckland Star*, 9 September 1937, p. 21.
49 Quoted in Palfreeman, *Aristocrats*, p. 170.
50 Some 100 Chinese nationals, mostly veterans of Mao's Red Army, are thought to have fought in Spain with the International Brigades.
51 *Dominion*, 13 July 1937, p. 10.
52 In the years after the war, however, this region of Extremadura was transformed into fertile farmland by an irrigation scheme fed from the Tagus River.
53 *Dominion*, 13 July 1937, p. 10.
54 Massons, 'Un any al servei de les Brigades Internationals (B.I.) com cap d'equip quirúqic', *Gimbernat* 28, 1997, p. 226. Translated from Catalan by Farrell Cleary and Saioa Polin Lopez.
55 Massons, *ibid.* Telge's real name was Zvetan Kristanov. Like many other International Brigaders, especially those from Eastern Europe, he used a *nom de guerre* in Spain.
56 Angeles Carceres, personal communication, 6 June 2014.
57 Massons, 'Un any al servei . . . ', p. 229.
58 *Ibid.*, p. 228.
59 Neugass, *War is Beautiful*, p. 10.
60 *Ibid.*, pp. 14–15.
61 Massons, 'Un any al servei . . . ', p. 228.
62 *Ibid.*, pp. 237–238.
63 *Ibid.*
64 *Ibid.*, p. 230.
65 Jolly, personal letter, 22 March 1937; Painter family collection.
66 Quoted in Wilson, *In the Margins,*. p. 217.

67 Trueta, *Trueta – Surgeon in war and peace*, p. 136.
68 Quoted in Wilson, *In the Margins*, p. 217.
69 This mysterious statement describes a geographic impossibility, since the Sierra Morena is 400 km south of Brunete. Dorothy is likely to have misnamed the range from which she and her colleagues viewed the battle.
70 *Press*, Christchurch, 7 May 1937, p. 14.
71 Massons, 'Un any al servei . . .', p. 230.
72 Video interview, JM Massons, 2011.
73 R. Sola Carrio, *Diario Personal*, quoted in Derby, 'Josep Trueta and Douglas Jolly', 2010.
74 Roderick Farquhar quoted in MacDougall, *Voices from the Spanish Civil War*, pp. 84–85.
75 *Press*, Christchurch, 7 May 1937, p. 14.
76 Massons, 'Un any al servei . . .', p. 231.
77 DM letter, ATL, 28 April 1938.
78 Elizabeth Ogilvie, personal communication with Michael O'Shaughnessy; M. O'Shaughnessy collection.
79 DM letter, ATL, 10 September 1938.
80 *Daily Telegraph*, 2 June 1937, quoted in Palfreeman, *Aristocrats*, p. 173 fn27.

3 Hospital Inglés de Niños

1 Wilson, *In the Margins of Chaos*, p. 189.
2 *Ibid.*, p. 173.
3 Roberts, 'Place, life histories and the politics of relief', p. 201.
4 Frida Stewart, unpublished memoir, p. 12; A. Jackson collection.
5 Wilson, *In the Margins*, p. 182.
6 Wilson, *Manchester Guardian*, 9 July 1937.
7 F. Wilson, quoted in Roberts, 'Place, life histories', p. 203.
8 Wilson, *In the Margins*, p. 183.
9 F. Wilson, quoted in Roberts, 'Place, life histories', p. 203.
10 F. Stewart, unpublished memoir, p. 4.
11 Roberts, 'Place, life histories', p. 210.
12 Coni, *Medicine and Warfare*, p. 33; G. Jirku, *We fight death*, p. 40.
13 F. Stewart, unpublished memoir, p. 5.
14 G. Murray, quoted in MacDougall, *Voices from the Spanish Civil War*, p. 102.
15 Wilson, *In the Margins*, p. 192.
16 Palfreeman, *Aristocrats, Adventurers and Ambulances*, pp. 188–189.

17 Quoted in Wilson, *In the Margins*, p. 217.
18 E. Farquhar, quoted in Fyrth and Alexander, *Women's Voices from the Spanish Civil War*, p. 206.
19 *Ibid.*
20 DM letter, ATL, 5 January 1939.
21 *Ibid.*
22 Quoted in Wilson, *In the Margins*, p. 217.
23 McDonald, 'Summer in Murcia in 1937', *Newnham College Roll*, p. 40.
24 Burchill, *The Paths I've Trod*, p. 60.
25 McDonald, 'Summer in Murcia', p. 43.
26 DM letter, ATL, 5 January 1939.
27 Quoted in Wilson, *In the Margins*, p. 217.
28 McDonald, 'Summer in Murcia', p. 44.
29 DM letter, ATL, 28 April 1938.
30 Wilson, *In the Margins*, p. 189.
31 Ruth Cope in Fyrth and Alexander, *Women's Voices from the Spanish Civil War*, pp. 215–16.
32 Gregory, *The Shallow Grave*, p. 54.
33 *Ibid.*, p. 55.
34 McDonald, 'Summer in Murcia', pp. 44–45.
35 DM letter, ATL, 28 April 1938.
36 F. Wilson, quoted in Roberts, 'Place, life, histories', p. 210.
37 McDonald, 'Summer in Murcia', p. 45.
38 Emily Parker to John Reich, 1 March 1938, quoted in Mendlesohn, 'Practising peace', p. 130.
39 Dorothy Davies, quoted in Fyrth and Alexander, *Women's Voices*, p. 203.
40 Pilar Barnés, *El Gozo de mis Raices y su Entorno*, p. 196. Trans. David Jorge.
41 I. Dodds interview, T4, S7.
42 *Ibid.*
43 *Ibid.*
44 *Ibid.*
45 DM letter, ATL, 2 September 1938.
46 DM letter, ATL, 28 April 1938.
47 *Ibid.*
48 DM letter, ATL, 28 April 1938. Underlining in original.
49 Jorge, 'Bill Jordan – A distant champion for Spanish democracy', p. 24.
50 DM letter, ATL, 2 September 1938.
51 Quoted in Wilson, *In the Margins*, p. 21; Palfreeman, *Aristocrats,* p. 142.
52 Esther Farquhar to Reich, 25 May 1938, FSC/R/SP/4. Friends Library, London, Handwritten marginalia to typed letter.
53 DM letter, ATL, 20 September 1938.

54 AFSC cables, 19 January 1938; M. O'Shaughnessy collection.
55 Florence Conard, quoted in Fyrth and Alexander, *Women's Voices*, p. 210.
56 Dorothy Davies, quoted in Fyrth and Alexander, *Women's Voices*, p. 203.
57 *Ibid.*
58 Roberts, 'Place, life histories', p. 97.
59 Dorothy Davies, *Women's Voices*, p. 172.
60 Information from Xavier Garcia i Ferrandis, personal communication, 11 November 2014.
61 Pretus, *Humanitarian Relief in the Spanish Civil War (1936–1939)*, p. 284.
62 F. Wilson quoted in Hale, 'Waging peace in the Spanish Civil War', p. 12.
63 Dorothy Davies, *Women's Voices*, p. 173.
64 DM letter, ATL, 10 September 1938.
65 *Ibid.*
66 DM letter, ATL, 20 September 1939.
67 *Ibid.*, 2 September 1938.
68 *Ibid.*
69 Wilson, *In the Margins*, p. 217.
70 *Ibid.*
71 *Ibid.*
72 *Ibid.*
73 Ruth Cope in Fyrth and Alexander, *Women's Voices*, p. 214.
74 DM letter, ATL, 20 September 1938.
75 *Ibid.*, 2 September 1938.
76 *Ibid.*, 2 December 1938.
77 *Ibid.*, 30 December 1938.
78 'En el Hospital Ingles de Amigos Cuaqueros', *Nuestra Lucha*, 28 December 1938, trans. Ruth Cope, AFSC archives.
79 *Ibid.*
80 DM letter, ATL 30 December 1938.
81 Dorothy Davies in Fyrth and Alexander, *Women's Voices*, p. 203.
82 DM letter, ATL, 30 December 1938.
83 *Ibid.*, 5 January 1939.
84 Pretus, *Humanitarian Relief in the Spanish Civil War (1936–1939)*, p. 281.
85 Jorge, *Haciéndose los sordos en Ginebra*, p. 775.
86 Wilson, *Advice to Relief Workers*, p. 11.
87 DM letter, ATL, 2 December 1938.
88 Roberts, 'Place, life histories', p. 220.
89 Quoted in Mendlesohn, *Quaker Relief Work in the Spanish Civil War*, p. 65.

90   DM letter, ATL 5 January 1939.
91   DM letter, 5 January 1939.
92   *Ibid.*, 2 December 1938.
93   *Ibid.*, 14 February 1939.
94   *Ibid.*, 14 February 1939.
95   New Zealand nurse Renée Shadbolt, a colleague of Isobel Dodds at the International Brigades hospital at Huete, fell in love with one of her patients, an anti-Nazi musician named Willi Remmel. When they met again in another hospital the following year, they married in a civil ceremony but the outbreak of the Second World War forced them to separate for the rest of their lives (Derby, *Kiwi Compañeros*, pp. 144–45).
96   E. Ogilvie, eulogy for Dorothy Morris; Ogilvie family collection.

4 With Horsebox and Lie-Low

1   DM letter, ATL, 28 April 1938.
2   *Ibid.*, 25 March 1939.
3   *Ibid.*
4   *Ibid.*
5   *Ibid.*
6   *Press*, Christchurch, 17 November 1983, p. 21.
7   DM letter, ATL, 25 March 1939.
8   *Ibid.*
9   DM letter, ATL, 16 April 1939.
10   *Ibid.*, 25 March 1939.
11   *Ibid.*, 16 April 1939.
12   *Ibid.*
13   Quoted in Hale, 'Waging peace', p. 14.
14   Edith Pye in Fyrth and Alexander, *Women's Voices*, pp. 327–28.
15   Muggeridge, 'Spain today and yesterday', in *Foster Parents Plan for Spanish Children*, p. 7.
16   Casals, *Joys and Sorrows*, p. 233.
17   Roberts, 'Place, life histories', p. 22.
18   Quoted in Wilson, *In the Margins*, p. 222.
19   *Ibid.*, p. 223.
20   Wilson, 'Spaniards in Exile the Civilian Camp at Argelés, Perpignan', *Manchester Guardian*, 9 May 1939.
21   *Ibid.*
22   *Ibid.*
23   May bulletin, Friends Service Council, UK, quoted in *NZ Herald*, 28 June 1939, p. 18.

24 M. Griffiths to E. Cox, 8 May 1940, box 15, folder 72, page 22, hereafter b..., f..., p..., AFSC archives.
25 Roberts, 'Place, life histories', p. 221, fn 103.
26 DM letter, ATL, 24 June 1939.
27 Quoted in Roberts, 'Place, life histories', p. 224.
28 *Ibid.*
29 *Ibid.*
30 DM letter, ATL, 19 August 1939.
31 Jane Lidderdale to Dorothy Morris, 7 July 1939, b. 15, f. 71, p. 40, AFSC archive.
32 *Ibid.*, b. 15, f. 71, p. 47, 24 July 1939.
33 DM to Dorothy Thompson, 4 July 1939, FSC/R/SP/3/4 [France] Perpignan office correspondence 1939–1940, Friends Library.
34 DM letter, ATL, 24 June 1939.
35 *Ibid.*
36 DM to Dorothy Thompson, 4 July 1939, FSC/R/SP/3/4 [France] Perpignan office correspondence 1939–1940, Friends Library.
37 DM to Dorothy Thompson, 26 May 1939, FSC/R/SP/3/4 [France] Perpignan office correspondence 1939–1940, Friends Library.
38 Hilton, *The Horror of Love*, p. 86.
39 Jane Taylor, personal communication, 4 May 2014.
40 DM letter, ATL, 2 June 1939.
41 N. Mitford quoted in Hilton, *The Horror of Love*, pp. 86–87.
42 *Ibid.*
43 DM letter, ATL, 24 June 1939.
44 *Ibid.*, 19 August 1939.
45 *Ibid.*, 19 August 1939.
46 A. Russell to DM, 26 August 1939, b. 15, f. 69, p. 38, AFSC archives.
47 DM letter, ATL, 2 June 1939.
48 *Ibid.*, 4 September 1939.
49 *Ibid.*, 12 October 1939.
50 Bailey, *Love and War in the Pyrenees*, pp. 49–51.
51 Marta Bétoin, La Coume, personal communication, 23 June 2014.
52 DM to E. Pye and Dr Clark, London, 14 September 1939, b. 15, f. 71, p. 66, AFSC archives.
53 *Ibid.*, 11 October 1939, p. 85.
54 *Ibid.*, 17 October 1939, p. 88.
55 L. Urmston, in Fyrth and Alexander, *Women's Voices*, pp. 342–344.
56 DM letter, ATL, 12 October 1939.
57 M Elmes to Miss Frawley, 21 May 1940, b. 15, f. 71, p. 31 AFSC archive.
58 Bernard Wilson, personal communication, 30 July 2014.

59 DM to E Pye, 6 February 1940, b. 15, f. 76, p. 4, AFSC archive.

60 M. Griffiths to E Hughes, 14 November 1939, b. 15, f. 71, p. 101, AFSC archive.

61 DM letter, ATL, 15 January 1940. This hospital, the Maternité Suise d'Elne, based in a large chateau, was founded by a Swiss nurse, Elisabeth Eidenbenz. She was later honoured by the Yad Vashem organisation for her work with Jewish mothers and children. The building is now a museum, visited by large numbers of Spaniards eager to see where they or their relatives were born – http://www.maternitesuissedelne.com/index.html.

62 *Ibid.*, 24 April 1940.

63 DM to E Pye, 6 February 1940, b. 15, f. 71, p. 3, AFSC archive.

64 DM letter, ATL, 15 January 1940.

65 *Ibid.*.

66 DM to E Odgers, 13 April 1940, b. 15, f. 72, p. 15, AFSC archive.

67 *Ibid.*

68 DM to E. Hughes, London, 29 November 1939, b. 15, f. 71, p. 104, AFSC archive.

69 M. Griffiths to FSC, London, 21 February 1940, b. 15, f. 76, p. 9, AFSC archive.

70 Annual report 1940, AFSC, p. 10, AFSC archive.

71 DM letter, ATL, 12 October 1939.

72 *Ibid.*, 24 April 1940.

73 DM to Richard Rees, International Commission for Aid to Refugee Children, 16 May 1940, b. 15, f. 72, p. 27, AFSC archive.

74 DM to E Pye, 23 May 1940, b. 15, f. 76, p. 50, AFSC archive.

75 DM to E Hughes, FSC, 30 May 1940, b. 15, f. 76, p. 56, AFSC archive.

76 DM to Helga Holbeck, 27 May 1940, b. 15, f. 72, p. 41, AFSC archive.

77 DM to Richard Rees, 1 June 1940, b. 15, f. 72, p. 51, AFSC archive.

78 M. Griffiths to R. Rees, 28 May 1940, b. 15, f. 72, p. 45; DM to Richard Rees, 1 June 1940, b. 15, f. 72, p. 51, AFSC archive.

79 DM to Richard Rees, 3 June 1940, b. 15,. f. 72, p. 62, AFSC archive.

80 DM to Richard Rees, 11 June 1940, b. 15, f. 72, pp. 79–81, AFSC archive.

81 DM letter, ATL, 21 May 1940.

82 Roberts, 'Place, life histories', pp. 248–9.

83 Quoted in Wriggins, *Picking Up the Pieces*, pp. 143–44.

5 Wearing the Snood

1 D. Morris to Jane Taylor, 15 March 1977; Jane Taylor collection.

2 Werth, *The Last Days of Paris*, 1940, p. 206.

3 Quoted in personal communication, David Worsfold, 19 August 2014.
4 de Marneffe, *Last Boat from Bordeaux*, p. 79.
5 *Daily Telegraph*, 21 June 1940, p. 5.
6 E. Pye, 26 June 1940, FSC/R/SP/3/4 [France], Perpignan office correspondence 1939–1940, Friends Library.
7 'From Nice to England – adventures of a refugee', *Western Morning News*, 29 June 1940, p. 7.
8 Information provided by National Maritime Museum Cornwall, 31 July 2014.
9 Hon. W. Churchill, *Hansard*, 18 June 1940, Commons sitting, pp. 58–60.
10 Lewis, *A People's War*, p. 66.
11 Jane Taylor, personal communication, 4 May 2014.
12 DM letter, ATL, 22 April 1941.
13 *Ibid.*
14 *Ibid.*
15 *Ibid.*
16 *Ibid.*
17 *Ibid.*, 2 May 1941.
18 *Ibid.*, 22 April 1941.
19 *Ibid.*
20 *Ibid.*, 24/25 December 1940.
21 *Ibid.*, 22 April 1941.
22 *Ibid.*, 2 May 1941.
23 Harris, *Women at War*, p. 111 *et passim.*
24 DM letter, ATL, 24/25 December 1940.
25 *Ibid.*, 22 April 1941.
26 F. Wilson to H. Holbeck, 24 April 1941; Bernard Wilson collection.
27 DM letter, ATL, 22 April 1941.
28 'Wednesday night's raid', *Tottenham and Edmonton Herald*, 21 March 1941, p. 41.
29 Air raid wardens' logbook, provided courtesy of Enfield Local Studies and Archive, 26 July 2014.
30 DM letter, ATL, 2 May 1941.
31 *Ibid.*
32 *Ibid.*, 22 November 1941.
33 *Ibid.*
34 Lewis, *A People's War*, p. 110.
35 Bullock, *The Life and Times of Ernest Bevin*, vol. 2, p. 12.
36 *Ibid.*, p. 23.
37 Williams, *Ernest Bevin*, p. 223.

38 Evans, *Bevin*, p. 189.
39 Chris Morris, personal communication, 26 July 2014.
40 DM letter, ATL, 2 May 1941.
41 DM letter, ATL, 2 May 1941 – underlining in original.
42 The organisation survives to the present day under the name Plan, as a global children's charity working in 50 countries.
43 Midgely, 'Anna Freud: The Hampstead War Nurseries', p. 941.
44 Freud and Burlingham, *War and Children*, p. 12.
45 *Ibid.*, pp. 116–17.
46 Midgley, 'Anna Freud: The Hampstead War Nurseries', pp. 948–50.
47 DM letter, ATL, 16 April 1939.
48 *Ibid.*, 4 September 1939.
49 Frank Morris, oral history interview, T2, S2; Morris family collection.
50 DM letter, ATL, 24/25 December 1940.
51 *Ibid.*
52 *Ibid.*, 21 May 1940.
53 *Ibid.*, 2 May 1941.
54 *Ibid.*, 9 August 1941.
55 DM letter, 22 November 1941.
56 Morris, Roger, 'War Diary', p. 24.
57 Rattray, *Great Days in New Zealand Nursing*, p. 174.

6 The Conscience of the World

1 Wilson, *Advice to Relief Workers*, p. 5.
2 Quoted in Fox, 'The Origins of UNRRA', p. 584. Italics in original.
3 Woodbridge (ed.), *UNRRA*, vol. 2, p. 31.
4 *Ibid.*, vol. 1, p. 4.
5 *Ibid.*, p. 88-90.
6 Personnel report for Dorothy Morris, UNRRA archives.
7 Woodbridge, *UNRRA*, vol. 1, p. 267.
8 Wriggins, *Picking Up the Pieces*, p. 86.
9 Corsellis, *War and Aftermath*, pp. 10–11.
10 *Ibid.*, p. 14.
11 J. Corsellis quoted in Bach, 'The memorial at El Shatt is silent'.
12 Jane Taylor, personal communication, 4 May 2014.
13 A. Cochrane, quoted in Adams, 'Douglas Waddell Jolly as a pioneer in the surgical treatment of trauma', pp. 253–256.
14 Quoted in Jane Taylor, personal communication, 4 May 2014.
15 Roger Morris, 'War Diary', p. 28.
16 Frank Morris, oral history interview, T2, S2.
17 Frank Morris letters, 18 June 1945.

18 Frank Morris, oral history interview, T3, S2.
19 *Ibid.*, T1, S1.
20 *Ibid.*, T3, S1.
21 Shepherd, *The Long Road Home*, p. 59.
22 UNRRA, *UNRRA's Work for Displaced Persons in Europe*, p. 8.
23 Shepherd, *The Long Road Home*, pp. 138–9.
24 *Ibid.*, pp. 136–7.
25 Corsellis, *War and Aftermath*, 7 June 1945.
26 Reinisch, 'We Shall Rebuild Anew a Powerful Nation', p. 470.
27 Doherty, *Letters from Belsen 1945*, p. 201.
28 *Ibid.*, p. 42.
29 Armstrong-Reid, *Lyle Creelman – The Frontiers of Global Nursing*, p. 90.
30 Shepherd, *The Long Road Home*, p. 168.
31 Armstrong-Reid, *Lyle Creelman*, p. 94.
32 *Ibid.*, p. 307.
33 Quoted in Armstrong-Reid, 'Soldiers of Peace', p. 113.
34 *Ibid.*
35 Shepherd, *The Long Road Home,* p. 67.
36 Armstrong-Reid, *Lyle Creelman,* p. 75.
37 Wilson, *Advice to Relief Workers*, p. 8.
38 Armstrong-Reid, *Lyle Creelman*, p. 89.
39 *Ibid.*, pp. 26–27.
40 Shepherd, *The Long Road Home*, pp. 143–45.
41 E. M. Thorne, quoted in Armstrong-Reid, *Lyle Creelman*, p. 97.
42 Series 0406, box 8, file 6, Acc. PAG 4/3.0.11.2.0.1; 1 April 1946, UN Archives.
43 Shepherd, *Lyle Creelman*, p. 157.
44 Reinisch, 'We Shall Rebuild Anew', p. 471.
45 Fisher, *Raphael Cilento*, p. 211.
46 Series 0406, box 8, file 6, Acc. PAG 4/3.0.11.2.0.1, UN Archives.
47 Shepherd, *The Long Road Home*, p. 140; Sereny, *The Healing Wound*, p. 25.
48 Reinisch, 'We Shall Rebuild Anew', p. 453.
49 L. Creelman quoted in Armstrong-Reid, *Lyle Creelman*, p. 100.
50 Doherty, *Letters from Belsen 1945*, p. 175.
51 Armstrong-Reid, *Lyle Creelman*, p. 99.
52 *Ibid.*, p. 183.
53 Pamela Wood, personal communication, 26 September 2013.
54 Jane Taylor, personal communication, 10 August 2014.
55 Doherty, *Letters from Belsen 1945*, pp. 153–162.
56 Personnel report for Dorothy Morris, UNRRA archives.

57 K. Hulme quoted in Shepherd, *The Long Road Home*, p. 174.
58 *Ibid.*, p. 50.

7 'Brazen and Tyrannical'

1 Jane Taylor, 'A significant older person', unpublished ms.
2 Jane Taylor, personal communication, 10 August 2014.
3 *Ibid.*, 17 August 2014.
4 *Ibid.*
5 G. Morris, personal communication, 12 September 2014.
6 Elizabeth Ogilvie, personal communication with M. O'Shaughnessy, 18 June 1998; O'Shaughnessy collection.
7 Jane Taylor, personal communication, 10 August 2014.
8 Michael O'Shaughnessy, personal communication, 19 October 2014.
9 *Press*, 17 December 1983, p. 21.
10 Jane Taylor, personal communication, 8 August 2014.
11 DM letter to Jane Taylor, 20 May 1969; Jane Taylor collection.
12 *Ibid.*
13 *Ibid.*, 25 May 1969.
14 *Ibid.*, 28 November 1974.
15 *Ibid.*, 8 December 1975.
16 *Ibid.*, 15 March 1977.
17 Ibid., 30 November 1978.
18 *Ibid.*, 16 March 1980.
19 *Ibid.*.
20 Personal communication, Mary Stapylton-Smith, 27 November 2014.
21 Roger Morris, personal communication, 5 April 2014.
22 Jane Taylor, personal communication, 8 August 2014.
23 *Press*, 17 December 1983, p. 21.
24 Ruth Morris, personal communication with Michael O'Shaughnessy, 27 February 1998.
25 Anne Morris, personal communication, 23 October 2014.
26 Jane Taylor, personal communication, 14 September 2014.

Bibliography

Published

Books

Armstrong-Reid, Susan, *Lyle Creelman – The Frontiers of Global Nursing* (Toronto: University of Toronto Press 2014).

Bailey, Rosemary, *Love and War in the Pyrenees* (London: Weidenfeld and Nicolson 2008).

Barnés, Pilar, *El Gozo de mis Raices y su Entorno* (Lorca: Ayuntamiento de Lorca 2000).

Belcher, M, *A History of Rangi-Ruru School* (Christchurch: Pegasus Press 1964).

Bullock, Alan, *The Life and Times of Ernest Bevin* (London: Heinemann 1867).

Burchill, Elizabeth, *The Paths I've Trod – Autobiography of an Australian nurse* (Melbourne: Spectrum 1985).

Casals, Pablo, as told to Albert E. Kahn, *Joys and Sorrows – Reflections by Pablo Casals* (London: Macdonald and Co. 1970).

Coni, Nicholas, *Medicine and Warfare – Spain 1936–1939* (Routledge/Cañada Blanch Centre for Contemporary Spanish Studies 2008).

Corsellis, John, *War and Aftermath – Letter-diaries of a humanitarian worker with the Quakers, British Red Cross and UNRRA 1944–1947*. Online accessed 21 August 2014.

Cox, Geoffrey *Defence of Madrid – An eyewitness account of the Spanish Civil War* (London: Victor Gollancz 1937). New edition published Dunedin: Otago University Press 2006.

De Marneffe, Francis, *Last Boat from Bordeaux* (Massachusetts: Coolidge Hill Press 2001).

Derby, Mark, *Kiwi Compañeros – New Zealand and the Spanish Civil War* (Christchurch: Canterbury University Press 2009).

Doherty, Muriel, *Letters from Belsen 1945* (NSW: Allen and Unwin 2000).

Evans, Trevor, *Bevin* (London: George Allen and Unwin 1946).

Fisher, Fedora G. *Raphael Cilento – A biography* (Queensland: University of Queensland Press 1994).

Freud, Anna and Burlingham, Dorothy, *War and Children* (New York: International University Press 1944).

Fyrth, Jim, *The Signal Was Spain* (London: Lawrence and Wishart 1986).

Fyrth, Jim and Alexander, Sally, eds. *Women's Voices from the Spanish Civil War* (London: Lawrence and Wishart 2008).

Gregory, Walter, *The Shallow Grave – A memoir of the Spanish Civil War* (London: Victor Gollancz 1987).

Harris, Carol, *Women at War 1939–1945 – The home front* (Stroud: Sutton Publishing 2000).

Hilton, Lisa, *The Horror of Love – Nancy Mitford and Gaston Paderewski in Paris and London* (London: Weidenfeld and Nicolson 2011).

Jackson, Angela, *British Women and the Spanish Civil War* (Barcelona: Warren and Pell Publishing in assoc. with Cañada Blanch Centre for Contemporary Spanish Studies 2009).

Lethbridge, David, *Norman Bethune in Spain – Commitment, crisis and conspiracy* (Eastbourne: Sussex Academic Press 2013).

Lewis, Peter, *A People's War* (London: Thames Methuen 1986).

MacDougall, Ian, *Voices from the Spanish Civil War – Personal recollections of Scottish volunteers in Republican Spain 1936–39* (Edinburgh: Polygon 1986).

Mendlesohn, F., *Quaker Relief Work in the Spanish Civil War* (New York: Edwin Mellen Press 2001).

Neugass, James, *War is Beautiful – An American ambulance driver in the Spanish Civil War* (New York: The New Press 2008).

Palfreeman, Linda, *Aristocrats, Adventurers and Ambulances – British medical units in the Spanish Civil War* (Eastbourne: Sussex Acdemic Press 2014).

Preston, Paul *The Spanish Holocaust – Inquisition and extermination in twentieth-century Spain* (London: Harper Press 2012).

Pretus, Gabriel, *Humanitarian Relief in the Spanish Civil War (1936–1939)* (New York: Edwin Mellen Press 2013.

Rattray, Joan, *Great Days in New Zealand Nursing* (Wellington: AH and AW Reed 1961).

Scotter, W.H., *A History of Port Lyttelton* (Christchurch: Lyttelton Harbour Board 1968).

Sereny, Gitta, *The Healing Wound – Experiences and reflections on Germany, 1938–2001* (New York: W.W. Norton 2001).

Shepherd, Ben, *The Long Road Home – The aftermath of the Second World War* (London: The Bodley Head 2010).

Josep Trueta, *Trueta – Surgeon in War and Peace*, trans. Meli and Michael Strubell (London: Gollancz 1980).

UNRRA, *UNRRA's work for displaced persons in Europe* (London: UNRRA European regional office 1946).

Welch, David, *The Lucifer – A story of industrial conflict in New Zealand's 1930s* (Palmerston North: Dunmore Press – Trade Union History Project 1998).

Werth, Alexander, *The Last Days of Paris* (London: Hamish Hamilton 1940).
Williams, Francis, *Ernest Bevin – Portrait of a great Englishman* (London: Hutchinson 1952).
Wilson, Francesca, *In the Margins of Chaos – Recollections of relief work in and between three wars* (London: John Murray 1944).
———, *Aftermath: France, Austria, Germany, Yugoslavia 1945 and 1946* (Harmondsworth and New York: Penguin Books 1947).
———, *Advice to Relief Workers: Based on personal experience in the field* (London: John Murray and Friends Relief Service 1947).
Woodbridge, George (ed.) *UNRRA – The history of the United Nations Relief and Rehabilitation Administration* (New York: Columbia University Press 1950).
Wriggins, Howard, *Picking Up the Pieces from Portugal to Palestine – Quaker refugee relief in World War II* (Maryland: University Press of America 2004).

Pamphlets

Christchurch Hospital nursing school, Pq 610.73071 CHR 1940 Alexander Turnbull Library, Wellington.
Jirku, Gusti *We fight death – The work of the medical service of the International Brigades in Spain* (Madrid: date unknown), Alexander Turnbull Library, Wellington.
Eric Muggeridge, 'Spain today and yesterday', in *Foster Parents Plan for Spanish Children* (New York: Foster Parents Plan for Spanish Children 1939).

Articles

Adams, D. B. 'Douglas Waddell Jolly as a pioneer in the surgical treatment of trauma', *Surgery, Gynecology and Obstetrics*, vol. 171 (September 1990), pp. 253–256.
Armstrong-Reid, Susan, 'Soldiers of Peace – Canadians in Germany's UNRRA nursing brigade, 1945-47', *Bulletin canadien d'histoire de la médecine – Canadian bulletin of medical history*, January 2010 27(1), pp. 101–122.
Bach, Nenad ''The memorial at El Shatt is silent', *Crown*, Croatian World Network, 13 February 2006, online http://www.croatia.org/crown/articles/6971/1/%28E%29-The-memorial-at-El-Shatt-is-silent, accessed 21 August 2014.
Fox, Grace, "The Origins of UNRRA", *Political Science Quarterly*, vol. 65, no. 4 (Dec., 1950).
Hale, Frederick, "Waging peace in the Spanish Civil War: The relief efforts

of the British Quaker mission", *Studia Historiae Ecclesiasticae* 31, 2 (October 2005) accessed online http://uir.unisa.ac.za/handle/10500/4364.

Jorge, David, 'Bill Jordan – A distant champion for Spanish democracy', in *Labour History Project Bulletin*, no. 57, April 2013, New Zealand Labour History Project, pp. 21–26.

Massons, J. 'Un any al servei de les Brigades Internationals (B.I.) com cap d'equip quirúqic', *Gimbernat* 28, 1997, pp. 225–238.

McDonald, Inez, 'Summer in Murcia in 1937,' *Newnham College Roll* 1937, Newnham College, Cambridge University.

Midgley, Nick, 'Anna Freud: The Hampstead War Nurseries and the role of the direct observation of children for pyschoanalysis', *International Journal of Pyschoanalysis* (2007: 88), pp. 939–59.

Reinisch, Jessica, 'We Shall Rebuild Anew a Powerful Nation': UNRRA, Internationalism and National Reconstruction in Poland', *Journal of Contemporary History*, vol. 43, no. 3, 'Relief in the Aftermath of War' (July 2008), pp. 451–76.

Veatch, R. 'The League of Nations and the Spanish Civil War, 1936–9', *European History Quarterly*, 20, 1990, p. 183.

Willis, Elizabeth, 'Medical responses to civil war and revolution in Spain, 1936–1939: International aid and local self-organisation", *Medicine, Conflict and Survival*, 24:3 2008, pp. 159–73.

Wood, Pamela J. 'Nursing the patient, the room and the doctor: assessing New Zealand nurses' practical capability, 1900–1945', *Nursing Education Today* 31 (2011), pp. 140-44.

Video
Interview with Dr Josep Maria Massons, 2011, Youtube, https://www.youtube.com/watch?v=zcDCemQT5Mw last accessed 3 December 2014, trans. F. Cleary, S. L. Polin.

Periodicals
Auckland Star, 1936–42.
Canterbury Times, Christchurch, 1930.
Press, Christchurch, 1930–83.
Telegraph, 1940.
Western Morning News, 1940.

Unpublished
Theses
Dunstan, Stephen A., 'The collective voice – where to now? Two depressions

– a comparative study of two unemployed movements'. MA thesis, University of Canterbury, 1995.

Jorge, David, 'Haciéndose los sordos en Ginebra: La Sociedad de Naciones y la Guerra de España', PhD thesis, Universidad Complutense de Madrid, 2014 (Published version forthcoming).

Mendlesohn, Farah, 'Practising peace: American and British Quaker Relief in the Spanish Civil War', PhD thesis, University of York, 1997.

Parsons, Gwen 'The Christchurch community at war 1914–1918: Society, discourse and power', MA thesis, Canterbury 2003, p. 141.

Roberts, Siân L. 'Place, life, histories and the politics of relief: Episodes in the life of Francesca Wilson, humanitarian educator activist', PhD thesis, Birmingham 2010.

Rodgers, J 'Nursing education in New Zealand, 1883 to 1930: The persistence of the Nightingale ethos', MA thesis, Massey University, 1985.

Manuscripts

Derby, Mark, 'Josep Trueta and Douglas Jolly – Surgeons in war and peace', conference paper *Historical Crossroads – Spain from the Second Republic to the 21ˢᵗ century*, Auckland University 18–20 February 2010.

Morris, Dorothy MS-Papers-9144, Alexander Turnbull Library (ATL), Wellington, NZ.

Morris, Frank, 'Frank Recalls', unpublished oral history 1994; Morris family collection.

Morris, Roger, 'War diary', unpublished manuscript transcribed by Geoff Morris; Morris family collection.

Archives and Records

AFSC (American Friends Service Committee), Philadelphia, USA.

Friends Library, London, UK.

Angela Jackson collection.

Morris family collection.

Oral History Archive, National Library, Wellington, New Zealand.

Michael O'Shaughnessy collection.

Jane Taylor collection.

UNRRA archives, Archives and Records Management Section, United Nations Library, New York, USA.

UNRRA archives, World Health Organisation, Geneva, Switzerland.

Index

Abraham Lincoln Brigade, 43
Abyssinia, 29, 31
Advice to Relief Workers, 151
Africa (*see also* South Africa), 7, 20, 86
Ah Foo, 13
Aid Spain campaign (UK), 31
Air France, 86
Albacete, 50, 56
Albert Hall (London), 32
Alberti, Rafael, 87
Albuñol, 39, 42
Alexander Turnbull Library, 1
Alexandria, 144, 159
Alfonso, Don (Dr), 60
Alicante, 37, 61, 71–74, 83, 88, 91–92,
    94, 95, 117
Almaden, 49
Almeria, 35–40, 42, 44, 47–49, 56–57,
    59, 61, 71
Alpujarras, 42
Alsatian refugees, 103, 108
America (*see also* US), 88
American Friends Service Council (AFSC),
    60, 72, 74
Andalucia, 164
Angel Road (London), 130
Anglo-Persian Oil Co., 29
Antarctic, 15–16
Aragon, 32
Argelés (detention camp), 98–101, 106,
    107, 111, 112, 113, 114
Aroha (name), 11, 12
Ascher, Gerardo, 99
Ashburton, 167
Assouan (Aswan), 163
Athenic, 14
Athens, 137
Auckland, 26
Aude, 116
Austin Reed (clothier), 136
Australasia, 14

Australia, 32
Avenue des Baleares, 113, 115, 119
Avon River (Christchurch, NZ), 20

Baltic University, 153
Barcarés, 98
Barcelona, 35, 38, 46, 50, 54, 56, 70, 71,
    97, 112, 124
Barnés, Pilar, 68
Beaufoy Institute, 124–126
Belalcázar, 53–54
Belgium, Belgians, 111, 116–117, 120,
    121, 131
Benevolent Committee (Canterbury
    Hospital Board), 24
Benidorm, 74, 99, 165
Bergen-Belsen (death camp), 149, 152,
    154, 156
Bethune, Dr Norman, 38, 40
Bevin, Ernest, 131–132, 133
Blitz (London, Second World War), 21,
    123–124, 127, 131, 134, 135
Boadicea, HMS, 38
Boer War, 128
Bordeaux, 115, 117–118, 121, 123
Bourg-Madame, 161
Bournemouth, 60
Bowers, Lt., 16
Brighton, 146
Britain, British; government's response to
    Spanish Civil War, 31, 70–71; Franco
    sympathizers in, 36; funding from,
    45–46, 106; medical volunteers from,
    41, 61–63, 67; navy, 17, 38, 94–95,
    98; high society figures in, 106–107;
    evacuation to, 177–123; wartime
    preparedness of, 96, 108, 123–125;
    manpower regulations in, 131–133;
    war nurseries in, 134–135; refugee
    relief by, 139–144, 147–154,
    156–157; politics in, 6, 7

British War Relief Society, 135
British Zone (Germany), 149, 150, 151, 152, 154, 156, 157
Broadstairs (Sussex coast, UK), 145
Brunete, 54, 55, 69
Buenos Aires, 105
Bulgaria, 50
Burchill, Elizabeth, 32, 33, 47, 48
Burlingham, Dorothy, 134

Cabeza del Buey, 50–53
Cadbury-Fry Co., 35, 73
Cadiz, 58
Cairo, 139
Calle de la Platería, 65
Calle de la Traperia, 65
Cambridge University, 127
Canada, Canadian, 38
Canterbury College (NZ), 19
Canterbury Hospital Board, 22–24
Canterbury (province, NZ), 13, 15, 23, 25, 122
Canterbury (dredger), 14–15
Canut, Angel, 113
Capa, Robert, 98
Caproni (bomber), 54
Carcassonne, 117
Cartagena, 37, 85
Casals, Pablo, 98
Castilla-La Mancha, 68
Catalonia, 35
Cathedral Square (Christchurch), 8–10, 18, 28
Catholic Church (Spanish), 30, 64, 73
Cavell, Sinclair, 36, 46
Cerbére, 108, 113
Chamberlain, Neville, 70, 71, 84, 86, 97
Children's Rest Centre, 134
China, Chinese, 10, 13, 48, 140
Chorleywood, 163
Christchurch (NZ), 6, 8– 10, 12, 14, 17–20, 23–27, 160, 165–166
Christchurch Hospital, 20–22
Christian socialism, 23, 41
Churchill, Winston, 123, 131–132
Cilento, Raphael, 152, 154
Clark, Hilda, 109
Colonie des Enfants Espagnola, 113

Commission for War Refugees in Spain, 130
Communist Party, French, 56
Conard, Florence, 72
Cope, Ruth, 85, 87, 104, 109
Cordoba, 48, 91, 164
Corinthic, 14
Cornwall, Cornish, 123, 146
Coromandel (NZ), 47
Corsellis, John, 142–144, 148
Costa Blanca, 164
Costa del Sol, 164
Cottle, Jean, 102
Cox, Geoffrey, 4, 122, 141
Creelman, Lyle, 152
Crete, 137
Crevillente, 99
Crichton, Margaret, 36
Crimean War, 11
Cromwell (town, NZ), 10–12, 13, 15, 41, 54, 86, 144
Cromwell, Oliver, 10
Cuidad Real, 49, 91
Curcia, Durshan, 142
Curie, Eve, 121
Czechoslovakia, 84, 96

Daily Express, 122
Davies, Dorothy, 72, 73, 74
De Llano, General Quiepo, 34–35, 37
Delmer, Sefton, 122
De Sousa Mendes, Aristides, 121
Denmark, 73
Devon, 36, 131, 137
Dieppe, 36, 37
Dodds, Isobel, 68–69
Doherty, Muriel, 149, 152, 156
Don Quixote, 48, 91, 92
Dordogne, 113
Dunedin, 43
Dunkirk, 123
Düsseldorf, 152

East End (London), 41, 123, 134
Ebola virus, 7
Ebro, Battle of, 55, 92, 161
Edinburgh, 133, 136, 138
Egypt, 25, 137, 163, 166

Elmes, Mary, 48, 72, 73–74, 88, 91, 93, 94, 102, 104, 112–113, 118–120
Elne, 103, 113
El Shatt (refugee camp), 139–144, 146, 148
Emilia (kitchenmaid, Torviscon), 45
Enfield (London), 130, 161
Escort, HMS, 94–95
Europe, European, 27, 29, 30, 31, 43, 47, 49, 52, 69, 84, 88, 108, 115, 118, 129, 141, 148, 160
Euston Station, 95
Evans, Lt., 16
Extremadura, 48, 50

Falmouth, 123
Farquhar, Esther, 62–63, 71
Federación Universitaria Escolar, 68
Fernandez, Don Amalio (Dr), 62
Flackley Ash (house), 12, 15, 19, 159
Fonteyn, Margot, 166
Forgasc, Käthe, 51
Foster Parents Plan for Children in Spain, 134, 135
Fournier, Sidney, 25
France, 31, 36, 89, 94, 97–119, 127, 129, 131, 147
Franco, General Francisco, 30, 89, 93–95, 105, 108; British sympathizers of, 36; covert supporters of, 85; troops of, 49–50, 54, 56, 59, 71, 72, 95, 102; regime of, 160–162, 164
Frawley, Margaret, 117–118
French (language), 19, 33, 50, 72, 103, 104, 111, 112, 114, 142
Freud, Anna, 134–136
Freud, Sigmund, 134
Friends House (London), 32, 94, 96

Gandia, 94
Garonne, River, 118
Germany, German, 11, 30–31, 34, 51, 52, 53, 56, 57, 70, 71, 73, 85, 86, 93, 94, 96, 99, 108, 109, 110, 111, 115, 117, 119, 121, 122, 127, 129, 135, 136–138, 139, 140, 142, 145, 147–148, 151, 159, 162, 165, 166
German language, 50, 111, 116

Gestapo, 93
Gibraltar, 108
Gibson, Helen, 18
Gillies, Harold, 152
Girls High School (Christchurch), 18
Glasgow, 34, 47
Gloucester, 146
Granada, 45, 164
Granville (Normandy), 147
Graves, Robert, 160
Greece, Greeks, 137, 139
Greek (language), 112
Greene, Graham, 122
Greene, Hugh, 122
Grosvenor Court Hotel, 28, 40
Guadalajara, 54, 69
Guadarrama, 41

Haganah, 162
Hamburg, 145, 153, 156
Hampstead War Nurseries, 134–136
Hanna, Elisabeth (later Ogilvie), 159–160, 166–167
Hanna, Jane (later Taylor), 159–161, 166, 167
Haras (detention camp), 106
Harbour Board, Lyttelton, 14–16
Heals (department store), 162
Heck, Suzanne (Dr), 61
Herault, 116
Hinojosa del Duque, 53
Hitler, Adolf, 71, 106, 110, 121, 130, 133, 154
Hohne (refugee camp), 150, 156
Holderness, Mina, 20
Holland, Dutch, 53, 111, 116, 165
Hospital Board (Christchurch), 21, 25
Hospital Board (North Canterbury), 21, 22, 23
Hospital Inglés de Niños (English Children's Hospital), 59– 65, 67– 68, 70–74, 84–90, 165
Hotel Regina (Perpignan), 101, 113
Hoyo de Manzanares, 55–56
Huete, 68
Hulme, Kay, 157

Iglesias, Pablo, 59

Institute of Labour Management, 127
International Brigades, 31, 42–45, 48–56,
  61, 63, 66, 68–69, 71, 84, 91, 92,
  93, 107, 162
International Brigades Association, 162
International Commission (for the
  Assistance of Child Refugees in
  Spain), 88–90, 94, 95, 99, 101,
  105–107, 112, 115–119, 130–131
  135, 137
Ionic, 14
Isitt, Evelyn, 29, 162
Israel, 162–163
Italy, Italian, 29, 30–31, 34, 53, 54, 56,
  70, 71, 86, 89, 94, 95, 138, 140

Jackson, Edna, 161
Jackson, Robert, 148
Jarama, Battle of, 61
Jensen, Dr Fritz, 48–49
Jolly, Dr Doug, 41–42, 54, 144
Jordan, Bill, 70
Julia, Doña (teacher), 86

Kaiapoi, 113
Karitane hospitals, 161
Kawerau River, 13
Kelly, Dr Thomas,122
King, Dr Truby, 150
Kitty, Aunt, 13
Klagenfurt, 148
Kruger, Pitt and Yves, 110–111, 114,
  116, 134, 140

Labour government (NZ), 6, 29, 69–70
Labour Party (NZ), 17, 23, 25, 29
La Coume, 109–111, 114, 116, 119, 140
Lady Superintendent, 24, 27
Laiks Latviesu Zurnals (*News for Latvian
  DPs*), 153
La Mancha (*see also* Castilla-La Mancha),
  48, 68, 91
Lambeth, 124
Langdon-Davies, John, 133–134
La Pasionaria Hospital, 61, 69
League of Nations, 29, 31, 70–71
Legion d'Honneur, 120
Le Verdon, 118

Limes Hospital, Christchurch, 24–25
Lithuania, 96
Liverpool, 34
London, 6, 28–30, 32–35, 38, 41 95–97,
  104, 123–137, 145–146, 160–164
London Universities Ambulance Unit,
  33–34
Lorca, Federica Garcia, 79
Lucky Lady (dredge), 11
Luneberg, 156
Luxembourg, 111, 116–117
Luxor, 163
Lyceum Club, 30, 162
Lyttelton, 12–18, 23, 128, 146, 159, 166

Maadi Camp, 136–137
MacDonald, William, 43–44
Machado, Antonio, 87
Madrid, 11, 51, 54, 56, 58, 83
Madrid, Battle of, 4, 31, 35, 36, 41, 56,
  122
Madura, SS, 119, 121–123, 141
Magazine Bay, 12
Majorca, 74
Malaga, 34–38, 45, 46, 47, 57, 58, 164,
  166
Malbin, Virginia, 46
Malecon, 66
Manchester Guardian, 30, 59, 115
Manolo, 102
Maori people, 12, 25, 26–27
Maori language, 11, 18
Mappin and Webb, 162
Marcelino, Don, 102
Marseilles, 91, 94, 95, 97, 115
Mas de l'Abat, 112
Massons, Dr Josep Maria, 50–56, 64
Mathison, Jock, 9
McCombs, Elizabeth, 17, 23, 25
McCombs, James, 17
McDonald, Inez, 67
Mediterranean, 30, 57, 64, 94, 98, 107,
  129, 136, 137, 139, 165
Meir (Israeli guide), 162–163
Memel, 96
Mennonites, 36, 89
Merivale (Christchurch), 167
Mexico, 70, 105–106, 119, 154

Middle East, 131, 136–137, 142, 163
Mills, Anson, 127
Mills Equipment Co., 127–133
Miramar (hostel, Devon), 131, 137
Mitford, Nancy, 106–107
Mongolia, 13
Montessori (schools), 110
Montgomery, Dr Gladys, 47–48
Montpellier, 115, 117
Morocco, 34, 50
Morris, Anne, 167
Morris, Dorothy, family background, 11;
    birth and childhood, 12–17; educa-
    tion, 18–19; nursing training, 20–22,
    24, 27; entry to Spanish Civil War,
    31–39; nurse, International Brigades,
    39–40, 42–46, 48–57; director of
    children's hospital, 62–65, 67–70,
    74, 84–87; aid administrator,
    International Commission, 88–90,
    94, 101–117; welfare worker,
    London, 126–133; nursery director,
    Edinburgh, 135–136; nurse,
    UNRRA, 138–158; love life, 91–92,
    160–161; fondness for gardening,
    164; final years, 164–165; character
    and personality, 5, 26–27, 84, 95;
    political views, 5–6, 29, 69–70, 71,
    94–95, 96–97, 160
Morris, Frank, 136–138, 145–146, 163
Morris, Geoffrey (senior), 11–15, 20, 146
Morris, Geoffrey (junior), 13
Morris, Geoffrey (nephew), 160
Morris, Roger, 131, 136–138, 145–146,
    163
Morris, Roger (nephew), 166
Morris, Ruth, 159, 165
Mosset, 109–111, 116
Motríl, 38, 39, 44, 47, 48
Muggeridge. Eric, 134
Muggeridge, Marianne, 166
Murcia, 37, 51, 57–74, 83–92, 94, 99,
    101, 102, 104, 113, 114, 133, 134,
    135, 162, 165
Muslims (Moors), 47, 65, 67, 83, 97
Mussolini, Benito, 29, 31, 71

Naples, 138

Narbonne, 115
Nas List (Our Paper), 142
National Joint Committee on Spanish
    Relief, 106
Nazareth, 163
News Chronicle, 122, 133
Nightingale, Florence, 20, 22
Nile, River, 163
Non-Intervention Agreement (Pact), 31,
    56, 70–71
Normandy, 147
Nureyev, Rudolf, 166
Nurses Registration Act, 1901, 21
Nursing Journal (UK), 32
Nursing School (Christchurch), 20–22, 24

Oates, Lt., 16
O'Donovan, Peter, 36, 57
Ogilvie, Elisabeth – *see* Hanna, Elisabeth
Ohio, 62
Operation Aerial, 123
Orgiva, 42, 45
Otago, 11, 13
Otago Medical School, 41
Oxford St (London), 28

Pablo Iglesias (hostel), 58
Palestine, 163
Pancho Villa battalion, 45
Paris, 56, 71, 86, 95, 98, 101, 103, 104,
    106, 107, 112, 115, 116, 117, 119
Parker, Emily, 67, 72, 89
Pedreno, Miss, 102
Pepita Sicilia (nurse), 51
Penarroya, 49
Perpignan, 37, 99, 101–104, 106–109,
    115–118, 129, 133, 142, 161
Perth (Scotland), 36
Petit Méridional, 117
Piccadilly (London), 30
Poland, Polish, 36, 61, 108, 109, 116, 138
Polop, 73–74, 83, 85, 102
Port Hills (Canterbury, NZ), 12, 15, 17,
    18, 23
Portugal, Portuguese, 39, 48, 139
Prades, 111
Press (Christchurch), 43
Preston, Prof. Paul, 2

Pretsch, Karl, 11
Pretsch, Rebecca (later Morris), 11, 12, 159
Pueblo Nuevo del Terrible, 49
Pye, Edith, 35, 88, 99, 109, 114, 116, 122
Pyrenees, 97–101, 109, 116, 119

Quakers (*see also* Society of Friends), 5, 35, 72, 84, 87, 89, 90, 93, 94, 99, 101, 102, 103, 109, 110, 111, 115, 116, 117, 122, 130, 141, 160
Quakers, UK, 32, 58, 59, 61, 63, 71, 72, 84, 88, 95, 96, 99, 142, 148
Quakers, US (*see also* American Friends Service Committee), 61–62, 85, 86, 87, 89, 91, 99, 115, 119, 129
Queen Elisabeth of the Belgians, 120
Queen Elizabeth II, 124

Rangi Ruru School, 18–19
Red Cross (International), 138
Red Cross (US), 116, 117
Red Flag, The, 9
Rees, Sir Richard, 117
Reid, Alice, 156
Requetes, 45
Retirada, 97, 106, 122
'Righteous Among the Nations', 120
Ripa Island, 18
Rivesaltes (detention camp), 119
Rodd, Peter, 106
Rodríguez, Dr Manuel Blanc, 73, 74
Rommel, Erwin, 138
Ronda, 164
Roosevelt, Franklin, 133, 140
Rothschild, Baron, 122
Royal Ballet, 160
Royal College of Surgeons, 41
Russell, Dr Audrey, 99, 108, 143
Russia (*see also* Soviet Union), 11, 34, 36, 142, 147, 155

Salazar, António de Oliveira, 122
Santander, 133–134
Santos (shepherd), 110
Save the Children Fund, 32
Schindler, Oskar, 120
Scotland, Scottish, 32, 36, 60, 128

Scott, Captain Robert, 15–16
Segura River, 65–66
Selfridge's (department store), 28, 29
Senge, 152
Séte, 106, 115
Seville, 58, 164
Shackleton, Ernest, 15–16
Shadbolt, Renée, 68
Sharples, Millicent, 68
Shaw, Nurse, 60
Shaw Savill, 14
Sierra de los Filabres, 37
Sierra de Mulhacen, 43
Sierra Morena, 48, 55
Sierra Nevada, 2, 39–40, 42, 46
Silesia, 11
Sinaia, SS, 106, 119, 154
Six Day War, 162
Smilg, Santiago, 102
Social Democratic Party (NZ), 17–18
Society of Friends (*see also* Quakers), 35
Society of Women Engineers, 124
South Africa, 21, 117
Southern Spanish Relief Committee, 32
South Island (NZ), 10
Soviet Union (*see also* Russia), 31, 56, 147, 149
Spain: Dorothy Morris's attitudes towards, 6, 67, 86, 90, 95, 125, 129; Muslim occupation of, 65; Francoist repression, 105, 161, 162; post-Franco conditions, 164
Spanish Civil War: outbreak, 31–33; Non-Intervention Agreement, 71; first months, 35–41; medical services, 40–42, 44–45, 50–51, 62; International Brigades, 48, 53, 56, 84; food supplies, 59; mail deliveries, 3–5; refugee crisis, 89; Republican retreat, 97–101
Spanish language, 33, 43, 44, 63, 69, 104–105, 112
Spanish Medical Aid Committee, 32
Stapylton-Smith, Mary, 166
St Cyprien (detention camp), 98, 107, 113, 114
Stewart, Frida, 33, 59, 60, 61
Stuttgart, 150

Sudetenland (German), 137
Sussex, 11, 12
Swan Lake, 160
Switzerland, Swiss, 11

Tatler, 125
Taylor, Jane, *see* Hanna, Jane
Telge, Dr Oskar, 50, 56
Tembleque, 54
Teruel, 71
Tet Valley (France), 161
The New Spain, 33
Theresienstadt (Terezin), 145
Terra Nova, 16
Thorpe, Captain, 15
Thurstan, Violetta, 36–37, 39
Times (London), 29
Tobruk, 144
Torremolinos, 33, 34
Torviscon, 42–46, 48
Toulouse, 115
Trades Hall (Christchurch), 9
Tramway Workers Union (Christchurch), 8–10, 25–26
Tramways Board (Christchurch), 8, 25
Transport and General Workers Union, 132
Trias, Dr. Joaquin, 50
Trinity College, Dublin, 72
Trueta, Dr Josep, 54

United Nations, 140, 157
United Nations Relief and Rehabilitation Administration (UNRRA), 4, 5, 140–144, 146–157

United States (*see also* America), 43, 147, 155
University of New Zealand, 19
Upham, Dr, 20

Valdepeñas, 91
Valencia, 33, 36, 49, 59, 72, 83
Valmy, 112
Vienna, Viennese, 49, 134
Villa Elena, 47, 48
Villa Maria, 37, 39, 46, 47
Villa San Juan, 47
Villalba, Don Ricardo, 85

Wales, 96, 146
Wallenberg, Raoul, 120
War and Children, 135
Wellington (NZ), 4, 16
Wellington Hospital (NZ), 22, 68
West End, London, 28, 136
White Goddess, The, 160
Wildflecken DP camp, 157
Williams, Mrs (matron), 24
Wilson, Dr Edward, 16
Wilson, Francesca, 58–62, 67, 71, 73–74, 83, 84, 88–89, 99–101, 129, 140, 141, 143, 151, 152
World War One, 9, 13, 15, 20, 25, 35, 36, 41, 126, 140

Young, Lady, 36, 38
Young, Sir George, 5, 32–36, 38, 41–48, 56–57, 59, 61–62, 90

Printed and bound by CPI Group (UK) Ltd, Croydon, CR0 4YY

09/06/2025

14685952-0001